Law and Power in the Islamic World

Law and Power
in the
Islamic World

Sami Zubaida

I.B. TAURIS
LONDON · NEW YORK

Reprinted in 2005 by I.B.Tauris & Co Ltd
6 Salem Road, London W2 4BU
175 Fifth Avenue, New York NY 10010
www.ibtauris.com

In the United States and Canada distributed by Palgrave Macmillan
a division of St. Martin's Press
175 Fifth Avenue, New York NY 10010

First published in 2003

Library of Modern Middle East Studies 34

ISBN 1 85043 934 6
EAN 978 1 85043 934 9

A full CIP record for this book is available from the British Library

Typeset in Minion by Dexter Haven Associates, London
Printed and bound in Great Britain by MPG Books, Bodmin

Contents

Acknowledgements

I have benefited from comments and discussions with friends and colleagues in the process of writing this book. Chibli Mallat and Khalid Masud read a preliminary essay on the subject and were generous with their comments and suggestions. I also benefited from discussions in seminars and conferences at ISIM (International Institute for the Study of Islam in the Modern World) in Leiden, Holland, directed by Khalid Masud. Mohammad Nafissi read some chapters and commented at length; I also found discussions with him on the issues of the book stimulating and challenging. Sami Daniel gave me the benefit of careful and critical reading of the introduction and some chapters. Anna Enayat read much of the book, and made many valuable editorial and substantive comments. She also supplied me with much material, mostly on contemporary Iran. Baudoin Dupret was always generous in sending me material, including his own valuable work, and directing me to sources on current developments in Egypt. Enid Hill kindly showed me her unpublished material, which was most useful on contemporary developments in Egypt. Grateful thanks to all.

INTRODUCTION

The idea of the *shari'a*, the holy law, is central to the Muslim religion and a major element in the discourses and institutions of Muslim societies over the ages. This law is believed to derive from the sacred sources of Islam: the Quran as the word of God and prophetic tradition as attested by reliable narratives of Muhammad's words and deeds. In practice this law and its applications have been developed over the Muslim centuries by scholars and divines, known as *'ulama* ('ulama' in what follows). The corpus they produced is *fiqh*, jurisprudence, defining the rules and methodologies of law.

There is a common view that the *shari'a* is fixed and clearly discernible from its sacred sources. For Muslim ideologists this fixity and clarity are functions of its divine origin. For many Western observers they are functions of the fixity of 'Muslim society', totally other from 'the West', with religion as its essence. We shall see in what follows that the *shari'a* is a product of articulations of legal discourses and institutions to varying patterns of society and politics. The holy law has co-existed and interacted with statute laws issued by rulers, as well as customary conduct, sometimes extending its vocabulary and concepts to cover these existing practices.

The modern era, starting in the early nineteenth century, witnessed a series of reforms in government, law and society in the Ottoman lands and elsewhere in the Muslim world, which included the institution of law as state law (as against jurists' and judges' law), and the adoption of European codes and procedures. These steps opened up avenues for political protest and contest in the name of divine justice as against the ungodly reforms. These contests of legal modernity developed and mutated over the course of the two ensuing centuries. While playing some part in the politics of most countries, Islamic advocacy became one element among many in modern political fields.

The 'Islamic revival' of the closing decades of the twentieth century (from the 1970s) featured the call for the application of the *shari'a* as the central plank of its advocacy. Its basic premise is that to live the good life as a Muslim one has to follow God's commands, and that this only becomes fully possible within a community of believers in which God's rules govern social relationships and transactions. It follows that governing authority must rule in accordance with what God has revealed. In its most radical form as stated, for instance, by Sayid Qutb, the Egyptian radical Islamist executed for conspiracy and sedition in 1966, it contends that all man-made laws are idolatry, and governments which hold them cannot be Muslim and must be combated as infidels. This has been the predominant creed of the militant Islamists in recent decades. Islam, it is argued, is a religion revealed by God for the whole of mankind and for all time. As such it covers all aspects of life of the individual, society and the state. The *shari'a*, according to this line of thought, is the revealed law of God and is, therefore, the perfect set of rules for human conduct, which needs no supplementation by man-made laws.

These ideas are at the base of the revolutionary doctrine of Ayatollah Khomeini, the leader of the 1979 Iranian Revolution and of the Islamic Republic it inaugurated. The task of the Islamic state was to implement the law of God, as interpreted by the leading *faqih*, the just jurist, in this case Khomeini himself. The constitution of the Republic enshrines the *shari'a* as the law of the state. Yet as we shall see in Chapter 6, by 1988 Ayatollah Khomeini found it necessary to release the government from the commands of the *shari'a*, with the following formula: '[The Islamic state] is a branch of the absolute trusteeship of the Prophet...and constitutes one of the primary ordinances of Islam which has precedence over all other derived ordinances, such as prayer, fasting and pilgrimage' (quoted in Schirazi 1997:213). That is to say, the government is free to abrogate the most basic provisions of the law if it judges it necessary to the public interest. This declaration came after a period of conflicts over public policy, with the conservative clerics obstructing legislation on the basis of its non-conformity to the *shari'a*. There is a good reason for this: the *shari'a* developed historically to rule mostly on the private affairs of the community, dealing with commercial and property transactions and family matters, as well as ritual performances. The public-law provisions of the *shari'a* have remained largely theoretical, to do, for instance, with the laws of war and the division of the spoils. We shall see that public authorities over the centuries of Muslim history, while declaring allegiance to the holy law, largely bypassed it in matters of state. The task of the Islamic Republic, then, was to derive public law and policy within the framework and vocabulary of legal discourses developed and applied primarily in private contexts. The vast bulk of laws enacted by the Islamic parliament were on matters of practical administration and regulation which had nothing to do with religion. Crucially, however, when it came to legislation on social and welfare issues, such as land reform and labour law, the conservative clerics obstructed the process. They argued that the *shari'a* protected private property and made no provision for the ruler to redistribute land. The labour contract, they argued, is a matter for the parties concerned, and the state had no business to intervene to regulate conditions, wages, safety and holidays. Khomeini had to make that declaration, then, to facilitate the processes of government and policy-making, by bypassing *shari'a* provisions when necessary. Khomeini's action in this episode is illustrative, in a modern context, of the adaptations of legal thought and enactment to contingencies of rule. We shall see how the concept of *maslaha*, 'utility' or 'public interest', used by Khomeini on this occasion, has been advocated at various times as a let-out clause for policy and legislation.

The example of the Islamic Republic would not conform to the commonly stated view that Islam is a total 'civilization', not just a religion but a political and social system, and the divinely revealed law is at its core. This view is advanced both by some Western commentators, holding the 'clash of civilizations' position, and Islamists, insistent on the totality and indivisibility of Islam. There is a kind of ideological symbiosis between the two. 'Muslim society' in this perspective is not amenable to analysis in terms of economics, politics or sociology, but has religion as its essence which moves it and determines its processes. The sacred law is the major part of this essence. It is not just a law, but a 'total discourse' determining family, morality, ritual and politics. That is why Ernest Gellner considered Muslim society, unlike any other in modern times, to be impervious to secularization. In this perspective, this essential quality explains the resurgence of Islamic politics in modern times, displacing the earlier superficial grafts of modern ideologies. After the abortive Algerian election of 1991/2, in which the Islamists scored highly in the first round, posters appeared in Cairo streets declaring 'Algeria returns to Islam'. It is a 'return' to an essence which had always been there. I have argued elsewhere against this essentialist view of Islam, and in favour of confronting the diversity and dynamism of the many societies and histories dubbed 'Muslim' (Zubaida 1993, 1995). Neither 'the West' nor 'Islam' are homogeneous entities. Each one comprises a great diversity of cultures, social formations and political organization historically and now. There are no civilizational totalities that clash or 'dialogue', but there are many clashes within so-called civilizations. There is a great deal in common, for instance, between conservative Islamic advocacy in the Middle East and that of the US religious right. Both advocate the supremacy of revelation over science, the moralization of society and the regulation and censorship of cultural products. And they are both engaged in conflicts and struggles with antagonists within their own societies.

This book underlines the historicity of Muslim legal discourse and practice and the trajectories of evolution and mutations in different historical contexts.

While holding on to the notion of the sacred origins of the law, jurists have often shown flexibility in fashioning their formulations in line with the constraints of their contemporary societies and the contingencies of power. Contrary to the insistence on unity and perpetuity, the *shari'a* has in fact displayed considerable variation over time and place. This book is not a history as such, but delves into history for significant formative episodes which illustrate the genesis and development of the law in the context of power relations, of conflicts and accommodations between significant actors. The most significant actors were the rulers and the religious scholars, the *ulama*, the authors and the guardians of the law.

Contrary to the notion that Islam is a religion and a state in one, we find that the elaboration of the *shari'a* was not, at its beginning, the work of state legislators and rulers, but that of pious private individuals, mostly traders and artisans, who sought to live by the rules of God and to avoid the sin and corruption of the rulers and their courts. We shall see in Chapter 1 how these individuals worked on the actual practices and rules of their society and endeavoured to derive religious formulae for subsuming and moralizing these practices. Rather than starting from the religious sources as such, they worked on practical matters with a view to Islamizing and systematizing the rules that governed them. We shall see that this process culminated over the early centuries in a corpus of texts with a high level of conceptual sophistication and a systematic methodology. They created a body of discourse with its own logic and rationale, divided into different schools and doctrines. Four schools or doctrines (*madhhab*, plural *madhahib*) of law emerged in the early centuries as canonical in Sunni Islam, accepted as equally orthodox: Hanafi, Hanbali, Shafi'i and Maliki, named after their putative founders. Each became predominant in some countries and regions. The Shi'a developed its own body of law, with many similarities to and parallels with the Sunni schools. In the process of this elaboration the scholars did not remain separate from the rulers and their institutions. Processes of political struggles and quests for legitimacy articulated the scholars' art into the institutions of the rulers and transformed both, as we shall see.

The political resonance of the *shari'a*, historically and at the present, is associated with its function as a language of justice. It is not just 'law' in the modern sense, but a total discourse of religion, morality and justice. As such it is always exploited as a medium of contest. Rulers seek legitimacy in its terms, and the establishment scholars comply. Challengers and usurpers indict incumbents for injustice and irreligion. Protests and rebellions demand the rule of the holy law against the injustice of their rulers. The processes of modernization and reform in the Ottoman lands and elsewhere (see Chapter 4) generated many upheavals and dislocations. While benefiting sectors of the population it deprived others, mostly among the lower orders and the religious classes. These discontents were easily directed to claims of justice and morality in terms of religion and the *shariʿa*. They also merged into a kind of Islamic proto-nationalism directed against Europe and Christianity, seen as a unified force hostile to Islam. This Islamic proto-nationalism at the popular level, but also encompassing some intellectuals, continued to be a factor in political sentiments in the region: hostility to the dominant West and seeking salvation in religious revival and the application of the holy law. In later decades and throughout the twentieth century such sentiments were only one factor among many in the formation of political ideology and action. They ebbed and flowed with events.

As we have seen, many Muslim and Western commentators see 'Muslim society' as being impervious to secularization, and view the recent Islamic resurgence as an indication that religion is the only ideology which can animate the masses. My argument is that the recently resurgent political Islam is directed precisely against the secularization and the secularizing reforms that have occurred extensively in the region for two centuries, and which are irreversible. In Egypt, Turkey, Iran and most other countries, we see this secularization in government and its institutions, in the law, in education, in the economy and, most important for our argument, in the cultural fields. Print media, radio, cinema, television and most recently the internet have all acted as secularizing media. Even when the media relay religious messages they contribute to this secularization, because religion in them features alongside news and music, films and soaps, and as such loses its aura of sanctity. It is 'banalized'. It is related that soon after the installation of the Islamic Republic in Iran and the Islamization of television, the most popular programme featured a senior cleric answering practical questions from viewers in terms of *fiqh* rulings. Viewers derived pleasure and amusement in getting the cleric to rule on obtuse questions of sexuality. Egyptian clerics currently broadcast homilies of morality and order, and warn of the torments of the grave, much like their Christian counterparts in the US. But these are not dedicated channels, and the sermons alternate with films and soaps.

The Egyptian cinema, popular all over the Arab world, exerted a grip over the popular imagination throughout the twentieth century and to the present. The popular classes, men and women, are avid consumers of media products, and the songs of the popular films are on many lips. All this is not inconsistent with religiosity, but would tend to compartmentalize religion, where it is followed, to one aspect of the life of the believer, insulated from the others.

In politics and popular mobilization many parties and ideologies contended for influence, and Islamic parties were one such strand, not always the most salient. Nationalism of various brands, sometimes overlapping religious sentiment, was the most common ideology of the twentieth century, and continues in many places. Communism and the left exerted great influence and organized grass-roots movements in Iran, Iraq, Sudan and to a lesser extent Egypt and Syria. The Palestine Liberation Organization (PLO), though with some Islamic roots, had a predominantly secular appeal, including many Christians among its adherents and leaders. The Islamic current was a late development, resulting in part from the failures and corruption of the secular nationalists and leftists in power, and above all their failure to confront Israel and the West, exacerbated by the collapse of the Soviet Union. In many ways it paralleled ethnic revivals and identity politics elsewhere. These factors continue to feed Islamism. But it is not a one-way process: in Iran, the country of the most spectacular success of Islamism, the new generations are massively rejecting Islamic rule and its constrictions.

The quest for the *shari'a* is multifaceted: social protesters seek justice from corrupt regimes in its terms, clerics seek to restore their authority by imposing it, conservatives seek patriarchal virtues in its commandments, nationalists see it as a marker of authenticity and identity, and those same corrupt rulers seek legitimacy in adopting it. In practice it is an ideological project which has highly variable manifestations in the politics and the legal systems of different countries, which will be explored in what follows.

The modern context, while occupying only a part of the book is, in effect, the real focus of the study. It is this context which raises the questions regarding the nature and the locations of the *shari'a* in texts, institutions and politics, and its various expressions over time and place. As such, the history in this book is a history of the present.

A HISTORICAL SKETCH

The following sketch of Muslim history will provide a framework for the reader. The Muslim calendar is dated from the Hijra in 622, the flight of Muhammad from Mecca to Madina and the founding of the first Muslim polity. The Prophet died in 632, to be succeeded consecutively by four of his companions, Abu-Bakr, Umar, Uthman and Ali. This period is known as 'al-Khulafa' al-Rashidun', the rightly guided caliphs (successors of the Prophet), and is regarded by all Muslims as a sacred history, when the community of believers was ruled in accordance with prophetic inspiration. It is also known as "asr al-sa'ada', the Era of Felicity. It ended in a civil war in 661, the year of the assassination of Ali (all these caliphs except for the first died at the hands of assassins). There followed the Umayyad dynasty (661–750), centred in Damascus. This is widely viewed by Muslims as the inauguration of *mulk*, kingdom, as against *khilafa*, succession to the Prophet's rule. Yet the term *khalifa*, caliph, was retained for the Umayyads and succeeding dynasties. Indeed, these early dynasts styled themselves *khalifat*

Allah, God's deputy, regarded as blasphemous by subsequent clerics. There followed the Abbasid dynasty (750–1258), with Baghdad as its centre. While professing piety and adherence to the holy law (which was in the process of being developed by private scholars in that period), the Abbasids adopted Persian styles of government and courtly culture, and promoted the Persian aristocracy to eminent positions of state. A rival caliphate arose in Egypt and North Africa, that of the Fatimids (969–1171), and others in Muslim Spain. A crucial transformation in the system of rule occurred with the rise of non-Arab but Islamized military dynasties which conquered and subordinated the lands of the caliphates: first the Persian Buyids (945–1055), then the Turkish Saljuks (1055–1194). Under these dynasties the Abbasid Caliph became a nominal sovereign, with the real power in the hands of the military usurpers. The Abbasid caliphate was brought to an end with the Mongol conquest of Baghdad in 1258. The Mongols were stopped in Syria by the might of the Mamlukes, another military dynasty consisting of slave soldiers, which ruled over Egypt and Syria 1250–1517. After the end of the caliphates, the Muslim world was ruled by a variety of military dynasties, some descendants of the Golden Horde of the Mongol conquerors, who also established the Mughal Empire in India (1526–1857).

The division between Sunni and Shi'i Islam originated in the first civil war of 661 which displaced Ali with the Umayyads. The Shi'a was the party of Ali, who contended that, being the cousin and son-in-law of the Prophet, he was the rightful successor to the caliphate at the death of Muhammad, and that the three who actually succeeded were usurpers. The Shi'a developed into a sectarian community asserting the holiness of the lineage of Ali and its right to rule over Muslims. There were many branches of the Shi'a, depending on which line of succession they followed, but the main branch historically and to the present is that of the Twelver Shi'a, so called after the 12 descendants of Ali they recognized, culminating with the disappearance of the twelfth in 874. The Hidden Imam remains the incumbent for all time, but the community is deprived of his leadership and guidance until he reveals himself in the fullness of time as the awaited Mahdi, a messiah ushering in an era of supernatural bliss. Shi'ism and Alid allegiances of various sorts gave rise to periodic rebellions and messianic movements. But the mainstream Shi'a after the occultation of the twelfth Imam became largely quiescent first as a sectarian community, then as the official religion of certain dynasties. The Fatimids were Ismaili, a different and at one time prominent branch of Shi'ism. The Safavids (1501–1722) converted Iran to Twelver Shi'ism, and it remained such till the present time.

The two Muslim dynasties that prevailed till the twentieth century were the Ottoman (1389–1922) and the Qajar in Iran (1779–1924). This latter was a decentralized and weak state, which lost much territory to Russia over the course of the nineteenth century. The Ottoman was the longest-ruling dynasty of Islam, and extended, at the height of its power, over vast territories including much of Eastern Europe, Anatolia, the Middle East and North Africa. It presided over many nationalities and religions and was a cosmopolitan empire. It left its traces, culturally and politically, over much of the modern Middle East.

PLAN OF THE BOOK

Chapter 1 considers accounts and constructions of the formation of the *shari'a*, its sources, locations, concepts and methods. It looks at these processes in two perspectives: that of exposition, the way in which the *shari'a* is presented by its practitioners, and the historical order of its development as advanced by modern historians. It considers the hierarchy of canonical texts and the evolution of the books of jurisprudence.

Chapter 2 is concerned with the institutional locations of the *shari'a*, as well as of judicial and administrative tribunals and personnel which bypassed the *shari'a*, and the relations between them at different moments and periods. It treats these institutions in two historical contexts: pre-Ottoman and Ottoman. It examines forms and developments of judicial procedure, as well as some aspects of the social and cultural contexts of legal practice.

Chapter 3 deals with the core issue of the book: law and power, the relation between rulers and jurists. Episodes in the development of these relations and the traces they left in the formulation and ideology of the law are examined. It is also divided between the pre-Ottoman and Ottoman periods. The latter is especially pertinent because of the high level of bureaucratization and centralization of religion and the law in Ottoman practice.

Chapter 4 is about the age of reform and the etatization of law. It concentrates primarily on the Ottoman lands in the nineteenth century, including Egypt. It examines the political and ideological contexts of the reforms, and the social and economic constraints and conflicts which enframed them. In particular, the processes of structural secularization which accompany modernity and reform are examined. Many of the issues and problems of our own time originated in these contexts.

Chapters 5 and 6 deal with the twentieth century and recent developments in the politics and ideology of the *shari'a*. Islamic 'resurgence' is primarily an attempt to subordinate modernity to religious authority, and the law is a central element in this advocacy. Chapter 5 traces these issues and debates in Egypt, looking in particular at the interaction between oppositional Islamic advocacy and the responses of the authorities in repression and co-optation, the latter resulting in problematic legislation and state Islamism. Chapter 6 considers the application of the *shari'a* in the Islamic Republic of Iran. The problems encountered in this enterprise and the ultimate licensing of the Islamic government to bypass the *shari'a* in the public interest proclaimed by Khomeini in 1988 illustrate the dilemmas of the holy law in relation to modernity.

1   CONCEPTS, ORIGINS
AND MUTATIONS

TERMS AND DEFINITIONS

The notion of *shariʻa* rests on a theological base: it consists of rules and commands which have divine origin, first in the Quran, which is the word of God, then in the *sunna* of the Prophet, also of divine inspiration. The formula is clearly expressed by Calder:

> The words and deeds of the Prophet Muhammad (his *sunna*), being an embodiment of the divine command and an expression of God's law (*shariʻa*), were preserved by the Companions of the Prophet, in the form of discrete anecdotes (*hadith*). These were transmitted orally through the generations and became the source of juristic discussion (*fiqh*). [Calder 1993:vi]

The *shariʻa*, then, rules of divine origin, is transmitted and developed through human agency. *Fiqh* is literally 'understanding', the effort of pious men to understand and formulate the divine will. The historical *shariʻa*, as it developed in texts and practices, is the work of *fuqaha* (plural of *faqih*, the practitioner of *fiqh*). The *shariʻa*, then, as it came down to us, is largely man-made, based on exegesis, interpretations, analogies, and extensive borrowing from customary practices (*ʻurf*, recognized as a source of law) and existing local Middle Eastern legal traditions, such as Babylonian, Jewish and Arab, as well as possible adaptations of Roman law. This hybrid formation poses interesting questions for modern contexts of reform and of 'fundamentalism': both try to rescue the divine message from the man-made historical accretions, but come to quite different conclusions regarding the essence of the divine message, as we shall see in subsequent chapters.

Another terminological problem is the common translation of '*shariʻa*' as 'Muslim law', which is not strictly true. The *shariʻa* is much more than law in the modern sense. So much of its contents cover ritual and religious practice of prayer, alms, pilgrimage, diet and food taboos, and 'purity' regarding ritual washing and bodily functions, including sexual intercourse. It also functions as a vocabulary of morality and justice, much used in political disputation over the ages and to the present. It is a flexible vocabulary of a 'moral economy' of claims and counter-claims between the classes and factions, and regarding the obligations of ruler and ruled. Messick, adapting a phrase from Marcel Mauss, characterizes the *shari'a* as a 'total discourse', 'wherein "all kinds of institutions find simultaneous expression: religious, legal, moral and economic"' (Messick 1993:3). It displays what Weber calls 'substantive rationality', one in which law, morality, religion and politics are not distinguished, as against the 'formal rationality', which he attributes to Western capitalism, the product of a chain of the unique development of the West, in which law is clearly differentiated from these other spheres, and proceeds according to its own principles and institutions.[1]

In practice, however, legal principles and institutions did become quite specialized and differentiated, as we shall see. Legal theory and its elaboration also became a specialized activity, often distinct in its institutions and practitioners from the practical applications of the law in courts and notaries. This is a characteristic which Weber attributes to Western law, which featured a distinction between the university or church academics, who did not practise law but engaged in the development of theories and methodologies of law, and the actual practitioners of law. This feature was clearly shared by the Muslim world. *Fiqh*, indeed, developed an elaboration of highly speculative discourses, often concerning hypothetical cases with no practical application, what has been termed 'casuistry'.[2]

In its aspect as 'law', the *shari'a* continued to be, until recent times, jurists' and judges' law, derived and elaborated in books of jurisprudence and commentaries, as against statute law, deriving from the edicts of rulers or state traditions. These latter were prevalent in the world of Islam, but always kept distinct from the *shari'a*, as we shall see.

THE ORIGINS OF THE *SHARI'A*: THE ORDER OF EXPOSITION

In the order of exposition of the bases of the *shari'a*, a hierarchy of sources are presented. Top of the hierarchy is the Quran, as the word of God, followed by prophetic tradition, the *hadith*, reports of the sayings of the Prophet, and the *sunna. Ijma'*, consensus, is authoritative, springing from the Prophet's pronouncement, 'my community cannot agree on an error'. *Qiyas*, analogy (strictly a method rather than a source), comes next in the hierarchy of sources, followed by minor and not always agreed sources, such as *istihsan*, preference of jurists, and the more controversial *'aql*, reason, and *ra'y*, jurist's opinion. This is the order of exposition, as distinct from the historical order of development, discussed in the following section.

The Quran is the ultimate source: it is the divine word. The Quran is spoken by God in the first person. The Old Testament, also considered the word of God, is spoken in a narrative voice referring to God in the third person: 'And the Lord said unto Moses ...'. It continues as narrations of God's address to the prophets, his word always mediated by their report. It also includes historical narratives, in which God is invoked in the third person. The gospels of the New Testament are narrations by saintly figures of the birth, deeds and sacrifice of the son of God, followed by sets of sermons by Paul, another saint, the whole forming a canonical corpus deemed to be a chronicle of the divine. In contrast, the Quran is addressed by God in the first person. He commands the Prophet, and through him, the believers: 'Recite: in the Name of the Lord who created...' runs the first revelation (The Blood-Clot XCVI), and down to the mundane details, 'O Prophet, when you divorce women, divorce them when they have reached their period' (Divorce LXV). Historical narratives, such as that of Joseph, are prefaced in the divine voice, 'We will relate to thee the fairest of stories...' (Joseph XII:2). These verses were revealed to Muhammad by the Angel Gabriel transmitting the word of God. This direct divine voice represents unmistakable authority, and gives literalists considerable advantage over subtle interpreters, as we shall see.[3]

The Quran, it is often stated, is not a book of law. Yet many verses are unmistakable commands in the nature of rules (such as the one on divorce above). Jurists agree that 500 verses have legal content (Hallaq 1997:3; Botiveau 1993a:46), which is a small percentage of the total text, although, Hallaq argues, the legal verses are much longer than the others (Hallaq 1997:4). It may be argued, however, that these prescriptions cover a limited range of human affairs in more complex societies. There is no question, however, that the intention is expressed in the Quran and in prophetic pronouncements that God has legislated rules for the believers. Speaking of Jews, Christians and Muslims, a verse announces: 'For we have made for each of you a law and a normative way to follow. If God had willed, He would have made you one community' (The Table V:48; translation quoted by Hallaq 1997:5). This same chapter (The Table) contains frequently repeated injunctions to 'Judge in accordance with what God has revealed' (an injunction which features prominently in the discourse of modern radical Islamists, only they translate *hukm* as 'rule' rather than 'judge' and apply it to government). Hallaq (1997:5–7) and others have also pointed out that Muhammad made it clear that Islam and the Quran contained a law and a path for the believers, and proceeded to institute such law in his conduct of the affairs of the community.

PROPHETIC NARRATIONS: *HADITH* AND *SUNNA*

Sunna means an exemplary mode of conduct, to be followed and imitated. Crone and Hinds (1986:58–62) have argued that the concept pre-existed Islam in Arabia, where the Arabs followed the *sunan* (plural of *sunna*) of leaders and charismatic figures. The example and the pronouncements of the Prophet have special sanctity, as he was the conduit and interlocutor of the divine voice, and as such the recipient of divine guidance. Add to that the frequent injunctions in the Quran for Muslims to obey the Prophet, 'And obey God and obey the Messenger, and beware' (The Table V:93), linking the Prophet to divine authority. As such, the Prophet is a privileged interpreter of the Quran, and his actions and pronouncements are canonical. The place of prophetic narrations as a source of the *shari'a* will be elaborated in the following sections and chapters.

Consensus

Consensus of the community is generally considered authoritative in Sunni jurisprudence, and as such a source of legal formulation and certainty. This view is based on one Quranic verse (Women IV:115) which threatens hellfire to anyone who opposes the Messenger, guided by revelation, or, crucially, 'follows other than the believers' way' (Hallaq 1997:75). While only a vague pointer, it is held by jurists as authoritative, and supported by a number of prophetic reports, notably the oft-cited 'my community shall never agree on a falsehood' (Hallaq 1997:76; Goldziher 1910/1981:50–52). The agreement of the community is, of course, impossible to establish, and the general view among jurists has been that the required consensus is that of qualified *mujtahids* (learned jurists), and not of the whole community. What is agreed upon, however, must have a basis in revelation (*dalil*).

Who should be counted in the consensus, and how we know that all qualified persons did agree at any point in time, are questions seldom raised and not considered problematic, despite some occasional disagreements. One such is a question of generations of *mujtahids*, and whether a consensus can be considered binding before they had all died, in case one will subsequently change his mind! (Hallaq 1997:77–80)

An important consequence for jurisprudence is that a consensus reached by one generation of jurists is considered binding on their intellectual descendants. This becomes a mechanism of 'traditionalization', of consolidating and maintaining continuity in schools of law, and in the so-called 'closure of the gate of Ijtihad' (see *infra*).

For the Shi'a, *ijma'* has an ambiguous and shifting status. In its early history, the imam was the source of all guidance and authority, and the question of consensus did not arise. The development of Imami Shi'ism as a sectarian community with the doctrine of the occultation of the imam Shi'i *ulama* assumed the functions of guidance and interpretation, and consensus between them became a relevant issue, though never elevated to the authority and certainty it had for most Sunnis (Goldziher 1910/1981:191). In the later phases of development of Shi'i *fiqh* since Safavid times, and especially with the establishment of the Usuli school at the turn of the nineteenth century, the authority of living and independent *mujtahids* is stressed. The ruling and judgement of a *mujtahid* are deemed to die with him, and each believer must seek a living *mujtahid* to follow. In this regard, while consensus is accepted by the Shi'a as one of the *usul* of *fiqh* (Algar 1969:7), its status is rendered ambiguous by the wide competence and autonomy assigned to the living *mujtahid*. The polycentric authority of the different *mujtahids*, and the admission of difference and even contradiction between their ruling, also devalues consensus as such. The concept and practice of a supreme *marja' al-taqlid* (the ultimate source of emulation, the supreme authority), only established in the later nineteenth century, may diminish this multicentrism, but hand authority to a central figure rather than a consensus of peers.

Qiyas

Analogy is employed when a novel case is presented to the jurist for which there is no clear resolution on the basis of text, *sunna* or *ijma'*. It is an inferential procedure, and as such its conclusions can only be probable and are subject to disagreement and alternative analogies. Hallaq (1997:83) elucidates the logic of the procedure: the constituents of the analogical argument are four: the new case that requires a solution (*far'*); the original case, in the canonical sources, to which the analogy is to be made (*asl*); the rationale (*'illa*) common to the two cases, which makes them analogous; and the rule (*hukm*), attached to the original case and transferable to the new one because of their supposed similarity. This is the most common form of legal argument in the books of *fiqh*, and the prototype for logical arguments in general (Hallaq 1997:83). A common example is that of the interdiction of grape wine. Its rationale is the harm of intoxication, and as such is transferable by analogy to date wine, and subsequently to all alcoholic beverages. Questions then arise about intoxicants other than alcohol, such as hashish or even tobacco or coffee, whose production does not involve fermentation.

Literalists, including some Hanbalis (more *infra*), have opposed the employment of analogy, as it depends on human judgement and departs from strict adherence to text and tradition. They argue that the Quran, by its own declaration, is a complete and perfect guide to every aspect of human conduct, complemented by the *sunna*. Their opponents have pointed out, however, that the objectors themselves employ analogical reasoning without acknowledging it.

For the Usuli Shi'a, given their admission of *'aql*, reason, and the authority of *ijtihad*, *qiyas*, though specified by the Shi'a as one of the *usul*, loses its specificity within a more inclusive framework of deduction and inference.

Maslaha

Maslaha is commonly translated 'utility' or 'interest', in the sense of public interest. It is generally considered a more pragmatic principle, controversial in some quarters, in terms of which rules are fashioned, in line with what brings benefit and avoids harm. Its rationale in terms of legal theory is perhaps best stated by Ghazzali (d. 1111), who postulated the aims of the law (*maqsud*, plural *maqasid*). The law, it is argued, is known to prohibit what is harmful and to institute what is beneficial for Muslims, in this life and the next. The aim is to protect life, property, mind, progeny and religion. The punishments specified in the law, for instance, have the aim of deterrence and therefore protection (Hallaq 1997:88–90). It is accepted, of course, that these criteria, based on rational deduction of the aims and from the aims, cannot override clear textual or Sunnaic rules. But they do operate in much legal reasoning, which involves derivations and interpretations, as well as the solving of novel problems and cases.

The full elaboration of the concept of *maslaha*, in the context of a detailed treatise on *maqasid al-shari'a*, the aims of *shari'a*, was effected by Abu-Ishaq al-Shatibi, an Andalusian jurist (d. 1388, see Khalid Masud 1995). Shatibi embeds his theory in a novel epistemology of law (Hallaq 1997:164–8), an 'inductive' approach. He starts from the postulated certainty of the premises of legal theory deriving as they do from revelation, but also from rational certainties and conventional knowledge of what is necessary, possible and impossible. The derivation and corroboration of legal premises and solutions must be based on a survey of all these sources, and it is in their agreement and mutual corroboration that the jurist achieves certainty (Hallaq 1997:165). The aforementioned aims of the *shari'a* – the protection of life, property, mind, progeny and religion of the Muslims – are not to be found explicitly stated in the Quran or the *sunna*. Yet, Muslims are certain of these principles, because they have been attested by a wide variety of pieces of evidence, which in their totality generate certitude (Hallaq 1997:166–7). Once these universal principles are established, legal reasoning must proceed by reference to them. Excessively harsh interpretations of the law, for instance, must be in error because they oppress Muslims, against the Quranic verse declaring the holy book to have been revealed as mercy to the world (*rahmatan lil-'alamin*). A good example is the so-called *'Araya* contract, which involves the barter of unripe dates on the tree against their value calculated in terms of edible dates. Such a contract goes against an important principle in the *shari'a* prohibiting speculative contracts. Yet jurists have allowed this exception in order to avoid hardship for growers and to facilitate their livelihood (Hallaq 1997:168). Shatibi, and other advocates of *maslaha*, insist that judgements on that basis must proceed according to legal premises and careful reasoning, and not arbitrary invocation of utility. It is a pragmatic principle, but not an arbitrary one.

We shall see in subsequent chapters how *maslaha* has been invoked by modern reformers to justify the recasting of the law in accordance with the exigencies of modern life. It was an important principle in Khomeini's ruling in 1988 empowering the Islamic government to bypass legal principles if necessitated by the public interest of Muslims (see *infra* Chapter 6:210–11), though this concept had not been favoured in Shi'i jurisprudence.

THE ORIGINS OF THE *SHARI'A*: THE HISTORICAL REGISTER

Fiqh as a systematic body of jurisprudence with distinctive modes of reasoning and argument developed at the hands of private scholars, mainly in the second and third centuries of Islam (though some would trace it to earlier decades, in the second part of the first century: Hallaq 2001). This became, in effect, the body of the *shari'a* as derived from the canonical sources, rationalized and expanded to deal with the matters which concerned Muslims in their worship and social relationships. *Fiqh* in this sense is the historically developed *shari'a* per se. *Usul al-fiqh*, the bases or principles, as developed in later periods, consists of methodological reflections on the process and validity and argument in legal discourse.

According to tradition, the four Rashidun (rightly guided) successors to the Prophet applied the maxims of the Quran, the example of the Prophet and common customary practice in their judgements. Tradition, however, ascribes to this early period the formation of the legal institutions of courts and *qadis* characteristic of later developments. *Hadith* and episodes are cited from the Prophet and his Rashidun successors to the effect that they not only acted as judges themselves but appointed judges to the provinces with instructions on procedure and probity which were to become the norms (Tyan 1960:18–25). Tyan (1960:67–82) throws doubt on these traditions, arguing that conceptions and procedures of justice of that early period were continuous with that of pre-Islamic Arabia, centring primarily on arbitration, *tahkim*, between private parties who themselves bring the dispute to a wise man with charismatic credentials. This Tyan calls 'private justice', with no conception of a public judicial authority. The Prophet himself, argues Tyan, was such an arbiter, as indeed traditions confirm. Judicial institutions and *qadi* courts, according to this argument, were products of later political and administrative developments, in which Byzantine and Persian practices were adapted and developed (Tyan 1960:83–99). Some of these issues will be taken up in the next chapter. For the present, it seems probable that the early caliphs had no systematic body of legal theory and no developed institutions for legal application: they delegated their governors and generals to rule, and law was not clearly demarcated from general administration. The Umayyad dynasty that followed the Rashidun perpetuated these practices. Governors and generals applied legal judgements and practices at their own discretion, resorting for the most part to local customary practices mixed with selected Quranic injunctions and authoritative precedents. Tyan (1960:81) recounts an anecdote from Kindi that the Umayyad governor of Egypt, Marwan one day questioned the Qadi of Cairo 'Abis Ibn Sa'id, 'do you have the Quran?' to which the *qadi* answered, 'no'. Marwan asked, 'do you know the rules of dividing inheritance?', to which the *qadi* also replied in the negative, as he did to the question on whether he could write. 'How, then, can you reach a judgement?' retorted the governor. The *qadi* responded, 'I judge according to what I know, and what I don't know I ask'. Marwan then patted him on the back and said 'Go! You are a good judge'.

Early jurisprudence started towards the end of the Umayyad period at the hands of private men, not government functionaries. There was a general perception of the Umayyads as worldly kings, with little regard for religion. Pious men in Mecca and Madina, as well as the new bourgeoisie of the garrison cities, set about trying to preserve and develop a way of life consistent with the divine commands. Some, like Abu Layla (d. 148), were judges (later, under the Abbasids), others, like Abu Hanifa (d. 150), remained 'theoreticians'. Initially, the schools of law followed the living traditions of particular localities, and were known by their local identification, such as Kufian, Basrian and Madinese. They had as their 'raw material' existing legal and administrative practices under the Umayyads: '... it is safe to say that Muhamaddan legal science started in the later part of the Umaiyad period, taking the legal practice of the time as its raw material and endorsing, modifying, or rejecting it ...' (Schacht 1953:190). Hallaq dates the beginning of this proto-legal development earlier, to the second half of the first Islamic century, in the cities of the Hijaz.

Schacht goes on to show how two processes were cumulatively at work in this activity: systematization and Islamization (Schacht 1953:283–87). Coinciding with and feeding the growth of legal tradition was the new science of *hadith*: the retrospective collection, sifting and validating the traditions of the Prophet, and to a lesser extent the companions. Increasingly, legal judgement and reasoning had to be justified in terms of this growing body of validated *hadith*. At the same time, the increasing body of judgements, arguments and disputations constituted a pressure for consistency and systematicity, and for making explicit the criteria of judgement and validity of argument. Schacht, and others have argued that Shafi'i (b.767), who lived and worked in Egypt at the turn of the third century of the Islamic era, was the most thorough systematizer. I shall turn to Shafi'i's achievements after examining more detailed characterization of the formative period of Muslim jurisprudence.

THE FORMATIVE PERIOD

Schacht's account, local traditions, gradually systematized and Islamicized over the first two centuries, and the role of Shafi'i in the process, is challenged in its detail, periodization and the 'mechanics' of the process by later scholars, notably Calder (1993), and in a different vein, Hallaq (1997). Let us examine some of these issues.

The development of the *shari'a* as a systematic body of texts and practices divided into schools and traditions was the product of the first three centuries of Islam (Schacht, Calder, Hallaq). The loci of these formations were the urban centres of Arabia, the Middle East, North Africa and Spain, in which Muslims and Arabs engaged in a cultural synthesis with the existing traditions, norms and practices. While these had pre-Islamic roots, the synthesis developed in the idiom of Islam, or in relation to it. Christians, Jews and Zoroastrians were participants in this urban life, springing from common Middle Eastern traditions. The parallels and common elements between Jewish and Muslim law, for instance, attributed by some to the Jewish influence on Islam, can be better understood as the development of common local traditions in a shared milieu (see discussion in Calder 1993:209–17. Calder also stresses the considerable differences).

Schacht, as we saw, argued that the early *fuqaha* worked on rationalizing and textualizing common practice, taken as 'raw material'. All the authors cited agree, more or less, with this general description. The constant endeavour of the early jurists was to inject religious content and authority into the common practices developing from a mixture of scriptural and prophetic precedents and local customary conduct. This injection took the form of attribution of principles and practices to sacred sources, increasingly those of prophetic narrations, designated *sunna*. 'This process of projecting legal doctrines backward, mainly from the Successors and the Companions, and ultimately to the Prophet, was a lengthy one; it began some time towards the end of the first century and continued well into the third' (Hallaq 1997:17). Hallaq goes on to show how with each generation the number of *hadiths* quoted and the degree to which rules are anchored to them increase steadily. Abu Hanifa (d. 150/767) and his contemporaries had a small number of *hadiths* at their disposal, and ones which were later considered weak by *hadith* critics. He and his contemporaries referred to the *sunna*, but the technical verification of the *sunna* in terms of reliable prophetic reports was not established at that point.

> ...Awza'i [a Syrian contemporary of Abu Hanifa] viewed the practice (= sunna) of his community as having been continuous since the Prophet, and as having been maintained throughout by the caliphs and the scholars. Awza'i, in other words, projects the entire body of doctrine, including the elements of provincial customary practice, back to the Prophet, without, however, feeling bound to adduce formal reports. [Hallaq 1997:17]

This backward projection continues, but with increasing insistence on 'formal reports' to tie the practices firmly to the sacred sources. Successive generations of scholars displayed a greater reliance on the prophetic narrations and the methodology of their verification. Al-Shaybani (d. 804) was the first to insist that no legal ruling can be valid unless it is based on a binding text of the Quran or a prophetic *hadith* (Hallaq 1997:18). This textual rigorism in the construction of the law was completed by al-Shafi'i (d. 204/820). Hence Schacht's attribution of the ultimate Islamization of the law to this figure.

Norman Calder (1993), critical of Schacht's periodization and characterizations of the early texts, gives interesting accounts of the development of ideas and texts in the urban social context of those early centuries, culminating in the 'canonization' and the establishment of authority of the competing schools.

In the earlier period, in the first two centuries, the scholars are not clearly identified in the juristic literature as a social group, and there were no systematic rules relating to the profession of scholarship, to training or qualifications: 'the inference seems permissible that the status of scholar was initially informal and undefined' (Calder 1993:164). Scholars were elders and notables who enjoyed dignity and respect in the community. They were from various walks of life, merchants, craftsmen, even soldiers, one mud-brick maker, but also judges and princes (Calder 1993:181). The discourse they conducted was predominantly oral, in line with the general character of literary pursuits of the time.

The picture which emerges from Calder's account (based on the biographical, *tabaqat*, literature of North Africa and the *adab*, *belles-lettres*, literature of Iraq) is one of informal gatherings (*majlis*, plural *majalis*, use of the verb *jalasa*, to sit together) in which legal issues were debated and in which authoritative voices were heard. The locations of these *majalis* were varied, from mosques to shops in the market, to the court of a scholarly prince (Calder

1993:168). Some princes and judges would gather people of opposing views in their *majalis* and encourage them to debate. Writing and books entered these milieus, indeed they constituted an important part of third-century culture. When it came to legal literature, however, they were mostly of a peculiar kind, as we shall see presently.

These *majalis*, while informal and mostly open, were not always egalitarian. Figures of learning and authority, including jurists such as Malik (d.795) and Sahnun (d.819), whose doctrines and works were later to become authoritative, were among the voices in these gatherings. Indeed, the word *majlis* was attributed to the figure of authority, sometimes referred to as *sahib al-majlis*, a participant is said to have 'sat with', *jalasa*, the figure of authority and reference. Some of the listeners kept notebooks, called *sama'* (auditions, that which is heard) of their discourse. In the biographical literature, a person is said to have *sama'* from Malik or some other authority (Calder 1993:172). The writer of the notebook would then verify with the speaker that his account was indeed an accurate and faithful version. He would do this by reading his *sama'* to the speaker, and upon confirmation of its correctness the note-taker would then be free to disseminate the contents. Others would acquire notebooks of auditions, then add to them what they have gleaned. Eventually major compendia of particular legal traditions emerged, based on collections of the *sama'*. The *Mudawwana* of Sahnun, which was to become a canonical source of Maliki *fiqh*, probably evolved from such compendia. Similarly, the *Muwatta'* of Malik was not authored by Malik, but spoken by him (Calder 1993:175). One listener, Abd al-Aziz b. Yahya al-Madani, heard from Malik the *muwatta'* and other things, then heard also from other figures in the Maliki tradition. Abd al-Aziz then recited these works 'from memory'. Those who heard from him made notes, and these notes are the 'books' of Abd al-Aziz. Calder sums up: 'It is likely that Abd al-Aziz heard from Malik and transmitted what he liked, or remembered, or thought he had heard: that those in turn who heard from him made notes and that these notes are the "books" of Abd al-Aziz' (Calder 1993:175).

Over the course of the third century the trends in legal discourse and practice were towards greater formalization, writing and authorship and the professionalization of a class of *fuqaha*, practitioners and theoreticians of the law. This process was partly due to the competition between the schools and, crucially, to the increasing integration of the law into political power and government, and its bureaucratization. The establishment of definitive schools (*madhahib*) of law implies canonical authority, and that in turn, is most likely to emerge in interaction with political authority. Calder cites *Kitab al-Kharaj* of Abu Yusuf (d.182/798), a treatise on taxation and administration, as an example of this interconnection with political authority. It is the participation of jurists in government institutions that led to the establishment of school authority and the canonization of texts. Calder cites the disappearance of the Malikis of Baghdad as an example of what happens when a school failed to integrate into the political institutions, while the influence of the Malikis of al-Andalus and Qayrawan (Tunisia) led to the canonization of the *Muwatta'* of Malik and the *Mudawwana* of Sahnun (Calder 1993:163–64).

To sum up, in Calder's words:

> The third century sees a movement from a jurisprudence which is a predominantly oral and socially diffuse informal process towards a jurisprudence which is a complex literary discipline, the prerogative of a highly trained and socially distinct elite. That movement (not transition, for the end of the process was centuries off), signalled by the terms professionalization and bureaucratization, was no doubt part of natural process but was also affected by school competition and government policy. [Calder 1993:164]

A parallel process is that of what Schacht called 'Islamization'. The competition between the schools led to the search for authoritative backing for each school's particular formulations and interpretations, initially derived from a variety of sources and circumstances, including some religious texts and narrations, now to be made more authoritative through a selection of prophetic narrations (*hadith*) and interpretations of Quranic texts. This process sharpened the hermeneutic skills of the jurists in confronting the actual principles and practice with canonical sources, and manipulating the latter to obtain authoritative backing. This is the process of development of legal methodology and reasoning, of *usul al-fiqh*, which is part of the professionalization of the jurists.

The chronology of the evolution of legal thought in the third century, according to Calder's account, is the following: the formulation of rules and reflection upon them comes first and is put forward in the terminology of *ra'y*, opinion. Eventually the justification of rules is sought in preceding juristic authority, such as Malik or Abu Hanifa. At a subsequent stage, and driven by competition between schools to justify their particular rules, arises the appeal to prophetic precedent, now developed in the discipline of *'ilm al-hadith*, the compilation and verification of prophetic narrative. At this point there is a polemic of *ahlu-al-hadith* against *ahlu-al-ra'y*, one compounded by other intellectual and political contests between philosophers and mystics on the one side and jurists on the other, challenging the legitimacy of opinion and speculation not fully backed by prophetic precedent. The advocates of *hadith* win, and it then becomes obligatory to justify rules and procedures by derivation from prophetic precedent. The last stage is the introduction of scriptural sanction, the articulation of the rules so far developed to texts from the Quran. 'Chronologically the last stage, this [scriptural sanction] became, ideologically, the first principle of Islamic legal justification … The Qur'an was an influence on the law, usually secondary and intrusive' (Calder 1993:218–19).

This chronology, then, is the opposite of the ideological and expositional order of the *shari'a*, which privileges the scriptures as the starting point and the ultimate authority, followed by prophetic narrations of *sunna* and *hadith*. This variance between the chronology advanced by some scholars and the ideological bases of faith in the divine origin of the law, is an important point in later and modern political debates on the *shari'a*.

SHAFI'I'S ACHIEVEMENT

Schacht (1953:11–20) assigns great importance to Shafi'i's *Risala* as a singular achievement in laying the bases of *usul-al-fiqh*, and many scholars, including Calder, largely concur. It lays down the basic structure and logic of legal epistemology and reasoning, to be developed by subsequent jurists. I shall turn to the nature of these achievements presently, but first, a note on periodization. The *Risala* is, naturally, dated within Shafi'i's lifetime, at the turn of the third century. Calder argues that the book should be dated to a much later period, c. 300, that is to say long after Shafi'i's death (Calder 1993:242). This fits in with Calder's argument on authorship: the text as we know it is the product of annotation and redaction of earlier collected pronouncements by the master. Part of Calder's evidence for this supposition is that the legal literature of the third century does not show any awareness of the advances achieved by the *Risala*. Hallaq attributes the neglect of Shafi'i's achievements in third-century legal literature to the conflict between 'traditionalists' and 'rationalists' (more presently) (Hallaq 1997:34–35). Shafi'i, according to this argument, achieved a unique synthesis and compromise between the two positions, which neither was prepared to concede. It was only the weakening of the rationalists that led them to approach the traditionalist position and the synthesis was achieved. We can only note these conflicting interpretations, while retaining the interest in Calder's argument on authorship.

Muslims, as recipients of revelation, argued Shafi'i, were duty-bound to follow the dictates of the scriptures, which were divine commandments. Revelations are all-encompassing and cover all aspects of life. It follows that Muslims are duty-bound to seek knowledge, *'ilm*, of the divine revelations, by which they must live. Shafi'i then establishes the authoritative bases of the *sunna*: prophetic narrative and precedent, for the Prophet was following the commands of God, and God made it incumbent upon the Muslim to obey the Prophet (Hallaq 1997:21–35). The *sunna* elaborates and clarifies the Quran, making rules explicit. Further, the Quran and the *sunna* provide indications, *dalalat*, which provides a rationale for *ijtihad*, or *qiyas*, the exercise of reason and the tracing of analogies, to arrive at rules not explicitly stated in the sacred sources. Shafi'i then proclaims the legitimacy of difference of interpretation, *ikhtilaf*. Knowledge is of two kinds: the certain, the rules explicit in the canonical sources, and the probable, *zann*, the product of deduction and analogy. This argument provided the basis for the mutual tolerance between the schools, proclaiming the legitimacy of difference (Calder 1993:242). This step establishes overall unity between the diverse geographically based schools. The notion of variation was built into the system, its consequences no longer disruptive. Shafi'i delimited the range of *ijtihad* to strict adherence to the limits of the text and what it allows. This is distinct from the free play of reason claimed by the contemporary *ahlu-al-ra'y*.

Shafi'i is also credited with the beginnings of hermeneutic rules and skills: how to reconcile apparent contradictions in the canonical sources; the idea of *naskh*, abrogation, when one verse in the Quran is said to be abrogated by a later one, such as the prohibition on wine-drinking coming after verses that allowed it, and the rationale of this abrogation. The *Risala* also provided the epistemological bases for the professionalization of the *ulama* by making a distinction between general religious knowledge available to all, such as that regarding the obligations of prayer and fasting, and the specialized knowledge of the scholars and their hermeneutic skills in arriving at rules and judgements. Calder (1993: 243) argues that this step also 'liberated the juristic tradition into aesthetic and intellectual play; also permitted the remarkable development of the juristic literature that is classical fiqh'. These developments included a continuity of debate, arising from the acknowledged uncertainty of knowledge. The debate further generated ever elaborate structures of text, argument and commentary. The *fiqh* literature increasingly acquires its own logic and structure, and its practitioners increasingly follow the logical imperatives of the system.

Finally a note on the contest, already mentioned, between 'rationalism' and 'traditionalism'. The early centuries of Islam witnessed a flourishing of philosophy and mysticism, influenced by Hellenistic and oriental traditions in the Middle East. The early Abbasid period featured a prominent philosophical school of the Mu'tazila,[4] embracing and elaborating the sciences, mathematics, as well as religion and mysticism. These were opposed by the religious 'fundamentalists' who tried to restrict knowledge and reflection to the boundaries of the revealed text, read literally, and the *sunna* (a movement that was to recur in Islam up to the present day). The 'rationalists' argued that reason was given by God and preceded revelation: knowledge of good and evil was part of this reason, and could be employed in the development of norms. Orthodox theology, closely associated with Ash'ari (d. 935) rejected this view, insisting that revelation was the only source of norms. No law could be valid unless contained in or derived directly from the sacred sources (Watt 1973:303–18). The philosophical trend in matters of law was towards the free play of reason, with reference to the sacred sources but not entirely limited by them; these were *ahlu-al-ra'y*, opposed by the traditionalists, *ahlu-al-hadith*. The latter ultimately won the battle and established strict adherence to the sacred sources as the bases of legal methodology. Hallaq argues that Shafi'i, in securing a place for *ijtihad* and *qiyas*, effected a compromise between the two sides. One can only remark that it was a heavily skewed compromise, incorporating all the canonical rules of the traditionalists, with a light leaven of strictly delimited reasoning, without which no legal system could function. Ghazzali at a later point incorporated the logic of Greek philosophy into Muslim legal and theological theorizing, while retaining the now orthodox insistence on the supremacy of the sources. This legalistic orthodoxy was to predominate in Muslim religious thought over the subsequent centuries, divorcing it from philosophy, which developed its own separate practices and discourses.[5] This orthodoxy, however, was increasingly subverted by Sufi mysticism, mixed with various heterodoxies (mostly Alid and Shi'i) such as Ismailism. Imami Shi'ism, to the present day, shares some of the rationalist positions. Its doctrines insist, for instance, on the justice, *'adl*, of God. God could not have pre-ordained all human actions and then proceeded to punish the actors for the sins they committed. It follows, then, that God must have created men with free will. This doctrine was one of the basic issues of conflict between rationalists (such as the Mu'tazila) and the traditionists. The latter insisted that God, being all-powerful and all-seeing had determined every-thing in the world, including men's actions, and it is not for us to reflect on his purpose or judgement.

THE GATE OF *IJTIHAD*: IS IT CLOSED?

It is commonly stated that in the Sunni schools, the 'gate of *ijtihad*' was closed at some stage, often assumed to be the third or fourth century. The formation of the four schools and the recognition of their canonical status (to the detri-ment of others), it is assumed, 'fixed' the main contours of *fiqh* and substantive law, and left no room for *ijtihad*. Jurists from then on would follow the authority of the founders (*taqlid*), their canons being contained in the major texts and early commentaries. Rather than independent *ijtihad*, arguments and rulings would have to be sought in the existing corpus. It is further argued that the authoritative *ijma'* of previous generations was binding on jurists, thus further restricting the scope of *ijtihad*. This feature of Sunni schools is often advanced as a distinction from Shi'i *fiqh*, which sanctioned and required independent *ijtihad*, recognizing the rank of *mujtahid* as the highest in the clerical hierarchy. This is also the position challenged by modern reformers and fundamentalists alike, asserting their right to practise *ijtihad* to arrive at novel formulations in line with their respective projects.

Contrary to what we may be led to expect from this proclamation of the closure of *ijtihad*, we find many jurists throughout the history of *fiqh* who exercised independent judgement to reach novel theoretical as well as substantive formulations. Hallaq (1997:143–61; 1984) traces the controversy which resulted in the generalization of this position to the sixth century, when some Hanafi and Maliki jurists argued that there were no longer any *mujtahids*, and that the practitioners of each school must follow authority. Their arguments were opposed by Hanbalis and some Shafiʻis, who insisted on the necessity of *ijtihad* at all times, indeed on the religious duty (*fardh kifaya*) of the learned to practise it on behalf of the community. At issue in this argument was whether *ijtihad* is a necessary qualification for *ifta'*, and that a mufti must be *ipso facto* a *mujtahid*. Hallaq states that until that point *ijtihad* was considered a necessary qualification, and one direction of the argument against the continuation of *ijtihad* was the denial of the necessity of this qualification for a mufti.

It seems, then, that the assertion of the closure of the gate of *ijtihad* became a common position in all the schools except the Hanbali. However, as Hallaq shows, this position cannot be sustained in the light of the actual legal developments in subsequent periods. He cites the case of the Andalusian jurist Ibn Rushd in sixth-century Cordoba, who issued a *fatwa* contradicting an actual judgement in a case of murder. The victim left young children and a brother with adult children. The rule that gives the 'heirs' the right to choose between demanding the execution of the culprit or their forgiveness against a monetary compensation was given by the judge to the brother and nephews, in view of the minority of the children, who were the primary heirs. This would be the ruling that would follow from the general rules and precedents of the Maliki school. Ibn Rushd's *fatwa* contradicted this judgement, asserting that the resolution of the case should await the majority of the children, backing this conclusion with arguments from Quranic texts and prophetic traditions as well as analogies. Hallaq concludes: 'Ibn Rushd's contribution can by no means be considered an exception, and when considered alongside many of the other juriconsults' fatwas in which ijtihad was practised, it becomes only too easy to dismiss the claim that the "gate of ijtihad" was closed' (Hallaq 1997:160). Why, then, is this claim so persistent and insistent? And why have the modernists found it necessary to refute it? The answers to these questions are probably to be sought outside the confines of legal theory.

The course of development of substantive law (as against legal theory) may give some support to the assertion of the 'closure of the gate'. It is generally agreed that substantive law, in the form of a corpus of positive legal rulings on the whole range of issues covered by the *shariʻa*, was set in its authoritative form in the first two centuries of Islam. Hallaq himself emphasizes this closure:

Of course, reformulation of the substantive legal rulings belonging to the early period in accordance with the systematic demands of later legal theory was out of the question. For this, if it was carried out on any significant scale, would amount to a grave violation of consensus. It would have constituted a deliberate and conscious departure from that law on which the early fathers and eponyms had agreed. More serious was the glaring implication of such a step, namely, an acknowledgement that the law that constituted the foundation of earlier Muslim society was wrong. [Hallaq 1997:130]

The task of legal theory thereafter was to set this substantive law within a structure of derivations, proofs and justifications. This is a history of ever-increasing systematicity, sophistication and elaboration of hermeneutic technique to harmonize these rules with the canonical sources and to solve new problems as they arise. Does not this fixity of substantive law, in its respective schools, constitute a kind of closure? There is, of course, a tendency of all intellectual, and certainly legal, systems towards closure. But the continuity of such tendencies and their resistance to innovation are not always successful. They are occasionally overcome with exigencies arising from political, economic and cultural changes, and Muslim legal thought and practice is no exception.

Baber Johansen, in an interesting study of the transformations of Hanafi law on land rent in Ottoman times, outlines two mechanisms of change in Islamic law: the *sharh* (commentary or exegesis), and the *fatwa* (authoritative ruling) (Johansen 1988, 1993). The dominant doctrines of the schools of law are recorded in the founding texts: these are the *mutun* (plural of *matn*). Each generation of scholars within the school add their contributions to the text in the form of *shuruh* (plural of *sharh*) written in the margins of the main text. These commentaries are often in the nature of explication and amplification of the text, which often involve innovation (Johansen 1993:31–32). Johansen demonstrates, however, that they can also make radical alterations of the rules in the text, even reversals. The *fatwa*, while supposed in theory to be consistent with the *mutun* of the school, do in practice alter or reverse some of these if there is a sufficiently authoritative body of opinion in its support (Johansen 1993:35–36).

Johansen's case study illustrates these processes of innovation. Early Hanafi law – up to the eleventh and twelfth centuries – regarded rent on agricultural land as determined by contract, which was the necessary condition for the payment of rent. At that point in time, there was a shift in legal opinion away from the necessity of contract and into recognition of the local customary practices of land use and share-cropping, and regarding these local rules as binding even without a contract (Johansen 1993:39–41). Later on, from thirteenth to sixteenth centuries, these and further changes were systematized to conform with the practices of Turkish dynasties, which regarded arable lands as state possessions, and tended to blur the distinction between rent and tax.

The dispossessed peasant became subject to coercive rather than contractual obligations to the authorities and landlords, and *awqaf*, endowments, in various relations to authority and to the land (Johansen 1993:42–47).

Johansen shows that the jurists are explicit in their recognition of the divergence of these laws, embodied in *shuruh*, *fatawa* (plural of *fatwa*) and judicial practice, from the *mutun* of the original texts:

> They do not, though, consider the new doctrine to be a substitute or replace-
> ment of the old doctrine. The validity of the old and the new doctrine is, rather,
> a matter of the literary genre in which they are applied. There is no doubt that
> on the level of the *mutun* – and for teaching purposes – the early legal doctrine
> remains dominant. But on the level of the *shuruh* and the *fatawa* – and for
> judicial practice – the new doctrine supersedes the old one. [Johansen 1993:46]

The picture we get from Johansen's study is one of pragmatic flexibility and the recognition of the necessity of change in line with the exigencies of power and administration. At the same time, the theoretical continuity with the founders is maintained at the academic and literary levels, as well as in some aspects of practice, in this case that of subsistence farming in some marginal cases (Johansen 1993:46). This flexibility is also a means of the jurists maintaining their authority over judicial and administrative practice, by narrating the new practices of power in the vocabulary of *shari'a* and *fiqh*. I shall elaborate on this theme in Chapter 3.

THE TEXT

The *shari'a* is located in texts, institutions and practices, which at various points of Muslim history constituted complexes of power and knowledge. Let us first examine the textual component of these complexes (institutions will be considered in Chapter 2).

The Quran stands at the apex of a hierarchy of texts. As we have seen, it is considered as the direct speech of God. It is the only text that is original and not derivative. As divine revelation it is the highest authority, the ultimate source, in terms of which other texts have to be validated. It constitutes the starting point in all religious and legal education. Children go to Quranic schools to be taught reading and writing so that they can read, memorize and recite the holy text. Every Muslim – even the illiterate – must memorize key verses in order to be able to utter his or her daily prayers.

An essential characteristic of the Quran, however, is its 'orality': The very word connotes 'recitation', from the Arabic *qara'a*, 'to recite' ('to read' in modern usage, which creates some ambiguity in translation; most scholars now agree on 'recite'. See Messick 1993:22). The manner of its revelation, *inzal*, was the angel

Gabriel's recitation of the verses to Muhammad, who memorized them to recite in turn to the Muslims. Muhammad was said to be illiterate (*rasulun umiyyun*), as a verse in the Quran declares. The Quran was preserved predominantly in the memory of the early Muslims, affirmed in repeated recitations, fragments written down in various forms, until collected in authoritative textual form by the Caliph Uthman (d.656). Though written, the essential medium for knowledge of the Quran is the voice of the reciter. The enunciation of the verses by the voice remains the most reliable form of knowing the text. Given the absence of vowels in Arabic writing, save for diacritical signs, often omitted, the written word can be ambiguous, only clarified by voicing it aloud. The study of the book is always through recitation and memorization. Memorizing the Quran remains a great virtue, and children and adults continue in this quest to the present day. In present-day Egypt, for instance, there are charitable societies whose sole objective is to help people memorize the book (*tahfiz al-Quran*). Recitation follows certain musical modalities, *maqams*, and is an elaborate art perfected by the professionals, recited on many occasions in different settings (now, regularly on radio and television, recorded on cassettes and CDs), and much appreciated by the cognoscenti.

The Quran sets a paradigm to all other texts, especially in the priority of oral recitation over the written word. Traditional (mostly pre-print, but the practice survived printing) teaching and learning of the books of *fiqh*, for instance, took the form of teachers reciting the text to pupils, in the form of dictation. The pupils wrote down the text, but mostly as a means to memorization, for one only truly knew what one committed to memory. Pupils then verified the accuracy of their noted text with the teachers, thus securing their own copies of the key texts.

Mitchell (1988) raises the question of the authorial presence in the text. The conventional assumption is that writing mechanically represents what is in the author's mind on the written page, ' ... if it can make an absent author present to a reader, this is because it is in the nature of words to operate as the representatives of singular meanings' (Mitchell 1988:150). These assumptions, argues Mitchell, did not fully prevail in Arab thinking on writing. He quotes Ibn Khaldun (Mitchell 1988:150–51) on the ambiguity of the written text until read aloud. Mute reading does not render the meaning: only the voice and the pronunciation can clarify meaning (related to absence of vowels). It follows that the reading of the text is always an interpretation. The author's presence in the text can only be guaranteed, it follows, if the author is reading. Indeed, Mitchell cites examples of how the only fully competent teacher is considered to be the author of the text. Failing that, the teacher should be one who has heard the author read or teach the text, or, at another remove, a teacher who can trace a chain of narrations, much like *hadith*, ending in the author. Mitchell quotes an example from the city of Nishapur in which those wishing to study the *Sahih* of

Bukhari (one of two canonical collections of *hadith*), 'travelled two hundred miles to the town of Kushmaihan, near Marv where there was a man who recited the text from a copy made from Bukhari's own dictation'.[6] Similarly, Messick quotes the example of a Yemeni scholar who travelled to Mecca in 1184 to hear the recitation of Muslim's *Sahih*. He returned to his home town to teach that text in the same recitational way by which he learnt it, then in turn licensed a number of local scholars to transmit to their students (Messick 1993:24).

Though writing constituted an essential part of Muslim religious and legal scholarship, this emphasis on orality and recitation as a privileged medium of truth continued until recent times, as we shall have occasion to note.

Second in the hierarchy of texts is *hadith*. In reality, *hadith* is the primary canonical source of *fiqh*. Rules contained in the Quran, however few or many, cover a limited area of social and economic life. *Sunna*, and particularly *hadith*, are considered decisive sources in interpreting and generalizing Quranic rules, as well as being essential sources for rules not contained in the book. We saw how in the process of the formation of *fiqh* traditions in the first three centuries of Islam, protagonists of different opinions and arguments appealed to prophetic narrations to support their arguments, a process that culminated with Ibn Hanbal, then Shafi'i, in the Islamization of the *shari'a*. Rigorous attribution and derivation from *hadith* became the ultimate criteria for the validity of rules and judgements. In the process many *hadiths* were invented or doctored to suit arguments.

This process led to the proliferation of *hadiths*, advanced to justify a variety of legal, political and sectarian interests. Some of what was put in the mouth of the Prophet were versions of Jewish, Christian or Greek materials, aphorisms and legends (and some of those persisted in the later canonical collections) (Gibb 1962b:51). Pious scholars, alarmed at this proliferation, sought to control it by introducing rigorous criteria of validity, that of *isnad* and of *'ilm al-rijal*. *Isnad* (from *sanad*, backing, support) consisted in a chain of transmission for each *hadith*, connecting the ultimate narrator, through intermediaries, to a companion of the Prophet: 'It was told us by Abdallah Ibn Yusuf who said, it was told us by al-Laith, who had it from Yazid, who had it from Abul'Khair, who had it from Uqba Ibn Amir – he said...' (quoted in Gibb 1962b:52), where this last Uqba was a companion. The question then arises, how was the scholar to know how reliable every link in this chain was? *'Ilm al-rijal*, the science of men, arose to cope with this demand: a compilation of biographies of the different generations after that of the Prophet. These biographies would establish the character, piety and reliability of the men and women constituting the chain of *isnad*. The compiler of *hadiths* could judge the probable validity of attribution by the reputation and probity of the narrators.

A crucial requirement for the compiler and the jurist was that the narration of the *hadith* be literal, word for word. Shafi'i insisted that a good narrator should be 'capable of transmitting the hadith letter for letter [*bi-hurifihi*] as he heard it ... If he transmits only the meaning and is unaware of what might alter its sense, he might unknowingly transmute the lawful into the unlawful and vice versa' (quoted by Messick 1993:26). Summaries and paraphrases supposed to convey the gist or the meaning were considered dangerous, the transmitted *hadith* must be a literal memorization of what was heard.

On the bases of these procedures, two canonical compilations of *hadith* emerged in the third century, both called *al-Sahih*, the accurate or sound, one by al-Bukhari (d.870), the other by Muslim (d.875). These two, especially the first, acquired canonical authority, only next to the Quran (Gibb 1962b:53). *Hadiths* not contained in them were considered weak and unreliable, while those included became authoritative.

Bukhari's *Sahih* is divided into 97 books, subdivided into 3450 chapters, adding up to 2762 *hadiths*, many repeated in different contexts. Each book contains *hadiths* pertaining to a particular subject, 'such as prayer, fasting, alms, testimony, buying and selling, surety, marriage' (Gibb 1962b:53).

These *Sahihs* furnished material for jurists and theologians to sustain arguments and judgements. The elaboration of the legal system in subsequent generations required further authoritative material not contained in the two compilations, and legal scholars collected further *hadiths* to cope with these needs. Of these, four compilations emerged as authoritative, though of lesser ranks than the *Sahihs*, those of Abu Dawud (d.888), Al-Nasa'i (d.915), al-Tirmidhi (d.892) and Ibn Maja (d.896) (Gibb 1962b:55).

While jurists working in the mainstream traditional schools have continued to treat the *hadiths* contained in the *Sahihs* as canonical, doubt and scepticism were voiced from various quarters. Sectarian Quranic fundamentalists, such as the Khawarij[7] did not go along with *hadith* attributions, while the Shi'a developed its own authoritative collections based on narrations by and of its 12 imams. In the modern period reformers trying to reshape the law in relation to modern exigencies have raised doubts about some *hadiths* which seemed to impede their task. In particular, the many *hadiths* considered inimical to women's status, their moral standing and their participation in community affairs have been questioned by reformers and feminists, trying to find in Islam a woman-friendly content. A notable writer in this vein in recent times is Fatima al-Mernissi. She questions many of the *hadiths* regarding women, especially those traced to the companion Abu Harira. She argues that the participation of the Prophet's widow Ayisha in the sectarian battles which followed his death motivated a campaign of vilification not only of Ayisha, but of women, raising doubts about their moral status and their right to participate in community politics, supported by invented *hadiths* (Mernissi 1991:49–81).

The texts coming after the Quran and the authoritative collections of *hadiths* are the founding books of *fiqh*, primarily those of the eponymous masters of the schools and their immediate disciples. For the Hanafi school, Abu Yusuf's *Kitab al-Kharaj* is one such source. Malik's *Muwatta'* and the *Mudawwana* of Sahnun are the main early references. Ibn Hanbal's *Musnad*, as well as a number of early Hanbali works and Shafi'i's *Risala* and *Kitab al-Umm*, are primary sources for their respective schools.

We have noted Calder's arguments on the process of authorship of these works, and the way in which oral recitations were noted, checked and written. Malik recited his *Muwatta'*, and disciples heard it, and some noted it down, checked it with Malik, then circulated it. Calder argued, from textual analysis and periodization of influences, that Shafi'i's *Risala* in its present form could not have been completed in Shafi'i's lifetime, and bears the marks of later developments. Given this process of authorship through recitation, dictation and selective writing, the setting of authoritative texts in the forms that came down to us must have undergone some evolutions and mutations in the process of authorship. Much of this process is one of systematization and Islamization noted by Schacht and others.

The centuries following the formative period of the schools of law witnessed many innovators who introduced new ideas and concepts. Ghazzali introduced Aristotelian logic to the methods of argument and deduction in *fiqh*. Ibn Rushd (d.1198) was another innovator, drawing on Greek philosophy and developing new theological ideas with an input into *fiqh*. Ibn Taimiya (d.1328) challenged the conventional division between *shari'a* and *siyasa*, as the respective realms of the jurist and the administrator, by putting forward the concept of *al-siyasa al-shar'iya*, the legal, *shar'i* bases of policy and administration. Shatibi (d.1388) introduced the concept of *maqasid al-shari'a*, the aims or intentions of *shari'a*. When combined with an elaborated notion of *maslaha*, interest or utility, it gave the jurist considerable scope for innovations adjusting rules to current needs and requirements.

All these texts offered the jurist resources for developing and elaborating rules and judgements and their backing in authority and logic. We considered Johansen's study above in which he shows how innovations arising from political and administrative exigencies are incorporated into the *mutun* of authoritative texts in the form of *shuruh*. Some of the innovations and elaborations, however, were not those arising from practical demands, but hypothetical questions invented by the authors, as exercises in juridical ingenuity. This is the form of discourse, designated 'casuistry', prevalent in *fiqh* literature, which will be considered in what follows.

The *shari'a*, we should remember, is primarily a body of working law, one that is applied in courts and notaries. For those functionaries engaged in the application of the law, theoretical sophistication and casuistic arguments were not of much use. For their needs, each school of law developed handbooks containing the rules of that school classified by subject-matter. These books had titles like *Minhaj*, programme, or *Mukhtasar*, summary or abridgement. These became handbooks for students to memorize (for, as we have seen, that was considered the most secure form of learning), and for judges to refer to in their everyday work. Some such works were versified to facilitate memorization and recitation (Messick 1993:26–27).

We should recall that every work of *fiqh* was composed within a tradition and had a 'genealogy'. A text belongs to a school, and each scholar composes text as a commentary or elaboration on his or her predecessors, from founding authorities to immediate teachers. The written page contains the traces of the process of transmission, in the form of commentaries, *sharh*, written in the margins and between the lines. These commentaries become an integral part of the text. In the process of teaching, teachers will recite passages from the text, then explicate it and elaborate on it to students: this is *sharh*. The written page parallels this oral transmission and explication. The commentary is integrated into the text, and gives it further meaning and clarity. This complex is transmitted in turn to the next generation, who may add further commentaries to the text. We have seen how the *shuruh* can constitute a medium of innovation. The process of commentary and explication is especially pertinent to the handbook genre of *mukhtasar*, which is so condensed that its bare sentences often require elaboration to be fully clarified.

EXAMPLE OF A JURISTIC TEXT: NAWAWI'S *MINHAJ AL-TALIBIN*

Al-Minhaj is a standard Shafi'i text much used as a textbook for students and as a reference book for judges and scholars. It was written by the Syrian scholar Muhyi al-Din al-Nawawi (d. 1277). The book was translated into French by one L. W. C. Van den Berg, and published in 1882 by the government of the Netherlands Indies (now Indonesia), for the purpose of facilitating the colonial administration and the application of the Shafi'i doctrine, predominant in those territories in the courts. Van den Berg wrote:

> From year to year European control over Muslim peoples is extending, so that it is unnecessary to insist upon the importance of rendering the two works that form the basis of the legal literature of the School of Shafii accessible, not only to a small number of Arabic scholars, but also to magistrates and political agents. [Quoted by E. C. Howard, the translator of Van den Berg's French translation into English. Minhaj al-Talibin 1914, *A manual of Muhammadan Law According to the School of Shafii*, London: Thacker and Co. Prefatory Note]

Howard's translation was for the purpose of its application in the territories of
Aden (south Yemen), colonized by the British, and following the Shafi'i school.[8]

Nawawi informs us in his introduction that he bases his work upon the
Moharrar of Abu Kasim al-Rafi'i (d. 1226), which he praises highly for its concise
and exhaustive account of the doctrines of the school. 'Its prolixity, however, is
an obstacle to this work being learnt by heart... and consequently it appeared
to me to be useful to compose an abridgement of it...' (xi). The necessity of
memorization as the true form of learning dictates the production of abridgements. Messick (1993:19–22) elaborates on this process in his study of the
learning and practice of law in the Yemeni town of Ibb, where two abridgements
were the standard texts: Nawawi's and the even shorter *al-Mukhtasar* of Abu
Shuja', dating to the twelfth century. Study by recitation and memorization
continued in the academy of Ibb until recent times, only challenged by the
advent of printing and modern educational institutions.

The *Minhaj* is divided into 71 chapters (or books), each treating a particular
subject. Book 1 is devoted to purity (*tahara*), specifying forms and causes of
impurity and the ritual requirements for removing them, the prohibitions
applying to the person in such a state. It covers bodily functions, the pollution
they engender and the prescribed forms of washing and bathing. The following
books treat prayer (*sala*), funeral ceremonies, alms contribution (*zakat*), fasting
and pilgrimage (*hajj*). These matters of worship and ritual cover the first eight
books and 122 pages of 558. The book then proceeds to transactions (*mu'amalat*),
with chapters on sale and barter, pledges, bankruptcy, partnership, companies
and related matters, land-holding, rent, share-cropping, hiring, succession and
the distribution of estates, and so on. There follow the chapters on marriage and
divorce, then on crime and penal exaction, then on miscellaneous subjects, such
as the poll-tax (*jizya*) for infidels, food prohibitions, hunting, competitions,
oaths and vows. There follow chapters on the administration of justice, court
procedure, witnesses and evidence. The *Minhaj* concludes with four chapters on
slaves and manumission.

The *Minhaj* gives an account under each of these headings of the rules
according to the Shafi'i school, exceptions, special cases and subsidiary prescriptions. It contains very little on the derivation or justification of these rules,
except by the authority of the founder and of precedent. The author is meticulous in noting disagreement of authorities, within and sometimes outside the
school on certain rulings, as well as noting Shafi'i's change of mind from the
early (Baghdad) period to the later Egyptian period. In these instances the
author notes the relative weight of the different opinions and gives his own
preference, with a rating of the degree of confidence in a particular preference.
The grounds of disagreement and the arguments for one position against
another are, however, not specified. Scriptures or *hadiths* are rarely cited,

presumably on the assumption that the founder and his successors derived these rules from the sacred sources, and an abridgement does not have to go into the arguments, merely to note disagreements and express preferences.

Many of the rules prescribed are straightforward and relate to clear cases, such as the rules for prayer, for a sale to be valid and what invalidates it. Some rules, however, pertain to highly hypothetical or obscure cases, such as the list of 'things impure in themselves' which includes: 'dogs and pigs; and any animal born of the copulation of a dog or a pig with any other – even a pure – animal' (Nawawi 1914:10).

The orality of *shari'a* culture is attested by the rules covering transactions, in which the participants are to utter particular formulae for the operation. A contract of sale is valid when mutual consent is expressed; the seller should utter an offer, 'I sell you' or 'I make you owner', to which the buyer responds 'I buy the object', or 'I accept the ownership'. Similar sets of declarations have to be uttered regarding the price. For a mute party, a sign will suffice (Nawawi 1914:123). The paradigm of the contract (and this applies to partnership, marriage, divorce and any transaction) is an oral agreement. There is hardly any mention of writing or records (although these were known though subordinate for much of Muslim legal history, as we shall see). If a dispute should subsequently arise, the evidence each party must advance is the oral testimony of witnesses to the declarations, and failing that, an oath by the plaintive.

One wonders what kind of actual social conditions in the past centuries led to the complex specifications of rules for conditional repudiation by a husband of his wife. We know that divorce and repudiation are complex affairs with financial implications. As we shall see, a husband can repudiate his wife at will, but there are degrees of repudiation: the ultimate and irrevocable is to repudiate thrice, as in the husband declaring 'you are thrice repudiated'. A husband can also swear an oath or make a vow that if certain conditions relating to third parties are not fulfilled, then he would divorce one of his wives. Such an oath can be undertaken without the knowledge of the wife. On the other hand, a wife who wishes for a divorce can only obtain it with the husband's consent, usually procured for a monetary consideration, 'buying herself back', as it were. These considerations make divorce and its condition a complex issue of domestic politics and financial arrangements. Does it, however, account for the casuistry of Nawawi's conditions and rules? Consider the following: 'If a husband calls one of his wives and another answers and he says to her, "You are repudiated", believing himself to be speaking to the wife he called, it is the wife that answers who is repudiated' (Nawawi 1914:342) (it is signalled in the text that other authorities hold different views). Is this another example of the primacy of orality and vocal declaration in contract? Consider further: 'The words, "You are repudiated if you eat a pomegranate, and if you eat the half of the pomegranate,"

result in a wife being twice repudiated if she eats a whole pomegranate'
(Nawawi 1914:342).

> When a woman has a date in her mouth and her husband repudiates her on
> condition she swallows it, and then changes his mind and makes it depend on
> her spitting it out, and then changes his mind again and makes the repudiation
> depend upon her taking the date in the hollow of her hand, and the woman on
> hearing these words quickly swallows half the date and spits out the other half,
> the condition is not considered to be fulfilled. [Nawawi 1914:343]

One wonders whether these games were ever a feature of domestic politics,
enlivening meal times, or whether these examples, which are multiplied in the
text with the more complex pomegranate and its numerous seeds, were part of
the casuistic exercises which intrigued the jurists.

Al-Nawawi's text shows how ritual acts and declarations constituted an
important part of legal procedure of contract, marriage and divorce. It also
entered into aspects of tax collection. The text prescribes the manner in which
the poll-tax (*jizya*), due from infidels under the protection of a Muslim ruler,
should be collected:

> An infidel who has to pay his poll-tax should be treated by the tax-collector with
> disdain; the collector remaining seated and the infidel standing before him, the
> head bent and the body bowed. The infidel should personally place the money
> in the balance, while the collector holds him by the beard and strikes him upon
> both cheeks. These practices however, according to some jurists, are merely
> commendable, but not obligatory, as some think. [Nawawi 1914:467]

There is no indication in the text as to what argument or authority would make
these practices commendable or obligatory. We must assume that these arguments
are conducted elsewhere, and the results reported in an abridgement.

The examples of ritual and casuistry in law should not obscure the fact that
most of the rules promulgated in relation to transactions are practical and
matter of fact, and constituted a working set of rules for the management of
business and domestic life. Ritual rules, are, of course, the substance of the
sections outlining the requirements of worship, devotions and purity. We can
see from the foregoing examples, however, that ritual elements enter into many
spheres of the law, mostly in the form of formulaic declarations in contract and
domestic transactions.

SUFISM, ORTHODOXY AND THE *SHARI'A*

A discussion of concepts and issues relating to the *shari'a* will not be complete
without a consideration of the challenges to orthodoxy posed by certain dominant
strands of Sufism. It is difficult to make statements about Sufism in general,

because there have been such wide variations in Sufi doctrine and practice, as we shall have occasion to show. We may, however, trace some general features, while keeping in mind that there are always exceptions to any generalizations made. In any case, I shall concentrate here on the aspects of Sufi doctrine which posed challenges to orthodoxy, mostly those crystallized in the work of Ibn al-Arabi and widely followed, with variations by many *turuq* (orders). The doctrines of Ibn al-Arabi (d. 1240) (Nicholson 1921:77–142) are pantheist, that is to say, hold a belief in the unity of all existence (*wahdat al-wujud*), all being emanations from God's essence. Before creating man and the world, God was pure essence, without attributes. He created Adam in his own image in order to make his attributes manifest. It follows that there is a certain divinity in mankind, but one that is hidden in external phenomena. Only certain men are gifted with the ability to explore the divinity in their own selves, and to regain consciousness of that divine essence. In Adam God had created the 'perfect man', *al-insan al-kamil*, who fully reflected his essence. All the prophets have been bearers of this perfection, none more so than Muhammad, who is the highest incarnation. Muhammad, in this belief, is not just a mortal man chosen by God for his message, but a supernatural creature, who pre-existed his time and message.

For the Sufis (as for the Shi'a), the incarnations of the Perfect Man did not end with Muhammad, but in every age, such a *qutb*, a 'pole' or 'axis', appears. For the Shi'a their imams had this character, now characteristic of only the Hidden *Imamul-zaman* (the imam of all time). For various Sufis, *awliya'* (singular, *wali*), friends or God, appear every so often and are distinguished by signs of saintliness, such as miracles, telepathy and the ability to see into the past and the future and into men's hearts. The great Sufi saints are not given these powers, though they may be disposed towards them by divine grace, but attain them through a path, *tariqa*, of hard spiritual exercise, ascetic practices, isolation and concentration on the attributes of the divine for many years (Nicholson 1921: 1–76, on Abu Sa'id Ibn Abi'l-Khayr). This 'path' culminates in an 'illumination', in which the divine essence is revealed. The self is transcended, *fana'*, then returns to earthly existence (*al-baqa' ba'd al-fana'*). The saint is then a source of wisdom, aid and felicity to his fellows and disciples. Many embark upon this path, under the guidance of a master, and attain various levels of ecstasy and even enlightenment, but few are endowed with the divine light and can attain the ultimate goal of *fana'*, and all the powers that come with it. The great masters, such as Abdul-Qadir al-Gaylani (d. 1166) or Jalaluddin Rumi (b. 1207) were deemed to have founded major orders, *tariqas*, or paths. These were to proliferate in different parts of the Muslim world, under local masters, but always tracing their spiritual descent (*silsila*) in a line from the Prophet and Ali, the line then passing through the founder and the major saints of the order. The supreme headship of the order was often claimed by the kin descendants of the founder, such as the Gaylani family in Baghdad, guardians of the shrine of Abdul-Qadir to the present day. To Qadiri lodges in distant lands such as Morocco, for instance, this claimed supremacy by the Baghdad family may not be of much consequence.

Lodges and convents of the major *tariqas* proliferated in most of the lands of Islam over much of its history. Many were endowed with considerable revenues, their masters (often a hereditary position) disposing of much influence and patronage, some of them holding official religious positions such as judgeships at the same time, as we shall see. Most of their adherents were ordinary persons with families and work to whom their order was part of their religious devotions and social networks. A few were devoted dervishes, engaging in prolonged spiritual and ascetic exercises, in a hierarchy of adepts, deputies and the ultimate master and guide. These engaged in the activities commonly associated with dervishes, of ecstatic exercises, dances, 'miracles' and magic. Ordinary members of the order also engaged in ritual exercises, dances and so on, but not so intensively and mostly on ritual occasions.

Sufi belief and practice posed an implicit challenge to orthodoxy and to the law, although in most instances of 'respectable' Sufism this challenge was muted and glossed over to make it compatible with orthodoxy. The very pantheistic theology of mainstream Sufism poses a challenge to the transcendent God of orthodoxy. *Tawhid*, the term asserting the uniqueness of God in Islam, is subtly subverted in Sufi usage to assert the unity of all existence with God. The Quran remains central to the Sufis, but its range of significance is enlarged in their beliefs. The recitation of the Quran, for instance, becomes part of the spiritual exercises of concentration on all things divine. The act of prolonged and repeated reading, the dwelling on particular verses and phrases, becomes a spiritual exercise, aiding in the achievement of illumination. The Quran is of course acknowledged as revelation, but for many Sufis it is not the whole of the revelation. Abu Sa'id bin Abi'l-Khayr, for instance, argued that the word of God went beyond the fixed quantity and extent of Quranic revelation, and indeed was infinite. God revealed some of his truths directly to the hearts of his enlightened servants. Nicholson (1921:59–60) elaborates:

> Here Abu Sa'id sets aside the partial, finite and temporal revelation which the sufis find in their hearts. As a rule, even the boldest Mohammadan mystics shrink from uttering such a challenge. So long as the inner light is regarded only as an interpreter of the written revelation, the supremacy of the latter is nominally maintained, though in fact any doctrine can be foisted upon it: this is a very different thing from claiming that the inner light transcends the Prophetic Law and possesses full authority to make laws for itself. Abu Sa'id does not say that the partial and universal revelations are in conflict with each other: he does not repudiate the Koran, but he denies that it is the final and absolute standard of divine truth.

Here Nicholson hints at the range of deviations from orthodoxy, but deviations there must be, implicit in the very Sufi notion of illumination. For that opens the way to revelation received into the heart of the saint, a communication from God, a revelation of truth. This goes counter to the central Muslim doctrine of the finality, the 'seal' of Muhammad's prophecy as conveyed in the Quran and amplified in the *sunna*. One Christian parallel is to be found in the so-called 'radical Reformation' in the sixteenth century of Muenzer and the Anabaptists, ancestors of modern evangelism, who asserted the 'prophethood of all believers' (as against Luther's Sunni assertion of the priesthood of all believers). God, in this view, is not dumb: he speaks to the hearts of those servants who are endowed with his grace, and who are tuned to receive his message. This belief is potentially subversive to religious authority of priests, *ulama* and churches, as it challenges their claims as guardians of a fixed and eternal truth. As such, it always has political implications.

As far as the *shari'a* is concerned, Sufi beliefs and practices pose even more serious challenges, ones that were appreciated and combated by many of the orthodox throughout history. The *raison d'être* of the *shari'a* as sacred law depends on Quranic prescription and prophetic example. The Sufi search for esoteric and intuitive reading of the Quran devalues its explicit commandments. The text has to be understood though the intuition of the initiated and the enlightened. Literal reading by the uninitiated is of lower value. And if revelation and prophetic example are only part of potential revelation that God can inspire into the hearts of his chosen and enlightened servants, then the law and the commandments are not fixed but open to addition and amendment. Many of the more orthodox and respectable Sufis have not drawn those conclusions, but continued to stress the duty of observing all the rituals and commandments. Orders such as the modern Naqshbandis in Turkey present Sufi devotions as a means of disciplined and richer observation of the 'pillars' of the faith. Others, however, such as the Mevlevis and the Bektashis, have tended to devalue and displace the orthodox observances in favour of their own rituals of ecstatic practices which often involve music and dancing, trances and miracles. The doctrines of Ibn al-Arabi, common to so many Sufis, are quite explicit in their subordination of the *shari'a* in a hierarchy of religious achievements. The *shari'a*, as a literal reading of the 'raw' sources, is a first stage of exteriority, *zahiri*, as against *batini*, or inner knowledge. The adept follows the *tariqa* under the guidance of a master, on the way to illumination, which, if successful, leads to the next stage of *ma'rifa* or knowledge, and ultimately, for the few chosen, to *haqiqa*, the Truth of God, the divinity within the self, which annihilates the self in *fana'*, but return the saint to the world as a superior being, maybe even the 'perfect man'. We shall see that these doctrines and practices became issues of political conflicts and struggles at various stages of Muslim history.

Finally, the orthodox had one more issue of contention with the Sufis, and that is the tendency of the latter to see the ultimate pursuit of truth by all religions, not only those of 'the book', but also of pagans, who were all trying in their own way to seek the same truth of the one God (Nicholson 1921:130–42). They recognized the superiority of Islam as a path to that truth, but were inclined to be conciliatory and sympathetic to the other faiths. The orthodox were always jealous of the absolute superiority of Islam and the error of the infidels, who were to be subordinated, despised and always reminded of their protected status.

CONCLUSION

This chapter has elucidated the conceptual and textual architectures of *fiqh* and the *shari'a*. The following chapters will consider the social and institutional frames for the operation of these concepts, with special emphasis on relations of power and political authority.

2 INSTITUTIONS: COURTS, *QADIS* AND MUFTIS

This chapter will survey the various judicial institutions in the history of Muslim societies. For the pre-Ottoman period it will draw primarily on the work of Tyan,[1] unique in its comprehensive coverage of these institutions, and not available in English. It will then proceed to a detailed consideration of Ottoman judicial institutions and practices, and conclude with examples of the operation of courts at various points in time.

HISTORICAL SKETCH

The earliest days of Islam, as we have seen, presented some continuity with pre-Islamic practices in matters of adjudication and legal judgement. Under the early caliphs, Rashidun and Umayyads, there was no set system of law and justice, but a mixture of ad hoc practices (Tyan 1960:67ff). Later histories attributed to the Prophet the institution of a judiciary system, but, argued Tyan, this assertion is in line with the Muslim historians' tendency to attribute institutions and practices of later periods to the earliest formative moments, thus bestowing upon them the sanctity of the Prophet and the companions.

According to Tyan's account, the early Muslims continued to resort to men of wisdom and charisma to judge between them, as they did before Islam. The example is given of the poet Al-Akhtal, who remained a Christian but who was called upon to adjudicate between Muslims in the mosque. This was mostly private justice, cases which the disputants agreed to refer to the judgement of an approved *hakam* (adjudicator). What about the justice of rulers?

The traditional histories have the Prophet and the caliphs appointing *qadis* to the provinces (Tyan 1960:18–27). There is a famous epistle quoted in these histories from the Caliph 'Umar Ibn-Al-Khttab to Abu Musa al-Ash'ari, whom he is supposed to have designated as Qadi of Kufa (Tyan 1960:23–27, 78–82).

This epistle is held by the traditionalists to be the paradigm of judicial ethics and responsibilities. Tyan challenges the validity of this document, and part of his argument is that it is not mentioned in the early *fiqh* books of Malik or Shafi'i, but only appeared in the early Abbasid sources, such as the *Kitab al-Kharaj* of Abu Yusuf, precisely at the moment at which judicial practices were being institutionalized.

Judges were appointed by the rulers in the early period. These appointments, however, were ad hoc, often made by the governors of the provinces. No corpus of law had formed at that stage, so the judges ruled according to a melange of customary rule, governors' edicts and some general ideas of religious righteousness, according to the Quran and holy precedent. At this point, the Umayyads and early Abbasids thought of themselves as Deputies of God on earth, and as such law-makers (more in Chapter 3). The judge, then, was merely the deputy, *na'ib*, of the sovereign, appointed by the governor as part of the local administration (Tyan 1960:100–1). In Chapter 1 we cited the example of the Qadi of Egypt questioned by the governor as to his knowledge of the Quran or basic principles of succession, to all of which he replied in the negative, but that if stuck he would ask, at which he was patted on the back and told to carry on. That reflects precisely the absence of a legal corpus and of the established legal institutions which were to come at a later point.

The formation of distinct judicial institutions and practices were to develop under the Abbasids, coupled with the development, already noted, of a legal corpus of the *shari'a*. The Abbasids made a great show of their piety, the right-eousness of their rule and their fidelity to the book and the *sunna* of the Prophet. Part of this public religiosity was the patronage and advancement of *fuqaha*, and the appointment of prominent jurists to courtly functions. Judges, then, were appointed directly by the caliph. Al-Mansur (r. 754–775) was the first caliph to appoint *qadis* directly, starting with the nomination of the Qadi of Damascus in 770 (Tyan 1960:124–25). Under Harun (r. 786–809) a veritable judicial bureaucracy and hierarchy was instituted in the office of Qadi al-Qudat, the judge of judges. Under the Abbasids the apparatus of state bureaucracy was vastly expanded, adopting and adapting Persian imperial practices and methods. Judicial institutions were part of this expanded bureaucracy, and the office of Qadi al-Qudat was the head of this bureaucracy and a court appointment. The first incumbent under Harun was his protégé and advisor the Hanafite Abu Yusuf (d. 798), author of *Kitab al-Kharaj*, which was written as advice and guidance for this caliph (Tyan 1960:125–27). This post, it is supposed by Tyan and others, developed from the previous Persian position of *mobedan mobed*, the chief judge and head of the judicial administration of the Emperor (Tyan 1960:128–29). Indeed, the term *siyasat al-qada'*, judicial administration, came into use at this point.

True bureaucratic delegation would imply that the head of the judiciary is given the power of appointment and revocation of his deputies and subordinates. This was not the case in the heyday of the Abbasid caliphate. The caliph himself retained the power of nomination of the *qadis* of the provinces. Their discipline was entrusted to the governors. When a corrupt Qadi of Egypt was exposed, his punishment was decreed by Harun and entrusted to his governor of the province to have the offender shaved of his hair and beard, beaten and paraded in public on a donkey (Tyan 1960:127). When Ma'mun (r.813–833) proclaimed the doctrine of the createdness of the Quran as the true creed (see Chapter 3), he ordered his governors to test the fidelity of the *qadis* of their provinces to this proclaimed doctrine (Tyan 1960:127). It seems, then, that the chief judge was a figure of great influence at court, close to the caliph, as was Abu Yusuf to Harun, or Abu Duwad to Ma'mun and his two successors, with a status comparable to the wazir, a chief minister and the highest functionary. Yet this eminence pertained to the person and the courtly office without being generalized into an institutionalized power of delegation. Later periods, in the decadence of the Abbasid caliphate and the splitting off of provinces, chief judges at various points did seem to have the delegated powers of appointment, as was that of the family of Abu Al-Shawarib in the early tenth century, which furnished to the Abbasids a succession of eight grand judges, all of whom enjoyed wide powers of delegation in the appointment of the provincial judiciary (Tyan 1960:146–47).

Judicial institutions underwent a number of transformations following the political fortunes of the Muslim empires and the changing social conditions. The process of fragmentation of empire and the development of provincial autonomies was reflected in the judiciary. The autonomous princes, such as the Tulunids (878–905) in Egypt, established their own chief judges, nominated by the prince independently from the caliph or the Qadi al-Qudat of Baghdad. By the same token, when Baghdad reasserted its control, the appointed governor, then the chief judge of Baghdad resumed the prerogative of judicial appointments (Tyan 1960:144–45). Of course, the rival caliphates of the Fatimids of Egypt and the Umayyads of Spain spawned their own judicial systems, with a chief judge appointed by their respective caliphs. The appointment of a Qadi al-Qudat was an attribute of sovereignty.

Another development in the institutional evolution of the judiciary occurred under the Fatimids (909–1171) and was consolidated under the Mamlukes – that was the appointment of a separate chief judge for each of the *madhahib*. The Fatimids, being Isma'ili Shi'a, appointed their chief judge from their doctrine, but then appointed Sunni chief judges, Shafi'i and Maliki to cater for the legal requirements of many of their subjects. Fatimids and Shi'a in general were suppressed under the Ayubids and remained marginal under the Mamlukes.

The Mamluke Sultan Baibars (r. 1260–77), however, initiated the practice of appointing a chief judge for each of the Sunni schools, with the Shafi'i judge having wider powers and competence than the others.

THE ISSUE OF JUDICIAL AUTONOMY

To what extent did there develop a 'separation of powers' in the Muslim polity? There certainly was no legislative authority: legislation was assumed to have been established by God in his revelation (an assumption which persists to our day, constituting a central issue for debates and contentions). In practice, various agencies assumed legislative functions. The early caliphs claimed a God-given power to decree laws, but their decrees, as we have seen, only survived as traces of the 'raw materials' upon which the early scholars were to work. The early scholars themselves were the most important legislators in developing the substance and the methodology of *fiqh*. Their law was then maintained in institutional niches of *madrasas* (religious seminaries), courts and *ifta'*, the issuing of *fatwas*. Judges themselves, insofar as they could formulate deductions and analogies in their judgement, also assumed legislative functions. In this process of legislation the question of *ijtihad* and its allowability is highly pertinent. The so-called 'closure of the gate of *ijtihad*' precisely attempts to put an end to the process of legal innovation in favour of a fixed corpus juris established by the founders. Yet, this oft-proclaimed doctrine seems to be contradicted by actual practice and frequent utterances, as we have seen in Chapter 1. Authorities at various points proclaim the status of *ijtihad* to be a necessary qualification of a mufti, and some require it of judges. In the theory of imama, such as that of Mawardi,[2] *ijtihad* is even stipulated as a qualification for the imam/ruler. There then seems to be an inconsistency or ambivalence by the orthodox authorities about the legitimacy and requirement of *ijtihad*: is 'the gate' closed, or is the practice required from any authoritative practitioner of the law?

To what extent, then, does this established legal corpus provide for the separation, or at least the autonomy, of the judiciary? In most pronouncements, historically and up to recent times, the judge derives authority from the sovereign, as deputy and appointee. In judgements, however, the judge is bound by the *shari'a* and his own conscience in relation to it. There, are, however, other formulae of representation, in which the *qadi* is said to represent the public or the community (*na'ib al'-amma*), or even God (Tyan 1960:105). These designations are, however, rare, and maybe related to absence or fragmentation of political authority. Under such circumstances it is known for a city to appoint its own *qadi* (Tyan 1960:155–59). What is important, however, whatever authority appoints the *qadi*, his brief remains that he should rule according to the *shari'a*.

While the ruler can add certain decrees, which must not contravene the *shariʿa*, the major corpus of law operating in the *qadi*'s court remains the *shariʿa*. Moreover, interpretations of *shariʿa* principles are governed by the *qadi*'s affiliation to one of the orthodox schools of law. Ultimately, the judgement delivered by a *qadi* is his own responsibility before God, and he will have to account for it in the next life. Juristic authority as such would seem to reside in the legal institutions and personnel, even though these institutions operate under the authority of the ruler. This independence of the rule of the *shariʿa* works in practice in relation to the affairs of the subjects, rarely of the rulers. Judgements in a *qadi* court, while not subject to appeal within the *sharʿ* system, can be taken to the *mazalim* tribunals of the prince, or to other administrative bodies, if the litigant is sufficiently influential and well connected. In theory, all Muslims are equally subject to the rule of the *shariʿa* and its courts. Unlike Europe, there are no estates and separate courts and jurisdictions for them. In practice, however, and especially in later (Ottoman) times, different corporate groups, such as the Ashraf (descendants from the Prophet) merchants and craft guilds, established their own court tribunals. As regards autonomy, we may conclude that there is a certain scope for judicial autonomy, but not in the face of political power and influence. This is especially the case given the dependence of the judiciary on the patronage and favour of the princes in appointments and supervision, and in the widespread practice of farming judicial offices, as we shall see presently. In this respect the Muslim world was no different from other complex pre-modern civilizations.

Legal Procedure

Qadi courts are presided over by a solitary judge who pronounces judgement on his sole authority. There are no judicial tribunals in Islam, no assembly of judges and no juries. The *qadi* may consult with a mufti on points of law (and this became common in Ottoman practice), or may employ experts, such as those on succession law, or those with special knowledge of buildings or women's bodies. The judgement, however, emanates from one single authority.

The court normally employs auxiliary personnel. A court clerk records proceedings. Persons so employed must have knowledge of the law, and such an appointment can be an early step in a legal career. In addition to the clerk, courts employ witnesses, *shuhud* or *ʿudul*. This is a peculiarity of Muslim courts, to have professional witnesses appointed by the court as functionaries, and stems from the requirements of standards of evidence.

Muslim legal procedures privilege oral testimony of witnesses over written documents. Testimony is proof *par excellence*. What is written is never proof by itself, but needs witness testimony to validate it (Tyan 1960:237). What is written can be faulty, or can be falsified. All documents and signatures have to be certified by the testimony of witnesses, and this includes the verdicts and decisions of the judge. When these documents are then invoked as evidence the witness who validated the signatures must be present to confirm that the document is indeed what it purports to be. This places a great weight on the honesty and reliability of witnesses. In the early stages of Muslim legal practice, the judgement on the witness's reliability and admissibility was left to the whim of the judge. Judges are said to have rejected testimonies on various – sometimes bizarre – grounds, ranging from receiving payment for teaching the Quran to the taking off of all clothes when performing conjugal duties (Tyan 1960:328). Eventually, a procedure for establishing witness's integrity was established, called *tazkiya*, in which the judge initiated an inquiry as to the moral conduct of the person in question. A *qadi* in Egypt in the middle of the second Muslim century is reported to have initiated a standardized procedure. It soon became common to designate a small number of persons, who had succeeded in establishing their moral standing, as official witnesses. Their testimony was straightforward when it came to witnessing documents, but problematic in establishing the truth of rival claims. This procedure led to considerable discontent among litigants, and to multiple avenues for corruption, as we shall presently see. While the institution of *shuhud* or *'udul* continued until recent times, we shall see that its operation varied over time and place. In recent examples, professional witnesses were employed as 'detectives' to verify the claims of litigants and the reliability of ordinary witnesses by conducting inquiries outside the court. Eventually, by the fourth Muslim century, these professional *shuhud* became court functionaries to whom various tasks were delegated by the *qadi* (Tyan 1960:248–9). Some were entrusted with guarding and overseeing court funds, and funds under court guardianship, such as those of orphans and minors, or indeed of *waqf* funds. Others specialized in particular legal functions, such as that of calculating portions in succession. Some were even deputized to act on behalf of the judge in certain jurisdictions.

It is commonly stated that advocacy by professional lawyers on behalf of clients, common in Europe, is alien to Islamic courts, in which the *qadi* assumes the function of interrogation and cross-examination. This is, strictly speaking, correct. At various points, however, we find the practice of a litigant appointing a *wakil*, an agent, to plead on his behalf. Persons assuming these functions, however, were not necessarily educated or qualified in the law, but were valued for their skills in pleading and persuasion, and above all for their influence and connections. Their pleading did not involve legal or literary oratory of the Roman and later European styles, but concentrated on the exercise of persuasion and influence. The jurists, while not outlawing the practice of *wakala* (plural of *wakil*) were not entirely happy with it, and considered it open to abuse and deceit. There was some debate on the nature of the fee payable and whether it could be conditional on the success of the case or specified by the judge (Tyan 1960:268–69). In general, the professional agents were considered to be of low morality, enriching themselves by deceit and corruption, and their practice was at times put under the supervision and discipline of the *muhtasib* (a qualified lawyer)[3] (Tyan 1960:271–75). Tyan (1960:262–75) describes these aspects of the practice, mostly in the Mamluke period.

After the early period of the judiciary in Islam, during which deputy judges in the provinces were appointed by governors, the predominant practice became one in which the chief judge appointed provincial deputies. The chief judge from each school appointed his subordinates. Under the Ottomans the Hanafi school was favoured as that of the ruling dynasty, and the chief judge of that school often had an important voice in the appointment of other judges.

As regards the location of courts, for much of the earlier periods until Ottoman times, the favoured location was the main Jami' mosque of the city. The *qadi* could also hold court in his own residence, or in a public space allocated for that purpose. Shafi'is, however, did not favour holding court in mosques, because villains and ritually impure persons could be among the litigants or witnesses, which would pollute the sanctity of the mosque. Shafi'i judges sat in other spaces, mostly their own residence. In seventeenth-century Ottoman Cairo, the chief Hanafi *qadi* held court at an official palace, designated as Al-Bab Al-Ali (the High Porte). All other courts were held in mosques or residences (El-Nahal 1979:12–14). Order in court was kept by a *hajib*, a court orderly, often with a stick or a whip. It also fell to this functionary to mete out summary punishment to those judged to be in contempt of the court for failing to answer questions or otherwise misbehaving.

The *qadi* had many functions other than litigation. In the classic books of administrative law, such as those of Mawardi and Ibn Khaldun, these functions are listed, and include the following: judgement in litigation, the protection of the incapable (see *infra*), the administration of *awqaf*, the execution of wills and testaments, guardianship of unmarried women without guardians, the application of *hudud* punishments as stipulated in the Quran, the police of public buildings and roads, and the control of *shuhud* and other court auxiliaries and the appointment of deputy *qadis*. Ibn Khaldun adds to this list the *mazalim* ('grievances', usually a function of the ruler or his governor, as we shall see presently), the conduct of *jihad* or holy war, and the control of the mint (Tyan 1960:350–51). Some of these specifications have been largely theoretical, such as the conduct of war; others, like the supervision of the mint, were limited to particular periods. The policing of public spaces, especially markets, commonly fell to the *muhtasib* (see *infra*), though complaints about immoral activities in particular neighbourhoods were often brought to the *qadi*. The functions of supervision of the *waqf*, the guardianship of minors and incapables, and the execution of testimonies commonly fell to the *qadi*.

REMUNERATION OF *QADIS* AND FUNCTIONARIES

In theory, and in the opinion of the jurists, the *qadi* is not supposed to profit from the performance of his duty. Some jurists advocated that the *qadi* should not receive any payment, and should subsist on other sources of income, others stipulated that he should be paid just enough to cover his family's living expenses (Tyan 1960:233–34). In this view, the act of *qada'* is a merit, performed in the service of God, and will be rewarded in the next world. The view that the *qadi* should be paid for his subsistence became current and was reported to be the practice of the Rashidun caliphs. The *qadi* was, in these early discourses, forbidden to charge any fees or commissions from the litigants or on the funds entrusted to him, such as those of minors or *awqaf*.

The practice, however, was at wide variance from the theory. We find in the periods of the dynastic caliphates that the *qadi* was paid a stipend by the state, and in addition received grants and gifts from the ruler on various festive occasions. In addition, he received salaries and fees for his other functions, such as the supervision of *awqaf* (Tyan 1960:337–41; Gibb and Bowen I 1957:82–83). The *qadi* was responsible for the remuneration of all court functionaries, so payments received from the public treasury had to cover these disbursements. A later common practice was for the court to charge litigants a fee or a commission to cover its expenses. All these legitimate sources of income, however, pale into insignificance in comparison with the revenues reportedly derived from corruption.

CORRUPTION

The books of *fiqh* and treatises on public morals are stern in the high standards they set for the magistracy. They envisage all the forms of actually occurring corruption and prohibit them: strict impartiality of the judge not to be compromised by gifts, intercession (*shafa'a*) by personal contacts (what in modern parlance is known as *wasta*), payment for procuring judicial appointments, the favouring of kin in appointments and judgements, and the strict moral standards of conduct in private and public for the judiciary. All these prohibited acts were, in fact, widespread in practice at certain times and places.

Corruption is, of course, endemic to legal institutions and practices in many societies and historical periods, often the norm rather than the exception. With regard to Muslim contexts we have a variety of reports and narratives. Some, as we shall see, stress the fairness of *shari'a* courts and *qadis* in litigation, and in particular their attention to the scrutiny of an informed public. These courts and their personnel, however, are, as we shall see, not confined to functions of litigation, but range into notary functions, supervision of endowments, matters of inheritance and guardianship over minors and incapables – functions often involving property and finance and open to manipulations. Many of the narratives of corruption revolve around these areas. It is also a question of time and place. We shall see that the higher and more powerful judicial appointments and practices feature more prominently in narratives of corruption, whereas everyday judicial functions are more likely to be conducted by working judges, themselves part of the local bourgeoisie and *ulama*, and more meticulous in their judicial functions under the scrutiny of local public opinion.

Tyan (1960:293–332) cites numerous reports by historians, poets and essayists detailing instances of judicial corruption. He is cautious in pointing out the tendency to exaggeration and satire by poets and essayists (Tyan 1960:294–95), especially in pursuit of personal vendettas and dislikes. He concludes, however, that the reports are too numerous and consistent to be ignored, especially those by serious historians. In any case, the Islamization of the magistracy cannot be expected to change judicial morality from its Byzantine predecessors, notorious for its corruption.

As early as the second century of Islam, we find Abu Yusuf in his *Kitab al-Kharaj*, advising the caliph to be careful as to whom he entrusts the funds of the orphans and the strangers, for most *qadis* are not to be so trusted, and that they and their auxiliaries do not hesitate to despoil the weak of their goods and rights of inheritance (Tyan 1960:295).

The farming of judicial and auxiliary posts was one of the principal forms of corruption. From the fourth century of Islam, argues Tyan (1960:302–3), corruption was no longer incidental but systematic. He quotes the Baghdadi eleventh-century historian al-Tannukhi, himself a judge, for many examples of the farming of posts. Tannukhi regrets the levels to which the magistracy had sunk in his time (the Buyid dynasty), exemplified by a chief judge, Ibn Furat, who sold judicial posts to persons of little knowledge and doubtful morals. Other public posts of Shurta, police, and *hisba*, market inspection, were equally for sale. The process of sale of offices became formalized and official, in that contracts of sale were drawn up, conditions stipulated, areas of competence (and profit) specified. These were written contracts registered in the official records. The contract was called *daman*, the term later applied to tax-farming.

The annalists report that in the year 932 a certain Muhammad Ibn al-Hasan Ibn abi al-Shawarib took the post of grand judge for an agreed sum. This family of Abu al-Shawarib was to hold judicial posts over several generations. In 961, Wazir Mu'izz al-Dawla farmed out the same post to a brother of the said Muhammad for 2000 dirhems per annum (Tyan 1960:303). These posts fetched what they were worth in income, and one in the capital much more than the equivalent in the provinces. The chief judge, in turn, farmed out subordinate posts of provincial judges and of auxiliaries, such as clerks and *'udul*. The judges and auxiliaries recouped their costs from the revenues they obtained from the public in gifts, bribes, extortion and embezzlement. The funds of orphans, the disabled and the mentally ill were particularly open to embezzlement by the magistracy and their auxiliaries, the supposed guardians. A typical example is the chief judge of Egypt at the turn of the fifth Muslim century, one Fariqi, who conspired to lay his hands on the fortune of a reputedly rich lady. He set up four of his *shuhud* to bring a case attesting that she spent her fortune recklessly, and that as a spendthrift she fell within the category of 'incapables' who were subject to judicial guardianship (Tyan 1960:317–18). Tyan cites many more examples from the annals of chroniclers and essayists.

On the question of the purchase of judicial posts, Tyan makes an interesting comparison with France. For there, too, as in many other parts of Europe, public posts and commissions were purchased – sometimes auctioned – by revenue hungry kings and high functionaries. Tyan argues that there is a crucial difference between the French practice and that of the Muslim world: in France the purchase of an office was irrevocable, and became part of the patrimony of the purchaser, transmitted and inherited. This security of tenure, in turn, assured the independence of the judiciary from political power. This was not the case in the Muslim world, where the purchase of office was for fixed terms, often revocable and subject to the vagaries of politics and finance (Tyan 1960:308–9).

Another theme in the literature on the magistracy is the moral conduct of judges in their private lives and affairs. A regular theme in the satires of the poets and essayists is that of the drunkenness and debauchery of judges. The chief judges were dignitaries of state, with considerable wealth and power. As such, they mixed with the rulers and princes, were often their friends and boon companions and partook in the same lifestyles and diversions of banquets, drinking, song and the company of pretty women and comely boys. Historians (Yaqut and Ibn Khallikan) reported the exploits of the *qadi* (and fellow man of letters) Tannukhi in twelfth-century Baghdad. He and a number of other magistrates and jurists assembled each week at the house of Wazir al-Muhallabi:

> They met at his [al-Muhallabi's] house, at night, twice a week, and putting aside all modesty, they abandoned themselves to the pleasures of the table and of the

senses. These persons were the Qadi Abu Bakr bin Fari'a, Ibn Ma'ruf, al-Tannukhi and others. They were all advanced in age, with long white beards like al-Muhallabi himself. After becoming intoxicated with pleasure, they succumbed to frolicking without modesty. Each took in his hand a deep cup, filled with drink…and after having plunged their beards in the drink, they drank deeply from their cups, then they splashed the rest over each other. They would then proceed to dance until daybreak. They would then put on their air of gravity and reserve, as suited their judicial functions. [Quoted by Tyan 1960:320]

This al-Tannukhi was himself a fine essayist, who chronicled the social and cultural life of Baghdad.

Kindi reported that Hashim al-Bakri, Qadi of Egypt during the years 809–10, held his court after the midday meal, at which he would drink three cups of wine. The same historian reported that another judge, Ibn Abi al-Layth, was a great lover of wine and song, and spent his nights at the house of a female singer. His expertise was such that he would correct any musical errors in the song. 'This judge of iniquity, he lamented, spends his nights listening to female singers, and drinking wine the colour of gold…O unhappy victims of a libertine judge!' (Tyan 1960:299). It would seem that the debauchery of judges was a favourite theme of annalists and poets alike.

We shall have occasion in the next chapter to narrate the struggles of Ibn Taimiya against what he saw as the corruption and impiety of his contemporaries. His adversaries, it will be seen, were mainly senior judges and shaykhs of Sufi orders, both functions being combined in some individuals. Ibn Taimiya lived at the end of the period covered by Tyan, at the height of Mamluke power in the thirteenth and fourteenth centuries. This is a period in which abuses of power and venality of rule were also far advanced. The Mamluke system of multiple centres of power and the competition and struggle for revenues heightened the drive for fiscal extortion of diverse and original forms, and of an administration oiled by bribes, gifts and tribute. Moral turpitude, by Muslim standards of law and ethics, became institutionalized in the state, with the licensing and taxation of brothels and taverns. No wonder that a purist and puritan Hanbali like Ibn Taimiya, who never himself assumed a judgeship, was so outraged by this situation and moved to his campaigns of reform, which bore so little fruit. Gibb and Bowen (II 1957), ever respectful of the *ulama*, note that

At certain times and certain places, notably the Mamluke Sultanate of Egypt, the intervention and control of the secular powers [over the *ulama*] had already gone a considerable way, tempered only by the characteristic fluidity of Islamic institutions, the *esprit de corps* of the *Ulama*, and the respect they inspired by their generally high level of rectitude. [II 1957:82–83]

'Rectitude' would seem to be at odds with the account given by Tyan, and by Gibb and Bowen themselves in their description of judicial institutions and personnel in Ottoman time (see *infra*). Yet as we shall see, other, contrary, images of *shariʿa* courts emerge from studies of later centuries, such as Marcus's account of eighteenth-century Aleppo, considered below. While the general corruption of rule in many societies including historical Muslim countries would dispose the judiciary to participate or perish, there were limits. It would seem that in the specific functions of litigation between adversaries, judgement was subject to close public scrutiny by the informed inhabitants of a locality, and would raise scandal if transparently corrupt, as we shall see. It was in the other functions of the judiciary, mainly those of supervision over property, that the scope for profiteering was wider.

To adopt a comparative perspective, the corruption of justice in Muslim lands was not strange or unusual: the theme of judicial corruption and venality is one common to most areas of civilization, including Europe. We should note that 'corruption' does not refer to individual moral failings but to a whole system, in which a virtuous individual would find it hard to survive. This theme continues to the present day, especially with regard to lawyers, the subject of much outrage and satire all over the world, but especially in the litigious US. In many parts of the advanced industrial world, however, we expect (but don't always get) honesty and independence from the judiciary. Historically, there must have been some honest and pious judges, but their existence and survival would depend on social conditions of their time. Many pious men refused the magistracy and considered it a conduit of sin and moral pollution. It is perhaps this factor which lends the Muslim reports of corruption more poignant than elsewhere: the intrinsically religious character of the magistracy and the law in Islam. Corruption, then, is not merely worldly venality, but a deep religious offence.

EXTRA-*SHARIʿA* JURISDICTIONS: *MAZALIM, SIYASA* AND SHURTA

The *qadi* assumed a judicial function with a religious commitment. He judged (at least in theory) according to the *shariʿa*, rules ultimately based, it is supposed, on revelation and sacred precedent. Even though the *qadi*'s authority was, it is most commonly stated, delegated from the sovereign, the law by which he ruled preceded any sovereignty and was theoretically binding on the sovereign. *Qadi* justice was the 'normal' or 'ideal type' of jurisdiction in Muslim theory. In practice, however, it co-exists with a number of other jurisdictions, not bound by the *shariʿa*, and as such 'extraordinary'. These extraordinary forms, however, are common throughout the history of Muslim government.

Mazalim ('grievances') was the most common of the extraordinary jurisdictions. It was ultimately a function of the ruler as such, in his sovereign capacity, with the connotation of righting the wrongs suffered by his subjects. Its paradigmatic form is that of the sovereign sitting in his court, aided by his functionaries, giving public audience to any of his subjects to plead for justice against, typically, powerful persons who have usurped his rights. The biblical example of Solomon dispensing justice according to his wisdom illustrates this kind of procedure. As such, *mazalim* was not only extraordinary but superior justice, as it emanated directly from the will of the prince that overruled all others. The word *mazalim* derives from *zulm*, meaning oppression, injustice. A tyrant is *zalim*, ruling arbitrarily without regard to ethics or law. The victim raises his plea against *zulm* and this act is described in the verb *tazallama*.

By what standard of justice, by what law, was an act deemed to be *zulm*? The institution of *mazalim* did not proclaim an explicit code. It did not, of course, explicitly renounce the *shari'a* as standard, but its judgements were not bound by the logic of *fiqh*, nor did it follow the procedures and the standards of evidence demanded by *qadi* courts. We may say that its standards of justice were ad hoc and 'common sense' based on common ethics and customary standards. Ghazzali, the great jurist and theologian, defines *mazalim* as the usurpation of the property of individuals, to harm their moral virtue (*'ird*, connotations of sexual honour) and to oppress them by bad treatment in their common life and relations (Ghazzali, *Ihya' 'ulum al-din* IV:375 quoted in Tyan 1960:435). In all these matters the reference is implicitly to the common people being oppressed by the powerful. Occasionally, in technical matters of the law, as, for instance, in relation to inheritance, a *qadi* or a mufti may have been consulted, and as we shall see, in some cases legal personages were included in the *mazalim* tribunals.

A prince holding court to arbitrate in pleas raised by his subjects is a common prototype of justice in most historical societies and in myth and fiction. In the case of the Muslim kingdoms the practice was institutionalized, and in later times bureaucratized. Under the Mamlukes it became a regular tribunal of justice, alternative to *shari'a* courts, which tried various cases and administered punishment. The tribunals of Ottoman justice were in continuity with these institutions and practices. Tyan dates the inception of *mazalim* tribunals to the early Abbasids, specifically to the reign of Mahdi, the third caliph in the dynasty (r. 775–785) (Tyan 1960:476). He and his successors were reported to be jealous in personally attending to the pleas of their subjects and zealous in appearing to right wrongs. This was one of the strategies of establishing the prestige of their dynasty and spreading a reputation for power and justice. We find Abu Yusuf giving advice to Harun on just rules agreeable to God, and includes a rigorous pursuit of *mazalim* as an essential task of a good king. He advised Harun to hold a *mazalim* audience at least once a month (*Kitab al-Kharaj*, quoted Tyan 1960:478). Some of the caliphs and wazirs were more prolific in their audiences, holding them as frequently as twice a week, while some princes, especially in times of decadence and decline, dispensed with them altogether. After Abu Yususf we find *mazalim* being featured as an essential institution of rule in all subsequent books of public administration, notably those of Ghazzali, Mawardi (d. 1058) and later Ibn Khaldun (d. 1406), as well as 'secular' advice to princes, such as that of Nizam al-Mulk (d. 1092) (quoted in Messick 1993:171). Note, however, that unlike *qada'*, magistracy, it is not obligatory as a necessary condition of any state/society calling itself Muslim. Many rulers, as we have seen, neglected the *mazalim*.

In time, the *mazalim* became institutionalized and even bureaucratized. First, the conduct of *mazalim* audiences was often delegated, usually to a wazir. The famous ministers of the early Abbasids are featured by the chroniclers as holding these audiences at regular weekly intervals. Such were Yahya al-Barmaki, wazir of Harun, and Abu al-Hasan Ibn al-Furat under al-Muqtadir, both said to have pursued their audiences assiduously. This did not exclude the caliphs as such: they differed in the extent of delegation. What was important, however, was that the delegate must himself be a man of great power, a 'man of the sword' able to pronounce and to act to redress grievances against powerful functionaries and individuals. Later, under the Fatimids, then the Mamlukes, we find chief judges being appointed to take charge of *mazalim*. Their capacity as *sahib al-mazalim*, however, remained distinct from their qadial functions. They assumed the *mazalim* in their capacity as powerful men of state, approaching the status of a minister, and as such having the power to override the powerful of the land.

The mention of a specialized office of *sahib al-mazalim* indicates a degree of bureaucratization, also exemplified in the institution of a department of state called *diwan al-mazalim*. At this point, under the Mamluke sultanates, the institution had evolved way beyond the open audience of plaintiffs presenting their case to the powerful, into one in which plaintiffs presented a written case, to be sifted and selected, then presented to the *mazalim* tribunal for an audience. Tribunals were elaborate affairs of state, but always presided over by the sultan himself or a powerful delegate. We have a description of such a tribunal under Sultan Ibn Qalawun (r. 1279–90). This sultan held his audiences in a special wing of his palace, itself designated as *dar al-'adl*, the hall of justice, and held his *mazalim* audience in the throne room. He himself was seated under the throne, on his right were seated the four chief judges of the respective schools, next to whom was the director of finance, then the *muhtasib*. On the left of the sultan sat the main secretaries of state. This assembly formed a semicircle. Behind the sultan stood the armed guards of honour (*silah-darya*) and other servants attached to the person of the sovereign. On the right and left of this assembly, at some distance, were sat other dignitaries, such as the senior amirs and the high dignitaries of state. Behind these stood the functionaries of the audience, the *hajib* and *dawadar*, sort of chamberlains, whose function it was to receive and introduce the requests and the plaintiffs (Tyan 1960:502). This gives some idea of the kind of pomp and ceremony in which these audiences were conducted as affairs of state. Of course, these arrangements varied according to time and place, and in many instances petitions were not dealt with in such exalted audiences, but by delegated officers, as we have seen. Some sultans were known to make a brief appearance at the commencement of proceedings as a symbolic gesture of justice, leaving the main business to their officers.

What were the issues dealt with by *mazalim* courts? We have seen that they were predominantly in the nature of complaints against powerful persons, often high functionaries of state. Examples are complaints of excessive and irregular taxation by governors or collectors, usurpation of land by officials or powerful neighbours and the non-payment of debts, of the agreed price in a sale or of wages owed. Peasants complained of being held in bondage for periods beyond the contractual stipulation. If the *mazalim* court found in favour of the plaintiff, then the powerful person is obliged to make restitution, and in some cases receive reprimands and punishment. Complaints and sentences were always against individuals, not institutions and offices of state as such. If the plaintiff was shown to be at fault, and his complaint baseless or unjust, then he could be punished with a beating or fine.

There was no strict classification or limits on which cases could be brought before a *mazalim* court. Ordinary litigation, no different from that dealt with by a *qadi*, was brought to the *mazalim*. These courts, being the direct expression of the sovereign's will, would never rule themselves incompetent to deal with any type of case. In some instances, ordinary litigation was accepted under *mazalim*, in others the court would refer the plaintiff to the *qadi* court, considering it a waste of the *mazalim* court's time. These examples and records are largely silent on considerations that were crucial for deciding which cases went to which courts. Clearly, there must be calculations on the part of litigants as to where they stood the best chance of success, and this in turn would depend on their circumstances, connections and what influence they could exert or mobilize. The acceptance or rejection of cases as appropriate or not to the *mazalim* courts must, at least in part, have depended on these considerations. In time, *mazalim* courts became general *siyasa* tribunals, considering cases of penal law, which were largely excluded from *shari'a* provisions and dealt with by executive authorities. In Ottoman practice, a hierarchy of *divan*, councils, headed by the Imperial *divan* of the Porte, assumed the functions of *mazalim/siyasa* tribunals (Gibb and Bowen II 1957:116, 129).

Another class of cases is that relating to judicial procedure and enforcement of judgements. Complaints could be raised to the *mazalim* against particular magistrates and judgements they rendered. This procedure, however, was not in the nature of an appeal. As we have seen, there was no allowance for an appeal in Muslim law, each *qadi* being deemed competent to reach a judgement, which may differ from that of a colleague in a similar case; this difference and variation was accepted. So the appeal to *mazalim* was not on points of law, but always of procedure and of injustice arising from corruption, influence and nepotism. Other cases arose from the failure of a *qadi* court to enforce a judgement it had rendered. It may have ruled in favour of a litigant, awarding payments or restitution of rights, but the litigant's adversary may not have complied, and had sufficient resources of power and influence to persist in his refusal. The *mazalim* court could order the enforcement of judgement if it found in favour of the litigant.

What is missing from these accounts is a 'sociology' of *mazalim*. Corruption, misrule, fiscal oppression, usurpation, dispossession and extortion by the powerful were all common for most periods in history, Muslim or other. It follows that there must have been numerous potential plaintiffs to the *mazalim*. Many would not have expected a hearing or justice from the procedure and would not have bothered. But many would have tried, and of those, how many were actually heard and how was the selection of cases made?

We have an example of the working of *mazalim* in more recent times in Messick's study of Yemen. Messick (1993) quotes official histories of the Imam Yahya, in the early decades of the twentieth century, portraying him as receiving oral *shakwa*, complaint or petition, informally as he walked in the city, as he performed his ritual ablutions before prayer, and then after prayer. Oral complaints to the imam or to governors could be more extreme, as desperate individuals would shout their petitions outside the homes of these notables, until heard (Messick 1993:172). This orality and informality is in great contrast to the highly formalized and ritualized *mazalim* tribunals we noted of the Mamluke type. These accounts, however, either described extraordinary forms, as in the shouting, or an idealized mode appropriate to the virtuous ruler. Most commonly in twentieth-century Yemen *shakwas* were written (Messick 1993: 173). There was an official machinery with offices of *shakwa* which processed petitions and selected the serious ones to pass on to the appropriate person, with comments on validity and possible actions. The petitioner in effect had to present a written document, and may have resorted to the services of professionals for appropriate presentation. One governor placed a barrel with a slot for hand-submitted petitions to be posted, thus getting over possible obstruction of access by soldiers. Or the petition could be posted, once postal services became operative. In the imam's *diwan*, *shakwas* were screened and summarized by secretaries, classified according to subject-matter and appropriate actions. The *shakwa* was then passed to the imam, who would append a note of refusal or permission, and a direction to an appropriate official for action (who could be a *shari'a* judge). The petition, with the appendix, was then returned to the petitioner, who would then have to pursue the matter with the appropriate officials. Further progress was at the initiative of the petitioner (Messick 1993:174–75).

In this instance, the level of bureaucratization of *mazalim* in modern or recent context dispensed with the co-presence of petitioner and ruler/deputy in a direct audience, which is the paradigmatic and ideal form of *mazalim*. This form was attributed to the Imam Yahya by laudatory chronicles, but its prevalence must have been limited in time and place. The general operation in more complex societies can only proceed with selection and the following of bureaucratic procedure.

Siyasa *and Shurta*

The notion of *siyasa* is diverse. In general, it refers to functions of government and administration. We have seen that it is distinguished from *shari'a*, in that judgements and procedures, including punishments, effected within the framework of *siyasa* are outside the provisions of *shari'a* (although, in theory, not in contradiction to it). We shall see in the following chapter that in the case of Ibn Taimiya's use of the term *al-siyasa al-shar'iya*, the title of one of his books, he was attempting to assert the hegemony of the *shari'a* in all matters, including *siyasa*. This same term is used in a different sense by most authors to indicate the administration of justice or discipline by agencies and tribunals other than those of a *qadi* proceeding in accordance with the *shari'a*. This *siyasa* form of justice and penal procedure was general to Muslim polities throughout their history. Princes and governors held court and decreed punishments in major cases, especially ones with political significance – of rebellion, subversion and other challenges to authority. But for the common everyday infractions of robbery, murder, injury, affray, drink, fornication and other moral infractions, it was the Shurta which was responsible for maintaining order and punishing the crimes.

Shurta, translated as 'police', was instituted in Muslim cities from earliest times, certainly under the Umayyads, and probably in continuity with pre-Islamic urban administration.[4] The chief of police, *sahib al-shurta*, was one of the main administrative appointments by the ruler, and the post carried wide, even arbitrary, powers. This police force was of a military form, and carried out the functions of repression of rebellion and any threat to public order or authority. It also carried out the day-to-day task of policing the streets, apprehending suspects, and receiving and proceeding with complaints from victims of robbery and violence. The Shurta, however, was in most instances empowered beyond police functions and assumed judicial and executive functions. The fact of the matter is that criminal and penal law, though in theory based on the sacred sources of the *shariʿa*, was in practice under the control of executive authorities, and particularly of the Shurta.

The *shariʿa* specifies fixed penalties for a number of criminal infractions, namely robbery, for which mutilation of the hand is prescribed, brigandage, punished by crucifixion, fornication, punished by lapidation or beating depending on marital status, calumny, punished by 100 strokes (all these supported by explicit injunctions in the Quran), and drinking, punishable by 80 strokes, in accordance with a tradition of the Prophet. All these are designated *hudud*, limits or rights of God. Another category of *qisas* (retribution) relates to the rights of humans who are injured or wronged, such as in murder or injury. In these cases, punishment is in the nature of retaliation, and the victim or his or her heirs are empowered to choose between inflicting equivalent injury or receiving compensation, *diya*. For the wide range of crimes and infractions beyond this classification, the *shariʿa* gives the judge wide discretion under the category of *taʿzir*, chastisement.

The *shariʿa*, however, also requires strict and difficult standards of evidence. To establish fornication, for instance, four male witnesses must agree that they actually witnessed the act of penetration. Add to that the risk for the witnesses themselves of being accused of calumny and punished with 100 strokes. The tendency in *fiqh* was also to retreat from the harshness of these punishments and to surround it with conditions and qualifications, to make their application even more remote.

Siyasa and Shurta justice was not limited by such strict requirements of evidence and proof. The Shurta had wide discretion in judgement according to suspicion, to circumstantial evidence, to knowledge of the character of the accused, and so on. In many cases in which the miscreant was caught in the act, as in the case of drunks, the police agent could proceed directly with the prescribed punishment without recourse to due process. In more complex cases, the chief or competent officer arrived at a verdict according to his judgement as to the balance of evidence. The Shurta were not bound by *shariʿa* procedures or penalties, their rule was quite arbitrary. Only in the matter of capital punishment were they, in most instances, required to refer ultimate judgement to the ruler or governor, who had the ultimate power to endorse or refuse such punishment. In addition to the range of corporal punishments, the Shurta could also use imprisonment and fines, neither of which are specified in the *shariʿa*.

An important difference between Shurta and *qadi* justice is that the latter could only proceed in matters brought by litigants: there was no public authority which can bring cases to *qadi* courts. One of the functions of the Shurta, however, was to apprehend miscreants and bring them to justice. As such they assumed the functions of detection, prosecution, judgement and execution. They combined judiciary and executive functions. The Shurta sometimes assumed the functions of execution of the judgements of *qadi* courts, whether in administering punishments or in the transfer of funds and goods.

It would seem, then, that at many points in the history of Muslim polities criminal and penal matters were dealt with predominantly in accordance with *siyasa* justice, by administrative authorities, typically the Shurta. Depending on time and place, it would seem that few penal cases were brought to *qadi* courts, as we shall see in examples to come. The process of criminal prosecution and punishment proceeded largely outside the framework of the *shari'a*. In most cases they were not covered by any explicit law, though no doubt by custom and local practice. Under the Ottomans, the *qanun-name* (book of ordinances) of the sultan was followed in matters of punishment, with fines (in addition to corporal infliction) as the most common specifications, as we shall see.

This largely arbitrary system of criminal justice, was, of course, wide open to corruption and the play of power and influence, and accounts of such incidences are legion.

Hisba *and* Muhtasib

The literal translation of *hisba* is 'accountability'. The origins of the term in religious and legal discourse pertain to the Quranic injunction of *al-amr bil-ma'ruf wal-nahy 'an al-munkar*, to command the good and forbid the bad. According to this injunction, each Muslim has the duty to intervene in the conduct of others, and as regards forbidding evil deeds, to remonstrate with miscreants (such as the drinkers of wine, the shirkers of prayer and fasting, those indulging in music and dance, and so on), and to stop them forcibly, if necessary. This injunction is reinforced by other pronouncement in the Quran, such as the verse: 'al-muslimun wal-muslimat awliya'un...', 'Muslims, male and female, are guardians upon one another...', which addresses each Muslim and empowers him or her to protect and direct other Muslims. As such, each Muslim must watch out to protect and enforce *huquq al-lah*, the rights of God, in his or her society and company.

If this injunction is observed in normal society, then it can lead to disorder and even rebellion, each individual taking the law into their hands and acting directly and forcefully to ensure conformity. This potential for disorder led the rulers, supported by the orthodox jurists, to interpret these injunctions as directed to the community of Muslims as a whole, to be enforced by their authorities, in accordance with another Quranic injunction to the believers to obey the God, the Prophet and *waly al-amr*, he who rules. As such, the function of *hisba* became, in legal terms, *fard kifaya*, an obligation to be discharged by qualified members of the community and not by everyone, such as military and legal functions. The ruler, then, assumed the functions of *hisba* and appointed a competent officer in charge.[5]

Hisba was instituted as a function of state from early Abbasid time. The post of *muhtasib*, appointed by the caliph or sultan, is an exalted one, coming just below that of chief *qadi* in the official hierarchy. In the earlier periods the *muhtasib* was someone qualified in law and jurisprudence, like a *qadi*, but in later times could be chosen from among the notables of state, including the military (Tyan 1960:628–30). While his functions had religious connotations, the *muhtasib* was in practice the chief of municipal administration and policing.

Chief among the functions of the *muhtasib* was the policing of markets. He and his assistants inspected weights and measures, the quality of the merchandise and inspected possible frauds, dilutions and mixing and the quality of workmanship. In some instances, the *muhtasib* appointed an agent in each craft and trade guild, known as *'arif*, to report to him on the conditions and problems of that trade (Tyan 1960:636). The legal manuals of *hisba* did not, in general, allow the *muhtasib* to fix prices, there being a presumption in Muslim legal thought in favour of private property and freedom of contract. In practice, however, *muhtasibs* did watch unusual fluctuations in price, especially of basic commodities, and intervened to correct what they saw as wide variations from the customary norms (Tyan 1960:637). Among the *muhtasib*'s powers was to ensure that professionals had the appropriate qualifications and experience for their practice. This included medics, pharmacists, teachers and even judges.

The *muhtasib* had the duty to monitor the state of the roads and buildings in the city. He had the power to order the repair or demolition of dangerous constructions and ruins. He also dealt with complaints about neighbours' transgressions in terms of space or overlooking private spaces. He dealt with obstructions to roads, the dumping of rubbish or other nuisance and dangers to health and hygiene. The *muhtasib*, however, could not deal with disputes and contests between different parties regarding sales, contracts, boundaries and so on. He could only put such matters right if there was no dispute. All disputed issues had to be settled in a *qadi* court, with appropriate procedures and witnesses.

Another area of *muhtasib* power was public morals. The *muhtasib* had to watch over public places, streets, markets and baths for infringements of rules such as drinking, drugs, prostitution and generally reprehensible conduct. He could, for instance, apprehend a man and a woman who stopped in the street for suspicious conversation (Tyan 1960:640). In these respects his competence overlapped with that of the Shurta, and in some instances the two functions came under the same office.

The conduct and public appearance of *dhimmis*, Christians and Jews, also came under the jurisdiction of the *muhtasib*. Their attire had to conform to the regulation of dress colour-code and distinguishing appendages they had to carry, as well as the rules regarding inconspicuous acts of worship, refraining from mounting horses and deference to Muslims in the streets and markets.

The *muhtasib* employed a wide range of sanctions and punishments in the enforcement of the rules. Reprimand was the lightest, then strokes of the whip, *tashir* (public humiliation) of miscreants, being made to ride a donkey backwards with colourful clothing and headgear, being paraded through the streets with derision (usually after beating) and, sometimes, imprisonment. Repeated offences could lead to disqualification from the practice of one's trade, and in the extreme, banishment from the city (Tyan 1960:649–50).

The functions of the *muhtasib*, while based on religious injunctions, proceeded in practice in the pragmatic context of administration. While *shari'a* principles are occasionally invoked, the rules which prevail in the *muhtasib's* spheres were largely ones of local custom and practice and the interests of public order.

THE *ULAMA* AND THE JUDICIAL INSTITUTIONS UNDER THE OTTOMANS

Organization of the Ulama

The Ottomans integrated the *ulama* and its functions into their elaborate state bureaucracy. Religious offices featured at every level of government, from the highest offices at court, to mosque functionaries at the local level. This hierarchy was tied to a system of education and qualifications. To that end *madrasas* were established in all the major urban centres, the highest rated being in Istanbul (the eight schools), Bursa and Edirne. Only graduates from these high *madrasas* could aspire to the more important posts and appointments. Qualification for high office included not only graduating at one of these schools, but also holding a professorship. By the time of Suleiman, candidates for high office had to pass through 12 schools in a fixed order, first as students, then as professors.[6]

The office of *shaykhulislam* was the highest religious rank, and its holders enjoyed great power at court, theoretically equivalent to that of the grand vizir. The *shaykhulislam's* functions were not judicial, but concerned issuing *fatwas*, responses to questions posed by government or by private persons. Important acts of government, such as declaration of war, had to be sanctioned by such *fatwas*. The *qanun-name* of the sultan required the sanction of a *fatwa* declaring it compatible with the *shari'a*. We shall see in Chapter 3 that Suleiman's shaykh, Ebussu'ud, set a precedent in this respect: his *fatwas* sanctioned fiscal practices and expressed them in terms of *shari'a* concepts and vocabulary. In extreme cases, manoeuvres to depose the sultan had to be sanctioned by a *fatwa* from the shaykh, which was forthcoming when it became apparent that the sultan was cornered and his deposition almost accomplished. The sultan, however, had the power to dismiss the shaykh and appoint a replacement more amenable to his wishes.

At court, the *shaykhulislam* maintained a considerable establishment and a household similar to the other grandees (Gibb and Bowen II 1957:85). Part of this establishment was the *fetva-hane*, an office specializing in receiving and answering questions from persons and groups outside the court. Ebussu'ud was credited with rationalizing the administration of this function. By the seventeenth and eighteenth centuries, when the sultans lost their absolute power in favour of other court centres, the *shaykhulislam* became one of these centres, now in competition, now in alliance with the harem, the grand vizir and the other grandees. The *shaykhulislam* levers of power included extensive patronage in appointments and favours, as well as the administration of extensive and rich endowments.

The other court positions of *ulama*, coming directly below that of the shaykh, were of the two *qadiaskars*, of Rumelia and Anatolia respectively. Below them were a number of high judgeships, of the major cities of the empire. Together with the *shaykhulislam* they constituted the class of high clerics designated as *molla*, meaning lord or master (a word which in Iran came to designate clerics in general). The *qadiaskars* sat in the imperial *divan*, one of whose functions was the administration of justice, much like the *mazalim* courts considered above, and assisted the presiding grand vizir in this task. The Qadiaskar of Rumelia was the more senior, and accompanied the armies in European campaigns. The functions of the *qadiaskars* included judicial administration and appointments to provincial judgeships (not the *mollas*, who were appointed by the shaykh) and mosque ministers (Gibb and Bowen II 1957:86–88). The *qadiaskars* dealt in their respective areas of competence with all personal status matters relating to the *'askeri* class, as distinct from the *re'aya* class, whose affairs were within the competence of ordinary judges. This distinction became less clear in the eighteenth century, when the janissaries became native Muslims and mixed with the urban traders and craftsmen. Judicial administration and appointments was carried out by a number of subordinate functionaries and clerks. In the course of the seventeenth century the *qadiaskars* lost much of their authority, as all matters of law and order were removed from the competence of *qadis*, though the Qadiaskar of Rumelia continued to deal with matters considered within his competence arising in the *divan* (Gibb and Bowen II 1957:87–88). A crucial and lucrative function of this latter was the placing under seal the property of all individuals dying in the capital, to preserve this property intact for the heirs. In practice the heirs had to pay for its release. The Qadi of Istanbul, as well as the three *qadis* of the Istanbul suburbs, also sat in the *divan* once a week to assist the grand vizir in the administration of justice.

The *ulama*, whether judges, muftis or teachers, were organized in hier-archical grades, with specified qualifications for appointment to each grade, and marked paths of promotion between them. We have already noted the rank of *molla*. Within this rank there were several grades, headed by the *qadiaskars* and the Qadi of Istanbul, followed by the *qadis* of the two holy cities, Mecca and Madina, then the two former Ottoman capitals of Bursa and Edirne, grouped with the two former seats of the caliphate, Damascus and Cairo, then the three suburbs of Istanbul, together Jerusalem, Izmir and Aleppo, and so on. In the highest order were also placed court *mollas*, such as the *hoca*, tutor of the sultan, the imam of court prayers, the court physician and the court astrologer, both reckoned as *ulama* (Gibb and Bowen II 1957:89–91).

Entry to the learned professions and its ranks was officially governed by educational qualifications. *Madrasas* were founded by the great sultans, the conqueror, Bayazid II, and Suleiman, and were usually attached to mosques. Istanbul *madrasas* were reckoned highest, and were ranked among themselves into a hierarchy of status. These had generous endowments to pay the salaries of the professors, stipends for the students, lodgings and food provisions, as well as servants and functionaries. By the time of Suleiman, the teaching and diplomas were organized into 12 grades. After the sixth grade, a student became entitled to teach while pursuing higher studies. *Softas*, as the students were called before attaining the sixth grade and becoming *danishmend*, men of knowledge, could leave after passing the lower grades and obtain posts of ordinary *qadis*, *na'ibs* or provincial muftis, and most students took this route. To attain the higher grades, students persisted in further study until they got to the ultimate grade, at which point they started on teaching grades, themselves stratified by rank and the status of the *madrasa*. To qualify for the high *meveleviyet*, 'mollaship', they had first to reach a high rank in the top school as professor (Gibb and Bowen II 1957:146–48). From the second half of the sixteenth century, nepotism and patronage predominated in the award of qualifications and appointments. Many of the top appointments were trans-mitted within families, others farmed for hefty payments. Professorship came to be regarded as sources of income and assumed by well-connected or rich persons who were incapable of teaching and were said not to even know the whereabouts of their *madrasa* (Gibb and Bowen II 1957:150). Teaching was then carried out by low-rank substitutes.

Lower-ranking *ulama* occupied a host of positions as ordinary *qadis* or *na'ibs* (deputies) or as mosque functionaries. These included the mosque imams (prayer leaders), *khatib* (who delivered the Friday oration) and *wa'iz* (preacher), as well as the *muezzin* and *qayyim* (in charge of maintenance).

This strict organization and hierarchy of the *ulama* did not always prevail in the provinces. Gibb and Bowen note that 'the freedom of the local corps of *Ulema* was roughly proportional to their distance from Istanbul' (Gibb and Bowen II 1957:98), with Cairo *ulama* as the most autonomous. The chief *qadi* of each provincial city was appointed from Istanbul on an annual tenure, as was the chief Hanafi mufti and Naqib al-Ashraf and the head of the local *ulama*. In practice, in most instances, Istanbul merely ratified local choices in the last three appointments. Muftiship and Naqib al-Ashraf were often held or rotated in local families, and the head of the local *ulama* was chosen by them. Appointees to these posts from Istanbul, if they ever arrived, were ignored or hounded out of the city, and in extreme cases, murdered (Gibb and Bowen II 1957:98–100). Al-Azhar in Egypt was also recognized and venerated as a seat of learning, and its diplomas as qualifications for local appointments, but never for Istanbul posts.

By the seventeenth century, appointments of the high *mollas* were largely restricted to a circle of families which constituted a religious aristocracy (Gibb and Bowen II 1957:105–13). *Shaykhulislams* and *qadiaskars* awarded diplomas and appointments to their children and relatives. This included the top professorships at the elite *madrasas* which qualified the holders for higher office. Soon office farming was added to nepotism, and members of the leading families paid considerable sums for high office. The large number of candidates for office and the lucrative trade in offices brought about a quick rotation of office, so that chief *mollas* held their office for no more than one year in some appointments and 18 months in others. At any one time, consequently, there was a large number of *mollas* awaiting their turn. These were given revenues from *aparliks*, nominal judgeships in some province from which they drew the income, a fraction of which paid for a deputy who did the work. Provincial high *ulama* and their families held estates and tax farms (*iltizams*). As we have seen, many of the high religious offices in the provinces tended to be transmitted within families.

In Istanbul and the provinces, then, from the seventeenth century to the period of the nineteenth-century reforms, the high *ulama* constituted a hereditary aristocracy, enjoying a high level of wealth and power. In one respect they had the advantage over their secular counterparts in the ruling classes in that their wealth was sacrosanct, not subject to confiscation by the ruler at, or even before, death. While the secular officials were considered slaves of the sultan, and their accumulated wealth forfeit at their death, the *ulama* could safely transmit wealth and position to their heirs. This aristocracy was naturally close to the rulers and to the secular sectors of the ruling class. As such, in terms of religious legitimation, the *ulama* were conciliatory and accommodating to the actions and policies of their secular counterparts (Gibb and Bowen II 1957:112–13).

Qadis *and Muftis*

The different ranks of *qadi*, ranging from the great *mollas* of the capital and the major cities, down to the ordinary *qadis* at local levels were nominated from Istanbul, by the Qadiaskars of Rumelia for the European provinces, and of Anatolia for the Asian provinces and Egypt. These constituted separate services and no transfer or promotion were possible between them. All appointments from the capital were of Hanafi *qadis*. *Qadis* of other schools were appointed locally by the chief Hanafi *qadi* in the area. Many *na'ibs* were appointed, some to deputize for the appointed *qadi* in sub-districts (*nahiya*), others as substitutes in the absence of the *qadi*.

By the middle of the eighteenth century these posts were held on annual tenures by Turkish-speaking judges. All the posts were farmed, with considerable payments to the *shaykhulislam* or the *qadiaskar*, depending on the post. The chief Qadi of Cairo, for example, paid 10,000 paras a month to the *shaykhulislam* as well as a sum to the Qadiaskar of Anatolia (Gibb and Bowen II 1957:123). *Na'ibs* were appointed by each *qadi* from among the local *ulama* who paid for their office to each new *qadi* on his appointment, thus maintaining some continuity of judicial administration. Judges appointed from the capital were originally required to be resident in the city of their appointment. The *qanun-name* of Suleiman also forbade a *qadi* to appoint a substitute. By the eighteenth century, however, these rules were mostly flouted. The Qadi of Cairo, for instance, was authorized by the *ferman* of his appointment to choose as many *na'ibs* as he saw fit (Gibb and Bowen II 1957:123). Many senior judges preferred to live in the capital, appointing substitutes in their place of appointment, paid from the accruing revenues. Retired *ulama* could hold sinecures as *aparliks*, in the form of revenues from a judicial appointment managed by a substitute (Gibb and Bowen II 1957:124). Qualifications and knowledge of the law were not always important considerations in the appointment of *na'ibs*, many of whom had scant acquaintance with legal matters, and in turn depended on clerks and muftis.

The rotation and farming of appointments ultimately rested on revenues of office. These were of different kinds. A *qadi* derived revenues from litigation fees, usually paid by the winning party at a traditional rate of 2.5 percent of the object of litigation. This percentage varied according to the status and wealth of the litigant, and could go up as high as 8 or 10 percent. Another source of revenue was from the farming of offices of *na'ibs* and clerks, some of which, such as that of *qassam*, the specialist in dividing legacies, were very profitable. Another source was from the supervision of the mosques and the endowments which supported them. Notary functions of signing and certifying documents constituted another source of fees (Gibb and Bowen II 1957:124–25).

Qadis were also charged with functions of supervision over the administration, such as those of custom officers, and certifying the accounts from various departments and mediating in disputes.

The system of office farming and of the annual rotation of the qadiships was clearly one that invited the judges to enrich themselves from the variety of possible sources. As such, it is difficult to classify these practices as 'corruption'. For the most part the judges were normally correct in their judgements, and instances of bribing judges by litigants, though known, were unusual. Gibb and Bowen (II 1957:126–33) conclude that there were a number of constraints on judges to be straight in litigation. One was the fact that local custom and usage often determined outcomes, and in more complex cases, the *qadi* merely endorsed a ruling by a mufti. Another constraint was the jealousy and censor of rival local *ulama* watching out for infractions and slips. This view is confirmed by Marcus's study of Aleppo courts (see *infra*). The scope for excessive profits came not so much from bribes as from the variable litigation charges.

We should note again that much of the administration of justice bypassed the *qadi* courts and the *shari'a*, in corporate tribunals of guilds, tribes, lineages and communities, and in the courts of rulers and their deputies, and summary judgements and punishments by police, soldiers and market inspectors. The law of Suleiman forbade the administration of any punishment without a *qadi*'s order, but this rule was largely flouted in later times.

Muftis were also involved in the judicial process, especially in the latter periods of the Ottoman centuries. As we saw, the highest religious office in the empire was held by the mufti of Istanbul as the *shaykhulislam*. He combined many functions and controlled vast resources. One of these functions was the issuing of *fatwas*, which, as we saw, was processed through a special *divan* with many clerks and functionaries, who received and reformulated the questions received for the attention of the mufti. This post was replicated in other cities and provinces, with the appointment of official Hanafi mufti for each location, and the confirmation of locally nominated muftis for the other schools where the adherence of the local populations required it. In the main Arab cities, such as Damascus, by the eighteenth century, the official muftiship became hereditary in particular families, but their continuation required confirmation from the *shaykhulislam* in Istanbul, with the usual gifts being delivered. Rival claimants tried to manipulate favour and influence in the capital, but local opinion was important in the acceptability of appointments (Gibb and Bowen II 1957:135–36).

Mufti appointments were not as hierarchical and controlled as those of *qadis*. Many scholars acted as muftis to loyal, often local, followers, informally. Many people in the provinces preferred to take their disputes to trusted scholars rather than go through the court system. Officially appointed muftis, however, especially those in the main cities, enjoyed many privileges and resources. Although they did not receive a salary, and were lower in the hierarchy to the chief *qadis*, they could charge a fee for each *fatwa*, its magnitude dependent on the status and wealth of the questioner. In addition, a mufti was given grants of pensions and various administrative posts. Some held *malikanes*, a sort of tax farm, later to become a type of possession of land. Like judges, the top muftis did not themselves discharge the *ifta'* functions but delegated them to subordinates and assistants (Gibb and Bowen II 1957:137). Muftis became involved in the judicial process, as it became common practice for many *qadis* to refer judgements to muftis. Lane, describing court procedure in Cairo of the early nineteenth century, says that the *na'ib*, having heard the case, required the plaintive to procure a *fatwa* from the mufti, which would be forthcoming for a fee (Gibb and Bowen II 1957:130–31). The mufti also sat on the hearing of important and complex cases, and it was his judgement which was endorsed by the *qadi*. It would seem, then, that at that point the mufti assumed a regular and lucrative role in the judicial process.

ENDOWMENTS

Awqaf or endowments were central to economic and religious life in most Muslim societies. They were closely involved in religious institutions, which were the main beneficiaries of charitable, *khayri*, endowments, as well as often being administered or overseen by *shari'a* courts and religious personnel. In most instances, endowments were open to considerable profiteering by their administrators and a whole range of proteges and beneficiaries, many of them in religious office.

To endow a property, usually land or urban buildings, is to restrain it from any alienation or transfer of ownership in perpetuity. The word *waqf* (plural *awqaf*) derives from the verb 'to arrest' or 'restrain'. The term used in the Maghreb is *habus*, which means 'imprisonment'. The original purpose of *awqaf* was charitable and religious. Typically, mosques, *madrasas, dervish tekkes* (Sufi lodges) and other religious functions were the beneficiaries. Kings and viziers and other notables of state were among the foremost benefactors, and grand religious monuments, such as the Suleimaniya complex in Istanbul, still bear their names. The holy cities of Mecca and Madina were maintained by such royal endowments. Religious endowments, however, did not have to be on such a grand scale, and many private individuals endowed mosques, charities to help particular categories of 'the poor', fountains and Quran recitals.

Another type of *waqf* was *ahli*, meaning private or family endowment, in which a designated group, usually the family and descendants of the benefactor, were the beneficiaries of the endowment. This was useful in consolidating property and giving it the sanction of religious law, so that it could not be alienated or confiscated by authorities, as well as being exempt from the mandatory sharing of inheritance law. In Ottoman times this type of *waqf* became widespread: notable beneficiaries were high functionaries of state, officially 'slaves' of the sultan, and as such their property subject to appropriation by him, if not in their lifetime then after their death.

Each *waqf*, of whichever kind, was usually registered in the *shari'a* court. With the Ottoman penchant for centralized organization, bureaus were established in the main provinces for registering and overseeing endowments (Gibb and Bowen II 1957:173). The vast properties and lands so endowed made them a central factor in economic life, state revenues and patterns of land-holding and labour. A person endowing property had to designate an administrator or *mutawalli*, as well as a supervisor, *nazir*. In many cases, and especially in private *awqaf*, the administrator was the benefactor himself, then his descendants. The *nazir* was often a religious functionary, such as a *qadi* or a mosque official. For the grand *awqaf*, a *nazir* may be a high functionary of state. The administrator had to submit accounts for approval by the supervisor. Neither was supposed to benefit from their respective function. In practice, however, *awqaf* became a source of considerable revenues for their functionaries.

The most lucrative *awqaf* for their supervisors were the grand endowments of the sultan, including those of the holy cities. By the seventeenth century the function of the administration and supervision of sultanic endowments was assumed, oddly, by the chief black eunuch, the *Qizlar Aghasi*. For this extensive administration and revenue many functionaries were engaged, including inspectors, *mufattish*, who were usually religious functionaries, often *qadis*. The benefits to the agha and his functionaries were so vast, that when, at a later date (under Mustafa III, r. 1757–74) one grand vizir succeeded in taking this function away from him, the increase of *waqf* revenue was enormous and the agha was compensated from the surplus (Gibb and Bowen II 1957:171). 'Corruption' in *waqf* administration was rife at all levels. All kinds of subterfuges were employed in extracting benefit, and in some cases in the conversion of a *waqf* into private property for the overseer. The co-operation of a *qadi* was needed in these transactions (Gibb and Bowen II 1957:177–78).

Religious and charitable endowments in a city or a province also constituted means of building up bases of local power and influence for aspirants to political or religious office and local notability. A *qadi*, mufti or tax-farmer, through endowing mosques, soup-kitchens and charities, could build up networks of patronage and influence. We see, then, that endowments played many parts in the political as well as economic life of Ottoman societies, and were closely involved with religious function and legal transaction.[7]

THE PROCESS OF JUSTICE: EXAMPLES

Litigation in *shari'a* courts was for the most part initiated by a plaintiff raising a *shakwa*, a complaint, against another party that caused him or her harm or injustice, failed to fulfil a promise or execute a contract. Public prosecution in *qadi* courts was rare: offences against public order, morality or the ruler were mostly dealt with by police and administrative tribunals, as we have seen. The plaintiff would state their claim. The defendant, if not present in court, would be sent for, usually through a court usher. Unless the defendant confessed to the charge, the plaintiff was asked for proof. This usually consisted of oral witnesses – at least two Muslim males (two women were equivalent to one man, non-Muslims were admitted, if at all, only when a non-Muslim was party to litigation). Relevant documentation was admitted, though it was mostly considered inferior to oral testimony, and only admissible if the notaries who witnessed the drawing up of the document were present to affirm its validity. Failing adequate evidence, the case was dismissed. A defendant making a counter-claim would be called upon to supply evidence. When cases were not clear-cut and neither party could supply adequate proof, the plaintiff could demand that the defendant swear an oath. Another alternative open to the court in complex cases was to appoint mediators, either professionals or notable figures in the trade, craft or neighbourhood of the litigants.

In Egypt in the seventeenth century, the *qadiaskar*, the chief judicial authority, would be appointed from Constantinople, and he would in turn appoint his *na'ibs*, deputies, from local *ulama*. The Hanafi doctrine was the official legal school for the Ottomans, and the *qadi* would be Hanafi, while his *na'ibs* represented the other Sunni schools. This arrangement was replicated in the provinces (El-Nahal 1979:12–14). The central Cairo court, called El-Bab El-Ali, was held in an official palace. All other courts were held in mosques, which underlined, in spatial contiguity, the connection between religion and justice.

The main court functionaries were notaries and scribes, in some places called *'udul*. These were the professional witnesses, as noted above. A large court employed several *'udul*, and al-Bab al-Ali court in the seventeenth century had

19 (El-Nahal 1979:18–19). Their notary function was to draw up and witness documents, such as those of sale, lease, marriage and other contracts. Crucially, these documents, when produced as evidence in litigation, were of little value without the oral affirmation of the *'udul* who witnessed it that that was indeed their signature. They also served as court investigators: they would investigate the probity of witnesses by questioning the notables and *ulama* of their neighbourhoods or guilds. Given that most litigation centred on the claims of a plaintiff against the denials of the accused, *'udul* could be dispatched by the court to investigate at the scene of the alleged events, mostly by questioning people in neighbourhoods and markets. Finally, the *'udul* acted as court scribes, who recorded the procedure of every case in the *sijil* (register).

The oath, an essential preliminary to a witness's testimony in modern legal systems, was an exceptional last resort for *shari'a* courts (as it was historically in many parts of Europe). When a plaintiff could not supply adequate witness evidence against the denials of the accused, then they could demand that the latter take an oath; by doing so the accused would be cleared. There were cases, however, where the accused refused the oath and, in effect, admitted the claim against them. Clearly an oath was not taken lightly, and divine retribution was feared.

Given that the great majority of cases heard by the courts in seventeenth-century Egypt were civil and family cases (El-Nahal 1979:25 counts only 3 percent in all cases in one provincial court to have been criminal, and this is quite general as we shall see), the court decision was binding on the parties who normally undertook to comply. In cases of non-compliance, the plaintiff could demand that the recalcitrant debtor or defaulter be imprisoned till they had discharged their obligations (El-Nahal 1979:41). Execution of court orders of detention, or of corporal punishments in criminal cases was entrusted to police and the wali (governor).

Abraham Marcus, in his social history of Aleppo in the eighteenth century, provides many insights into the workings of legal institutions and processes (Marcus 1989:101–20). He shows that the *qadi* court was one of a number of media for adjudicating disputes – but the most prominent, and often an ultimate recourse. Corporate bodies, such as some guilds, especially those of merchants, employed their elders and notables to adjudicate members' claims. So did the ashraf (descendants of the Prophet) and the janissaries (Marcus 1989:108). Given the cost of litigation, many claimants first resorted to informal and communal adjudication. The most important tribunal besides that of the *shari'a* court, however, was that of the pasha (governor) sitting as an administrative judge (*hakim al'-urf*, or *hakim al-siyasa*). Officially, his jurisdiction was restricted to cases of public order and state security over which the *shari'a* did not rule. In practice, however, all kinds of claims of property, marriage and crime were taken to this court. The governor and his functionaries welcomed such litigation as a source of income through fees and fines, often extortionate. This court was open to much corruption and miscarriage of justice, in contrast to the *qadi* court, which, in Marcus's judgement was generally fair and consistent, did not favour the rich and powerful, sticking to the rule of law, and open to the constant scrutiny of an informed public (Marcus 1989:112). Victims of the administrative court could take their case to the *qadi*. While often powerless to get them restitution from the government, the *qadi* could and did order their false accusers to compensate them for losses. Litigants unhappy with the verdict of the *qadi* could also take their cases to the administrative judge, with whom influence and money were more effective.

Money, of course, was also central to the functioning of the *qadis'* court. The *qadi* had to pay in Istanbul for his appointment, and had to generate sufficient revenues to recoup his outlay with profit, as well as pay his deputies and functionaries. The revenues were generated from fees paid for drawing up and notarizing documents, as well as the fees paid by litigants. It was usually the winner in a litigation who had to pay, which detracted from the benefit of winning and led to abuses in mischievous litigation.

The overall picture of eighteenth-century Aleppo which emerges from Marcus's study is one of multiple jurisdictions and legal institutions in which the *qadi* court, ruling in accordance with the *shari'a* as well as *qanun* and customary law, was the most prominent, as well as the most accountable and consistent. The others were the governor and his functionaries, the police, the janissaries, the communal courts of the religious minorities, as well as many adjudicators ruling within their corporate units ranging from tribes to guilds to ashraf. None of these, however, was exclusive, and any claim could be taken to the *qadi* or the governor.

Marcus's characterization of the Aleppo *qadi* court as consistent and predictable in its procedures and judgements goes against a regular theme in Western discourses on the subject on the wide discretion enjoyed by the *qadi* and the apparent arbitrariness of his judgements. Max Weber, in his typology of legal forms, designates the most arbitrary and discretionary as 'Qadi justice'.[8] Of course, over the many centuries in a variety of territories and social contexts, there must be a great variety of forms and procedures of such courts. However, it would be safe to assume that under conditions of social stability and continuity, a *shari'a* court, under the scrutiny of an informed public, would tend to operate consistently and predictably with its particular combination of *shari'a*, government statutes and custom relating to time and place. These issues are taken up by Lawrence Rosen in an anthropological study of law and its operation in a Moroccan city in the 1950s.

On the question of the apparently wide scope of court discretion, Rosen writes: '[strict Islamic law] ... sets substantive standards on relatively few practices, leaving within what the Quran repeatedly calls "The Limits of God" considerable scope for the varied practices of humanity' (Rosen 1989:27). This is particularly true of penal provisions: explicitly specified punishments for five or six offences, but little on the large array of possible offences which normally crop up before the courts (Anderson 1976:37). These are classified as *ta'zir*, which leaves penalties to the discretion of the judge, who often proceeds according to customary law.

Another reason for the apparent arbitrariness is that the *shari'a* is not codified: indeed, traditionally, codification was ruled out (see Chapter 4). In theory, each case is different, and the *qadi* must find an appropriate ruling for that particular case, drawing on the canonical sources and the principles distilled from them by the authoritative founders of the schools and subsequent commentators. Precedent is also ruled out as a systematic justification for judgements, precisely because no case is like another. In practice, however, the *shari'a* position on a range of issues, such as marriage and divorce, is clear and predictable. Equally, cases that were taken to *qadi* courts are unlikely to have been straightforward questions of application of well-known rules; rather, they were usually disputes regarding facts and circumstances which determine the applicability of one rule and not another, as we shall see presently from Rosen's examples. Rosen argues that *qadi*-court decisions may have been arbitrary in terms of formal law, but followed distinct patterns and rules which are derived from the basic cultural motifs of Moroccan society.

Rosen's research was carried out in the 1950s in the Moroccan town of Sefrou. It is important to note that by then the independent Moroccan state, in common with many other governments in the region, enacted modern European-style law codes to regulate most civil and criminal affairs, and retained a *shari'a* court with a *qadi* to deal with family and personal status matters, but also in civil affairs where the documents (such as those relating to property) were previously drawn in a similar court. Morocco, however, unlike Egypt and many other formerly Ottoman territories, had not, at that point, codified the *shari'a* rules on personal status, leaving the *qadi* courts their traditional latitude and autonomy (it was subsequently codified in 1957/8). Examples of the kind of cases which Rosen observed included a woman complaining that her husband had thrown her out of the house and had failed to provide for her and their children, a man wanting his wife back after she had left to live in her father's house, and where she and her father contended that the husband had divorced her, a woman petitioning the court to order her husband to procure an independent residence for the family away from her in-laws, with whom she had endless troubles and disputes; a man complaining that a new window opened by his neighbour looked onto the private quarters of his house and invaded the privacy of the women of the house; a man demanding payment from his neighbour for building on a boundary wall which he had erected entirely at his own expense. Rosen shows how the inquiries and procedures instituted by the *qadi* were in accordance with cultural knowledges, conceptions and values. His first concern was to determine the status, relationships, origins and places of residence of the litigants and their witnesses, and to allow the litigants freedom to remonstrate with one another in court so that he could obtain insights into the nature of their relationships. The *shari'a* tradition, as we have seen, assigns great weight to oral testimony, and little if any to material evidence. It was imperative therefore to determine the reliability of the witnesses in terms of their relations to the litigants, and on whether their places of residence allowed access to the kind of information about the case to which they were testifying. Witnesses were vetted in procedures of *tazkiyah* and *tajrih*. The first involves an examination of the character of the witness to establish reliability, the second is for the opposing party to impugn the witness's character. We should note that this system may work in small communities with a high density of interaction and mutual knowledge between members, but difficult – if not impossible – in the large conglomerates that characterize most modern contexts. In the case of Rosen's Sefrou, notaries, as professional witnesses were entrusted with taking the testimony of large groups of witnesses outside the court, separately or in pairs, to determine the degree of agreement between them. 'Experts', such as men with close knowledge of particular quarters and their history, and the disposition of buildings and neighbourhoods, or women with special expertise on women's bodies and complaints, were employed by the court to verify evidence. In cases of contradictory assertions between two litigants, the accused would be required to take an oath, a solemn affair in the local mosque, a procedure so awesome that few take it lightly.

We should note that, as illustrated by Rosen's example, three methods of proof were accepted: confession, witness's testimony (with stress on oral as against written testimony) and oath, this being taken not as a matter of course, and not by witnesses, but by the accused as a last resort. Material evidence, if accepted, was subordinated to oral testimony, and circumstantial evidence not normally sought or presented. Witness's testimony was accepted or rejected on the basis of the character of the witness as established by the court, rather than subject to any procedure of cross-examination. Documentary and forensic evidence, the mainstay of modern justice systems, remained secondary.

CONCLUSION

In this chapter we have explored the relation of law to power in the context of the array of judicial institutions characterizing historical Islamic polities. In the application of law, as much as in the scholarship of *fiqh*, the law was formally entrusted to religious personnel in the form of *qadis* and muftis. The institutions and personnel of the law, however, were mostly part of government and of the power structure, and subject to their exigencies, constraints and networks. As a general rule, the power of judicial personnel derived primarily from their place in these power structures and their social (primarily family) networks, rather than from the judicial institutions themselves. At the same time *shari'a* courts were only one in a plurality of judicial tribunals, operating mostly outside *shari'a* framework and procedure, directed by the ruler and his agents, with or without the participation of religious personnel. We shall consider the transformations of legal institutions and practices in the context of the transition to political and legal modernity in the chapters which follow.

3   THE *SHARI'A* AND POLITICAL AUTHORITY

We have seen that the *shari'a* as it has come down to us is a body of rules deriving its legitimacy from the theological premise that it is God's law. This law was developed by scholars, recognized and institutionalized by rulers. Within its confines, however, these rulers cannot play a part in legislation: in theory this is already established from the sacred sources, and only the *ulama* have the competence to interpret and elaborate it. Rulers' edicts, rather than making an input into the *shari'a*, sat side by side with it in various political and legal arrangements. This chapter will probe the relationship between the ruler and the scholar, its evolution and variations, and historical episodes of conflict and accommodation.

The ruler was not always excluded from the process of legislation within the *shari'a*. It would seem that in the first century of Islam, the Umayyad and first Abbasid caliphs were endowed with supreme religious authority, including in matters of interpreting and elaborating, even promulgating *shari'a* rules.[1]

These early caliphs were accorded the title *khalifat Allah*, the Deputy of God. This is controversial, because according to subsequent usage, the term *khalifa* is used in the sense of 'successor', the caliph being the successor to the Prophet (*khalifat rasul Allah*), rather than the Deputy of God. Crone and Hinds (1986: 20–23) argue that traditions indicating the latter usage in the early period were invented by scholars at a later stage to justify their view and project it to earliest times, this issue having implications for their own authority, as we shall see.[2] Crone and Hinds produce dense textual evidence from letters, proclamations and court poetry and, crucially, from inscriptions on the coinage of the period, to show the generality of the Deputy of God designation. This title, they argue, is supported by a theory of prophecy and the caliphate enunciated by the Umayyads and their supporters. God sent messengers as prophets to call the people to the true religion and guide them to the rules of the good life. Muhammad was the last of these prophets, the seal of prophethood. With his death, the era of the caliphs began: 'God raised up deputies to administer the legacy of His prophets' (Crone and Hinds 1986:27). Their task was to see to the implementations of God's ordinances, punishments and rights. It was then the duty of all Muslims to obey and support the caliph. The performance of ritual such as prayer, fasting and pilgrimage would only benefit the worshipper within the community and order established by this deputy. Disobedience is a sin to be punished in this world and the next. Caliphs are successors to the prophets (in the plural), but not necessarily subordinate to them. Some of the pronouncements in court poetry and letters from governors cited actually raise the caliphs in status and merit above the prophets (Crone and Hinds:28–34). The caliph is the guide to righteousness, and a sort of redeemer (mahdi, but without eschatological associations this term later acquired), for it is only through his guidance that the worshipper can achieve salvation (Crone and Hinds:37–38).[3]

But why did God choose the Umayyads as his deputies? It is because of their kinship to Uthman, the third caliph, companion of the Prophet, compiler of the Quran, a martyr, unjustly assassinated. In this story, Ali (the fourth caliph) was the usurper, benefiting from Uthman's death and refusing to avenge it. Mu'awiya, and with him bani Umayya, emerged victorious in the battle with the usurper, in which the final step consisted of the adjudication to the holy book.[4] In the contest of ancestors and kin, however, nothing could beat descent from the Prophet himself, which was the claim of the Alids. It is for this reason, argue Crone and Hinds (1986:32–33) that the first Umayyads (the Sufyanids) downplayed the role of Muhammad, and subsumed him under the plural 'prophets'. Direct kinship to the Prophet, on the other hand, was to be used by the Abbasids to legitimate their deputyship.

This account is subversive of the classic view of Muslim history, held by many Muslims, that the Umayyads were worldly, even cynical, usurpers from the righteous Ali, and that their rule ushered in an era of non-religious *mulk*, kingship, to end the sacred history of the caliphate under the first four Rashidun, rightly guided caliphs.[5] According to the Crone and Hinds account, the Umayyads' view of the caliphate was thoroughly religious: they saw themselves as the rightful successors of Uthman and ultimately the Prophet, as deputies of God. They are no different in this regard from Ali and the Shi'a, who proclaimed Ali and his line of succession to be the only rightful imams of the Muslims. Crone and Hinds argue that the authority claimed by the Umayyad caliphs was little different from what the Alids claimed for their imams, including the special religious charisma which attributed to them a special relation to God and knowledge of his law – even *'isma*, infallibility and immunity from sin. In their view, the Umayyads and the Alids were political rivals, and the choice between them was a religious one. This is against the conventional view of the Alids as legitimists for a line of descent and charisma, as against the Umayyads as worldly kings.

The scholars, as we have seen, were active in their pursuit of the law from late Umayyad times, and mostly in tacit opposition to Umayyad claims. According to Schacht, they worked on the 'raw materials' of Umayyad practice and local custom, and tried to harmonize them with the sacred sources. The most important source and concept in the process of Islamization of the *shari'a* is the *sunna*, with the later specific meaning of the *sunna* of the Prophet, and to a lesser extent, that of his companions (the 12 imams for the Imami Shi'a). Crone and Hinds contend that at that early period, the term '*sunna*' had different meanings, and was often used in the plural '*sunan*' (Crone and Hinds 1986: 58–62). In pre-Islamic usage, goes the argument, outstanding charismatic figures were each attributed with their *sunna*, an example and a precedent for others to follow and to invoke. This usage continued in Umayyad and into early Abbasid times. There were the *sunan* of the prophets, but then, each caliph in his turn established an example and a precedent, and therefore a *sunna*. Subsequent caliphs invoked the *sunan* of their predecessors, as well as those of the prophets, and were praised for following those *sunan*. The concept of the Prophet's *sunna* was, it would appear, known and used, but only rhetorically, and in contexts in which figures of authority were calling dissidents and rebels to compliance and obedience in accordance with the book of God and the *sunna* of his Prophet. There was no specific concept of a determinate *sunna*, nor of its specific content, let alone the means to verify the correct reporting (*isnad*) which was to emerge in later *fiqh*. The prioritization of the *sunna* of the Prophet, and the establishment of a methodology for its study and verification was to emerge in the work of the *fuqaha* which was starting then. This emergence has profound implications for legal authority. If the prophetic *sunna* is the ultimate source of the law, then it is the scholars who have the authority of enunciation. This would challenge the politico-religious absolutism claimed by the Umayyad caliphs. It is precisely such a shift from caliphal to scholarly authority that took place under the Abbasids.

The early Abbasids continued to claim religious authority and divine guidance, styling themselves deputies and trustees of God, much like their Umayyad predecessors, but with the added legitimacy of kinship to the Prophet (Crone and Hinds 1986:80–82). They invoked the *sunna* of the Prophet more frequently than their predecessors, but, initially, without the specificity of attribution of the *fuqaha*. The *sunna* continued to be used as an honorific designation of correct conduct and judgement, and to be invoked alongside the plural '*sunan*' of prophets and selected caliphs. At the same time, however, the scholars had been at work in developing a much more precise and determinate concept of the prophetic *sunna* and the methodology of its reporting and verification. The Abbasids, in their propaganda against the Umayyads, and their claim to righteousness and guidance, patronized the scholars, recognized the law they were developing, and brought them into the government and the court as dignitaries and even functionaries (Goldziher 1910/1981:44–47). The prophetic *sunna*, in the specific sense of the *hadith*, came to more prominent usage in caliphal discourse. The Abbasid Caliph Al-Mahdi (r. 775–785) is reported to have resorted to reasoning in terms of the *hadith* in a public letter (Crone and Hinds 1986:88). His successor, Harun (r. 786–809), took the first step in formal recognition of scholarly law: he appointed the Hanafi Abu Yusuf a chief *qadi* (Crone and Hinds 1986:88). Abu Yusuf was the author, as we have seen, of *Kitab al-Kharaj*, a treatise on taxation, outlining rules and practices deriving from traditions of the Prophet and other early figures. Senior *fuqaha* were being brought into the process of government, forming a corpus of expertise, status and authority.

How did the authority of the *faqih* relate to that of the caliph, and did it pose a challenge? It would seem that the occupation of scholars in developing law from the *sunna* was generally accepted and not considered to be a problem or a challenge by the Abbasids (Crone and Hinds 1986:85) until Ma'mun (more later). Al-Mansur (r. 754–775) continued to style himself as deputy of God while patronizing the scholars and accepting their jurisprudential functions. Ibn al-Muqaffa' (d. 756), his advisor, while taking for granted that private scholars were engaged in the definition of the law, was nevertheless concerned at the multiplicity of opinions and judgements. He thought it right that the caliph should intervene in the process to make the law clear and uniform. He should review the various judgements, select the ones he favoured and proclaim them as uniform and binding codes. His advice was not followed, and the plurality of enunciations prevailed and was eventually institutionalized. The main unifying principle was that of *ijma'*, consensus, of the scholars (and more remotely of the community), rather than that of caliphal authority.

We should ask, at this point, what consequences followed from the status of the early caliphs as 'deputies of God', and in that designation, law-givers and exemplars whose *sunan* were to be emulated? What traces, if any, survived of 'caliphal law' in subsequent *shari'a*? As we saw, the schools of *fiqh* in their classic formation make no reference to the Umayyad caliphs or early Abbasids as sources or authorities, except insofar as the early ones may have been narrators of prophetic tradition. This latter source became the overriding canon for the *shari'a*. The only type of input that caliphal law or precedent may have had was in constituting Schacht's 'raw material' of legal practice upon which the jurists acted in the processes of systematization and Islamization which occurred in the formative period. It is necessary for the ideology of the *shari'a* that this 'raw material' remains unacknowledged.

In Crone and Hinds's view, the *sunna* in the sense of the traditions of the Prophet, traced through reported *hadith* was established from the reign of Harun

(Crone and Hinds 1986:90). Shafi'i's formulation of a rigorous methodology of validation of rules in terms of *hadith*, Schacht's 'Islamization' noted above, further confined the *shari'a* to the competence of the jurist. From this point on the character of the *shari'a* conformed to the textbook version of scholar's law, into which caliphs and their functionaries had no input.

While the scholars were ever respectful of the caliphs and preached obedience, or at least acquiescence in authority, they were clear that the law was their province and that it was theoretically binding on the caliphs and their servants. Law derived from prophetic *sunna* posed an implicit threat to caliphal authority. Only Ma'mun identified this threat and acted to counter it by restoring caliphal claims to divine guidance and taking on Ibn Hanbal in the *mihna* episode (to be discussed in what follows). For the rest, the Abbasids and their successors in the dynasties of Islam accepted the scholars' claim to be the custodians of the law and facilitated their work through patronage and official institutions. At the same time, rulers felt free to disregard the elements of the law which claimed competence on public affairs, crucially on taxation and the laws of war. The scholars, for the most part, acquiesced in this separation, and developed political theories which enjoined obedience to the Muslim ruler. In their capacity as administrators and judges they enforced the sultan's edicts side by side with the *shari'a*. We shall see that scholars at various points in Islamic history endeavoured to clothe the prevailing legal practices and the sultan's edicts in terms of concepts and vocabulary of the *shari'a*. This was not only in subservience to the kings, but also a way of maintaining the scholars' authority and competence in all matters legal. In effect, from this point on, political power was separated from law-making, though not from law enforcing, as the *shari'a* judge derived his authority from the sovereign, while his law was derived from revelation through the *sunna* of the Prophet.

The Shi'a, in their different branches,[6] never gave up the idea that the imam was the legitimate law-maker, inspired by God. This charisma was one of descent from the Prophet in the Alid line. For them the caliph/imam remained God's deputy and the heir to the function of the Prophet. This position was – and is – retained by the Ismailis, who became largely sectarian. The modern Ismailis maintain this belief in the charisma of their Agha Khan as a hereditary position. The mainstream Imami (Ithna'ashari) Shi'a held the same view of their imam. After his occultation, however, the believers were deprived of his guidance: Imam-ul-zaman was only accessible, if at all, through dreams and meditations. In practice it is the *ulama* and the *mujtahids* who were the guardians of the law and the guides of the community. Shi'i legal reasoning and institutions are not very different in these respects from their Sunni counterparts. Only the *sunna* for them is that of the Prophet and of the 12 imams.

In their conclusion, Crone and Hinds speculate on the consequences of this separation of the law from political authority for society, polity and law in

Islam. They argue that it led to a separation of state from society: 'The state was thus something which sat on top of society, not something which is rooted in it: and given that there was minimal interaction between the two, there was also minimal political development: dynasties came and went, but it was only the dynasties which change' (Crone and Hinds 1986:109). This, in their view, leads Muslim society and polity to be archaic and static (in implicit comparison with Europe).[7] The argument is only viable in an over-religious view of Muslim society and history. It is as if this separation of *ulama*-based law, followed by the community of the believers, from state practice, constituted the determining and unvarying essence of the whole of Islam. It is true to say that in most times and places in the Muslim world the institutions and practices of *shari'a* were *ulama* based, and maintained the view that the law was of divine origin, and not open to state legislation. Yet this trait co-existed with a wide variety of institutions and state–society relations, which altered its significance. Many other legal rules, institutions and practices, originating in state or society, co-existed and interacted with the *shari'a* and its institutions. *Shari'a* concepts and vocabularies were extended to cover actual practice in state and society, as we have seen in Chapter 1, and will consider in what follows. It should also be pointed out that religion was not confined to the law and the jurists. Various forms of Sufism became widespread throughout the Muslim world, often instituted in state and society, bringing elements of the two together, and often embracing the *ulama* and the jurists themselves. I shall return to these arguments about state, society and religion in the conclusion of this chapter.

In principle, there is a tension between the theoretical sovereignty of the sacred law, and the reality of its co-existence with profane law, and often its confinement in relation to it. The *shari'a* from its earliest stages contained rules pertaining to public administration, such as the laws of war, fiscal matters of taxation and the administration of the treasury, as well as the qualifications of the ruler and his conduct. In practice, these elements of the *shari'a* were widely disregarded. Taxation, for instance, always exceeded the *shari'a*-specified categories of *zakat, kharaj, 'ushr* and *jizya*, with a variety of taxes on land, trade, tolls and many other spheres. Administration and statecraft soon adopted and adapted existing practices in the defeated states of Persia and Byzantium, as did fiscal practice and the conduct of war. Although the *shari'a* contains many explicit penal provisions, punishment and retribution were often taken over by administrative or military authorities and personnel, in accordance with their own rules, or whims. These issues will be further elaborated in what follows.

The power of the jurists and the degree of their dependence on the ruler varied over time and place, depending on their place in the social and political structures. The Maliki jurists of al-Andalus in the Nasirid period (fourteenth century), for instance, enjoyed considerable power in relation to the ruler by virtue of being recruited from aristocratic families with powerful networks, and being involved in the constant intrigues and conspiracies of power (Masud 1995:33–47). They employed these powers in their struggle to suppress religious challenges to their legalism, in the form of philosophical works and Sufi trends, a form of contest which recurs in Muslim history. The ruler shared with the orthodox *ulama* an interest in suppressing heresy, as this is often accompanied by political subversion. This common interest led to a degree of interdependence between the ruler and the jurist. In some situations, as in that of Baghdad in early Abbasid times, the jurist could also count on the support of the populace in agitations against infidels and heretics. Popular wrath and fear of disorder could act as a further incentive for the ruler to support the *ulama* in combating heresy. However, popular sentiment can work in other ways. Sufi devotions, and the supportive social organization of the *turuq*, have, in various contexts, proved to be highly popular. The persecution of Sufis, recurrently demanded by the *ulama*, could also alienate the populace and lead to intrigue and disorder. These factors, and the intellectual attractions of mysticism, led to the spread and dominance of Sufi manifestations throughout the Muslim world, and the ultimate integration of Sufism into the religious sciences and even *fiqh*. This occurred first in the work of the great theologian, philosopher and jurist Ghazzali, in his treatise *Ihya' 'ulum al-din*,[8] which, among other advances, incorporated Sufi thought into mainstream religious discourse. Nevertheless, attacks on Sufism recurred at various points in Muslim history (notably in the modern period). The form of the contest and its outcome depended on particular political contexts, examples of which will be presented in what follows. At this point we should note that in most periods and regions, Sufi *turuq* were established as institutions and networks with considerable support and power, enjoying extensive resources secured by *waqf* endowments. As such, they were a power to contend with for both jurists and rulers. Their leaders, often descendants of charismatic founders, became integrated into urban power elites. This salient Sufi presence, although it often included jurists, nevertheless presented an implicit challenge to their legalistic interpretation of religion and to the supremacy of the *shari'a*. This is the reason for the recurrent 'purist' movements of orthodox jurists and their supporters against Sufism, and the struggles which followed.

SCHOLARS AND SULTANS: EPISODES FROM ISLAMIC HISTORY

In this section patterns of relations between rulers and *ulama* will be examined, with respect to religious authority and the law. First, the episode of Ibn Hanbal's confrontation with Ma'mun and his successors between 833 and 849, which passed into a legend of *ulama* independence, reinforced in historical memory by the much later episode of another Hanbali *'alim*, Ibn Taimiya (d. 728) and his confrontation with his Mamluke masters. In both episodes we examine political struggles in which the *shari'a* and aspects of *ulama* power in relation to the state are exhibited. They feature charismatic, orthodox *ulama* fighting to uphold religious righteousness and their autonomy against princes and their servants. In these struggles they were facing other *ulama* and religious functionaries ranged against them in political struggles. What distinguishes Ibn Hanbal and Ibn Taimiya in the annals of *ulama* is precisely that they stood up to princes and suffered the consequences – a stance only too rare, but one that illustrates the issues of conflict and resolution.

THE *MIHNA* OF IBN HANBAL IN ABBASID POLITICS

Ibn Hanbal (780–856) is identified as the prototype of the 'fundamentalist' *'alim*, a literalist in scripture, a rigorous follower of tradition (a tireless compiler of *hadith*), rejecting all elements of reason – even *qiyas* – philosophy and theology as innovation (*bid'a*) and impious meddling in what does not concern the believer. The famous inquisition (*mihna*) to which he was subjected by three successive Abbasid caliphs, and his ultimate but ambiguous rehabilitation by a fourth, constitute a formative episode in the history of Islam, one concerned with the relation of scholarly to political authority. It was part of a history that culminated in a *modus vivendi* between the two, resting on a separation of authority which was to take different forms in subsequent history. Let us consider the background and events of this episode.

The Abbasid caliphate came into being in 750 through a 'revolution' or civil war, in which the dynasty utilized legitimist propaganda against the Umayyads.[9] These latter, as we have seen, were widely perceived in the early Islamic world to be deficient in religious piety, worldly kings pretending to religious authority as deputies of the Prophet (actually, of God, see above). The Alids and their sympathizers viewed them as usurpers. It is on this particular issue that the Abbasids concentrated their propaganda. The clandestine movement which they started, primarily in Khurassan in eastern Iran, agitated for the overthrow of the Umayyads in favour of a descendant from the family of the Prophet, understood by followers to be a descendant of Ali. It was only at the hour of their triumph that the claimant, until then a veiled figure, was revealed to be Abu'l-Abbas, from the lineage of al-Abbas, the Prophet's uncle. Disappointing the Alids and many other supporters, the Abbasids strove to advance their religious credentials, upholding the Quran and the *sunna* of the Prophet as the bases of rule and justice (Goldziher 1981:44–47; Crone and Hinds 1986:83). Goldziher goes as far as characterizing Abbasid rule as 'a theocratic regime' with an ecclesiastical policy, supplanted the Umayyads, whom pietistic circles had condemned for worldliness [...] The Abbasids ... proclaimed that they were establishing a regime in harmony with the sunna of the Prophet and the requirements of divinely revealed religion. [Goldziher 1910/1981:45]

The Abbasid caliphs, while engaged in this pious posturing, were, at the same time, modelling themselves on the pomp of Persian kingdom, assuming its courtly culture, its luxuries, costumes and titles, including the theocratic assumption of unifying church and state under their authority. Yet they did not follow the logic of this theocracy by promulgating the law, and were content to leave this task to the *fuqaha*. The stock of the *fuqaha* rose in the court of the Abbasids, and they were recognized and patronized as the researchers and upholders of revealed and prophetic norms. The office of *qadi* acquired greater definition, and was occupied by prominent jurists, such as Abu Yusuf under Harun. Ibn al-Muqaffa', advisor to Abu Ja'far, was, as we mentioned previously, alarmed by the seeming autonomy of the scholars in promulgating law, and while taking their function for granted, he advised the caliph to assume legal authority in establishing a code of the correct laws and enforcing them, an advice which was not followed.

There followed a period, until and including the caliphate of Harun al-Rashid, during which the *fuqaha* continued to develop and advance their legal norms and arguments. Indeed, this was the period of the early flourish of *fuqaha*'s law, with figures such as Abu Hanifa (d. 767), and his disciple, Abu Yusuf. Their attitude and relation to authority varied. While Abu Hanifa was reported to have been reluctant to have any 'truck' with authority, considering it a source of impiety, and to have refused the position of *qadi* offered by the caliph, for which refusal he was flogged, Abu Yusuf did become a judge, and a notable of the court of Harun. He wrote his *Kitab al-Kharaj* as a guide to the caliph on fiscal matters in accordance with the *shari'a*. All these early Abbasids, however, left the scholars alone in the development of the law, without interference or assertion of caliphal authority.

This autonomy of the scholar in matters of religion was to come to a temporary halt during the reign of Ma'mun. To understand this shift, and the *mihna* episode, let us survey the political and intellectual scene.

The politics of early Islam, including that of the Umayyad state, was that of Arab factions and tribes. The conquered territories of the Persian and Byzantine empires became home to Arab soldiers, who were, however, insulated from the local populace in garrison cities. The cities were divided into quarters, each inhabited by tribally identified segments, and these constituted the bases for solidarities and factions. It was from the Iraqi garrison cities of Kufa and Basra that the agitations against Uthman started, intrigues that were to culminate in his assassination and the subsequent civil war. These Arabs were not involved in the agricultural economy of the territories, which remained largely in the hands of local peasantries, some converted and some not. Eventually the caliphs and their families established control over land revenues, the land still tilled by native peasants, and made grants of land to governors and generals. (Crone 1980:51).

The fiscal system was such that the Arab elite and the garrisons were funded from the taxes (*kharaj*) levied on the native populations. This consisted of *jizya*, poll-tax on non-Muslims, and the land tax (divided into *'ushr*, tithe, levied on Muslims, and *kharaj*, on non-Muslims). The burden of taxation induced many peasants to convert to Islam, and even more to abandon the land and flee to the cities. This loss of revenue led to many of these conversions not being recognized by the authorities, on the grounds that they were financially motivated. Peasants would then be rounded up and returned to their villages (Hawting 1986:5). One way to avoid this fate was to acquire an Arab patron, through the bond of *wala'*, thus becoming a *mawla* (plural *mawali*), a subordinate and dependent. This was to change under the Abbasids.

The Abbasid 'revolution', as we have seen, was planned and organized from Khurasan, a turbulent province, remote from Syria, the centre of Umayyad power, with a lively political and religious scene, combining Persian aristocracy and discontented Arab soldiery, and one in which religious heterodoxy, with traces of Persian religion and Alid sympathies, flourished. Abbasid agitation and intrigue, advanced by their able agent Abu Muslim al-Khurasani, in the name of the family of the Prophet (assumed by followers to be an Alid imam), fell on fertile ground. These were to transform the political field under the Abbasids, and bring the *mawali* into prominence, as secretaries, aristocrats and soldiers, as well as intellectuals and philosophers.

What happened, then, to the Arabs of the garrison cities? Most of them ceased to be soldiers, took up urban occupations of craft and trade, and constituted an urban bourgeoisie. It was in this milieu that the pursuit of the law, of *shari'a* and *fiqh*, flourished, at the hands of this very bourgeoisie, and the *shari'a* was stamped with their distinctive preoccupations of piety and commerce. This bourgeoisie had an ambivalent attitude to government: a distrust of power, considering it polluting by its impiety and corruption, and a desire to institute virtue, in the form of the sacred law, in government and public life. The caliphs, for their part, patronized the scholars and the religious classes, in pursuit of religious legitimacy among the populace, but also, it would seem, for their own edification. Harun al-Rashid and his successors were known to call preachers to their courts, inviting them to speak freely of the straight path and the dangers of hell fire. Harun was known for the luxury of his court and harem, and his patronage of the musical arts and singing slave girls, accompanied by indulgence in wine and good company. He was also known for his cruel tyranny in dealing with subjects and perceived enemies. At the same time, he liked forthright preachers. It is related that he once invited the famous preacher Ibn al-Sammak to preach to him, which he did, saying that in the afterlife there were only two states, no more: the choice was between heaven and hell. At this the caliph wept, wetting his beard. On another occasion, al-Rashid is said to have fainted from the severity of the preacher's warnings of the torments of hell. On recovering he awarded the preacher 1000 dinars (Wardi 1954:58–59).

The corruption of government, as seen by the pious bourgeoisie, had intellectual and religious dimensions. Philosophy, theology, and poetry, as well as luxury, illicit sex, music, dancing and drink, were associated with the court. The personnel of these activities included many Persian aristocrats, scribes and artists. The Arab bourgeoisie, for the most part, resented this courtly society and its urban counterpart, and this resentment had its religious components: upholding the *shari'a* and prophetic authority against the innovations of philosophy and its input into religion. Ibn Hanbal ultimately became the martyr and the champion of this advocacy.

The Abbasid *dawla* (loosely, 'state') comprised an expanded and sophisticated bureaucracy, manned by secretaries and courtiers who were drawn, for the most part, from the converted Persians, many coming from Khurasan. The Barmakids were the most prominent family supplying court secretaries, mainly during Harun's reign. In addition to politics and statecraft, this courtly aristocracy patronized the arts and philosophy. In matters of religion, they were inclined to the liberal and syncretistic and were soft on the Shi'a. In all these respects they fell foul of the *ulama* and the traditionalists, who saw it as impious and heretical. There was also an 'ethnic' dimension, of Arab against Persian. This is exemplified by the satirical verses of Abu Nawas, the famous court poet in Harun's time, known for his adventures and verses on wine and boys. He mocked the Arab preoccupation with Bedouin virtues, the desert, the romance of tents and horses, and the drinking of fermented milk, with which he contrasted fine wine, symbolizing urban living. One mocking verse enjoins the listener to piss upon milk if it should ferment, and to seek instead the amber nectar of aged wine.

The Abbasids faced challenge and opposition from the various Shi'ite sects and forces. The mainstream Shi'a and their imams were for the most part quietist, abandoning open defiance and revolt after the first days of the Abbasids. Their fortunes fluctuated: they enjoyed some sympathy and patronage, to the extent that the Caliph Ma'mun designated the contemporaneous Alid Imam al-Rida as his successor (Kennedy 1981:157–58) (which was not to pass, as Ma'mun outlived the imam). Basically, the logic of the Abbasid claim of religious legitimacy in terms of kinship to the Prophet bolstered the claims of the Alids, who were after all direct descendants in the prophetic lineage. So despite the general quiescence of the Shi'a, the authorities were always nervous about their potential claims. Indeed, sundry rebels at various points in Abbasid history made Alid claims of descent for their leaders.

Kharijites were another source of intrigue and rebellion. They were the Jacobins of early Islam: opposed to any sort of kingly rule or any authority outside that of the book. They strove for an egalitarian community of Muslims ruled by chosen amirs who ruled strictly in accordance with the book. As such, they rejected all caliphates. It was they who assassinated Ali and rebelled against Umayyads and Abbasids alike.[10]

In this religious context, the Abbasids inclined towards the Sunnis and their *ulama*, for those were against rebellion and preached acquiescence in caliphal rule, even when judged to be impious. The price they sought for this acquiescence was for the caliph to recognize and enforce the *shari'a*, and to combat heresy. That is to say, they sought for their specific religious authority to be upheld, in return to keep quiet about political authority and the reasons of state. This was to be the general pattern in Sunni Islam through medieval times and in many instances until recent times. But at the time of Ma'mun it was in the process of being set, and the *mihna* of Ibn Hanbal was a formative episode.

Ma'mun consolidated his caliphate after a civil war with his brother al-Amin, both being designated by their father Harun to share the caliphate, Amin in Baghdad and Ma'mun in Khurasan. After his triumph in the civil war, Ma'mun retained Marw in Khurasan as his capital, and was in general favourable to the Persian culture of his mother. His patronage of scholars and intellectuals favoured the philosophers. A central theological controversy of the time was that between the Mu'tazila, who favoured reason and logic in the understanding of God and his book, and the traditionists, who insisted on the authority of the book read literally and the *sunna* of the Prophet. One major issue was that of free will versus determinism and predestination (Watt 1973:209–52). The traditionalists held on to the absolute power of a God who foresees and determines everything. The rationalists objected that such a determinism would contradict God's basic attribute of justice: how could he cause men to sin and then punish them for it? No, they asserted, God had given man free will and choice, and would judge him on his actions. This presupposed standards of justice and morality outside revelation, part of reason with which God endowed mankind. To the literalists, this was heresy.

A related issue was that of the 'createdness' of the Quran: whether the Quran was the direct speech of God, his word and breath, or was created by him, caused to be spoken (and subsequently written) by the angel to the Prophet, and the Prophet to his people? The implications of the respective positions was that if the Quran was created and spoken through human agency, then it was open to the exercise of human reason, and therefore interpretation. The traditionalists insisted that the Quran was the breath of God, to be read and understood in its literal meaning, not susceptible to reason or interpretation. A side issue here was that of *tajsim*, anthropomorphism: if the Quran speaks of the hand of God or his head, it follows for the literalists that God is shaped in human form and is thus embodied. The rationalists argued that this literal interpretation was heresy, and that we cannot presume a body of God. It was on these issues that the *mihna* or inquisition was conducted. Ma'mun, siding with the rationalist Mu'tazila, ruled that the Quran was created, and required all the *ulama* to subscribe to this doctrine. His reasons for taking this position may have included a determination to assert the religious authority of the caliph as against the *ulama*, perhaps on the model of Persian kingship which combined political and religious authority. Ibn Hanbal, the arch-literalist, refused.

Ahmad Ibn Hanbal was born in Baghdad in 780, a descendant from a captain in the Abbasid army in Khurasan, but, it is said, of pure Arab stock.[11] He started studying and memorizing the *hadith* at 15 years of age, attending on scholars residing or passing through Baghdad (Patton 1897:11–18). Like students and scholars in general throughout the history of Islam, Ahmad then travelled to different centres of learning: Kufa, Basra, Mecca, Madina, Yemen, Syria and Mesopotamia (Patton 1897:12). We are told that he studied *fiqh* with prominent scholars such as the great Shafi'i himself, as well as Abu Yusuf, the Qadi of Harun. His great passion, however, was not *fiqh*, as he was disinclined for any speculative pursuits, but the collection of traditions.

Ma'mun is said to have been an avid student of theology, the Quran and traditions, and to have been thoroughly tutored in these sciences from early childhood. He subsequently widened his horizons into philosophy, and was much influenced by the Mu'tazila, the main school of rationalist philosophy, whom he favoured in his court. His chief *qadi*, Abu Dowad, was one of the main protagonists of the doctrine of the createdness of the Quran and an instigator of the *mihna*. Until the time of Harun, this doctrine was considered heretical, and philosophers holding it had to dissimulate their views or hide from the wrath of the authorities. So there may have been an element of reaction and revenge when Ma'mun was converted to that view. It is significant that Ma'mun and his supporters also expressed Alid sympathies, and declared their preference of Ali over the first three caliphs (Patton 1897:54) – a view offensive to the orthodox. As earlier indicated, at one point Ma'mun appointed the Alid Imam al-Rida as his successor to the caliphate. This lends credence to a political analysis of these stances: Alid advocacy insisted on the combination of political and religious authority under an imam with the charisma of lineage. To the Shi'a, their imam is the ultimate authority, and their *ulama* only assumed religious authority in subsequent centuries after the 'occultation' of the imam and his inaccessibility. So, in both stances, the Alid and the philosophical, Ma'mun was asserting the religious authority of the caliph over the *ulama*. The supremacy of traditions and a literalist reading of the Quran, culminating in a legalistic religion favoured the authority of the *ulama*; that of philosophy, reason and, paradoxically, the charisma of lineage favoured the caliph.

Ma'mun's claim to the stewardship of the true religion is contained in his letter to his governor in Iraq, written in 218, a few months before his death (text quoted in Patton 1897:56–61). In it he commands his governor to summon all the *qadis* and traditionists in his province, to read the letter to them, then test them on their views of how the Quran came about. His claim to ultimate authority and stewardship of religion is expressed in the opening of the letter:

> That which God has laid upon the imams of the Muslims, their Khalifs, is to be zealous in the maintenance of the religion of God...in the inheritance of prophecy which he has granted them to inherit...to act justly, also in those interests of his subjects over which God by his grace and bounty has appointed him to have rule. [Quoted in Patton 1897:57]

He then goes on to lament and decry the ignorance of the vulgar and their laxity in the assertion of the unity of God by putting him on an equal footing with the things he has created (that is to say, the Quran: this was a common argument at that time to damn the opponents with the charge of *shirk*, polytheism or erecting other gods). Then it goes on to rehearse the textual evidence for the createdness of the book, quoting verses such as 'wa-ja'alnahu qur'anan arabiyan', 'we made a Quran in the Arab tongue' (the argument then revolves on whether to make is to create).

Ma'mun then instructs his governor to report back to him on the confession of the assembled *qadis* and *ulama*, after testing them as to their confession of the true doctrine. He was also to instruct them to test legal witnesses before them and not to accept the testimony of anyone not confessing to the true doctrine. Any who did not assent was no longer to be engaged in the service of the Commander of the Faithful.

There followed a series of episodes of imprisonment and inquisition against recalcitrant *ulama*, chiefly Ibn Hanbal. At one point, he was taken in chains to be tested by the caliph, then on campaign in Tarsus in Asia Minor, but Ma'mun was to die before Ibn Hanbal arrived. Ma'mun's two successors, based in Baghdad, were to continue the inquisition. Ibn Hanbal was steadfast, continuing to assert that God is 'as he described Himself', and that the Quran was the word of God (Patton 1897:72).

Al-Mu'tasim (r. 833–842) eventually summoned Ibn Hanbal to the palace, to which he was taken in chains. There he was required to debate the Quran and matters of faith with a court notable. The adversaries rehearsed the stock arguments, Ibn Hanbal maintaining that the Quran was the knowledge of God imparted to man, and as such uncreated. The accounts of this interrogation upon which Patten draws (and with which he clearly sympathizes) are of those of Ibn Hanbal's biographers and hagiographers, and from these accounts he appears to be getting the better of his interrogators. This process went on for three days, during which disputations were interspersed by threats and cajoling from the caliph and the notables for Ibn Hanbal to recant, but to no avail. On the third day, after further disputations, he was ordered to be scourged with the whip (Patton 1897:107). Ibn Hanbal only protested that the punishment was unlawful, as the Prophet had given security to any man who professed the faith. The chief *qadi*, Abu Dowad, is said to have urged the caliph to execute Ibn Hanbal, which he refused to do. The punishment stopped when the victim collapsed. He was subsequently released and returned to his home.

In the meantime, the crowd outside the palace were getting very angry at news of the scourging. Ibn Hanbal apparently enjoyed considerable popularity among the common people of the city, who were, in any case, resentful of the caliph and his soldiery. It is said that the punishment ceased in fear of the mob attacking the palace. Indeed, the caliph called Ibn Hanbal's uncle and made him address the crowd outside to assure them of their imam's safety.

Ibn Hanbal was then left alone by al-Mu'tasim, who died in 842. The next caliph, al-Mutawakkil (accession in 847), eventually put a stop to the *mihna* in 849, abandoning the doctrine of the creation of the Quran, and forbidding anyone to profess that doctrine on pain of death. Patton, ever faithful to orthodox sources, tells us that 'there was a great rejoicing everywhere' (Patton 1897:123) at this proclamation, which gained this caliph much blessing and praise from the populace, despite impious acts such as granting his Turkish soldiery permission to sack Damascus, and his destruction of the tomb of al-Hussain (again, we see orthodox zeal closely coupled to anti-Alid sentiment) – a near sacrilege.

There then followed what seems like a rehabilitation of Ibn Hanbal at the hands of al-Mutawakkil. After initial suspicion of Ibn Hanbal's independence and aloofness, the caliph then tried to overwhelm the doctor with gifts, favours and invitations to his court to tutor his young son. Ibn Hanbal quietly resisted these overtures, ridding himself of all cash gifts in disbursements to pious purposes, selling gifts of valuable costumes for the same purpose, and forbidding his sons from receiving the gifts when the caliph diverted his favours to them (in which they disobeyed their father). Eventually the caliph realized the futility of his attentions.

Finally, on his deathbed, we are told, great crowds were said to flock to Ibn Hanbal's house and neighbourhood, eventually stopped by guards mounted at the gates. In his final illness, it is reported, he would not groan with pain, because groaning could be construed as a complaint against God (Patton 1897:170). He was happy when his son reported to him that, after discharging debts and obligations, he only had a small coin left in his purse. Great crowds assembled for his funeral, some say 600,000, some as high as 2.5 million (there couldn't have been anything like as many people in Baghdad of the time). It is said that there were 10,000–20,000 converts to Islam at his death. These are familiar features of the hagiography of saints and martyrs.

A note on Ibn Hanbal's 'puritanism', a characteristic attributed by some to all of orthodox Islam.[12] His asceticism in matters of comfort, dress, food and money are legendary, as is his aversion to any form of speculative thought as an avenue of disobedience and sin (see letter to Caliph, quoted in Patton 1897: 155–63). Yet we learn at one point, in passing, that he had children from a concubine (Patton 1897:175). Clearly, in orthodox Muslim piety, asceticism did not include sexual restraint, providing it was within the legal framework and supported by the *sunna* of the Prophet and the companions.

Of the founders of the orthodox schools of law, Ibn Hanbal stands out as the uncompromising literalist. However, his basic stance of the supremacy of the text and the traditions, and the rejection of philosophy and even theology, were to become regular features, with various degrees of strictness of the whole of Sunni Islam.[13] After the *mihna* episode, the authority of the *ulama* in matters of law and faith was rarely challenged in the Sunni world. At the same time, the *ulama* accommodated political authority, for the most part without question, and extended their tolerance to the sultanates that held the real power with the decadence of the Abbasid caliphate.

MILITARY USURPERS AND THE POLITICAL THEORY OF SUNNI REALISM

As a preliminary to a consideration of the notable impact of Ibn Taimiya in Muslim political and legal history, this section will explore some issues in Muslim political thought regarding the imama and *khilafa* (caliphate). These two terms are used almost interchangeably, with connotations of dual political and religious authority over the Muslim community. *Khilafa* and *khalifa* came to be the general designations of supreme authority in the Sunni world, while imama and imam prevailed as Shi'i designations. Imama, however, continued to be used by Sunnis as a more general designation of religio-political authority, and is the prevalent term in juristic discourse. Concepts of power and authority were further complicated with the rise of military 'usurpers' who imposed their rule over a now powerless Abbasid caliph, starting with the Buyids in 946. The jurists had to find conceptions and legitimations for the forms of rule which followed. I shall return to this question after considering the background of the historical disputes over the imama.

All Muslim thought concerning the imama naturally harks to the example of the Prophet and his rule in Madina, followed by his faithful companions, the four rightly guided caliphs. Yet it is generally agreed that this period ended with the Umayyads in 684, and came to a more decisive end with the eclipse of the Arab caliphate. At the same time, practically all the Muslim branches, with the possible exception of the Kharijites, agree that imama, rule by a unifying commander, is an essential condition for the Muslim community. The central question, then, is what are the conditions and attributes of this imama, after the age of the Prophet had passed?

Two different answers are given in the two dissident sects of early Islam: the Shiʻites and the Kharijites. The Shiʻite answer insisted on continuity with the prophetic period in the imamate of the descendants of the Prophet. They contend that the Prophet designated Ali as his successor, a designation abrogated by the first three caliphs. The designation of Ali was infallible, given that it was made by one with divine inspiration. As such, Ali and his descendants, each designating his successor, were equally infallible, and enjoyed special divine guidance. They could lead and instruct the community of the faithful with divine guidance. The imam, for the Shiʻa, is *maʻsum*, without error or sin. The founding Shiʻi theologians, such as al-Hilli (d. 1325), argued that the designation of an imama was a duty of providence, an obligatory grace (*lutf wajib*), an obligation with the same logic as that of sending prophets (Laoust 1939: 279). That is to say, God is obliged to designate and inspire imams to guide the faithful. As it happened, the Shiʻite community escaped the rigours of such infallible theocracy with the 'disappearance' of the twelfth imam in 874. Thereafter, Twelver Shiʻism continued, for the most part, as a sectarian community. When it became the official religion of Iran from the beginning of the Safavid dynasty in 1500, the claim of the early Safavids to the imamate was not sustained, and the doctrine of the occultation of the imam continued as a messianic creed to the present day. Ismaʻili dynasties, notably the Fatimids, had no such inhibition, and claimed the status of imam for their caliphs. In practice it made little difference.

The second answer to the problem of the imamate was that of the Kharijites (Watt 1973:9–37). In their view, there was nothing in the Quran or the *sunna* to require an imamate with a special religious status. Rule in the Islamic community was by the book and the law, not a special person. After the Prophet, there was no sanctity in the ruler, only in the community. A leader was no more than a practical necessity, and as such was to be elected by the community, and he was to rule by the book. Kharijites as such were always rebels, always combated by the authorities. Few survived in sectarian communities (the Ibadis of Oman and Algeria). Their spirit, however, survived in many Muslim contexts. We shall see presently that Ibn Taimiya had a certain sympathy with these views, and many of the radical Islamists of our time invoke similar notions. In a sense, Kharijism is very 'modern'.

The Shi'a and the Khawarij had clear answers to the question of the imamate: what about mainstream Sunnism? Sunni theorists agree on the obligation of the community to have a supreme leader. They don't entirely escape the genealogical conditions of the Shi'a. After a dictum attributed to the Prophet and the companions, *al-umara' min Quraysh*, the amirs are from Quraysh (the tribe of the Prophet and the Arab caliphs), Qurayshi descent becomes a condition of the imamate. In addition, the qualities required in an imam were enumerated: a male (potent) Muslim of sound body and mind, intelligent and learned, indeed some specify the learning and ability for the practice of *ijtihad*, deducing judgement and rule from the sacred sources. Needless to say, justice, probity and virtue form part of the catalogue of merits necessary for the caliphate.

How is this caliph to be chosen or designated? According to the precedent of the succession to the Prophet (in the Sunni version), a caliph is elected by a consensus of the community, which then pledges allegiance in a contract of *bay'a*, in return for righteousness and justice of rule. Who, then, are the electors? After the early days of the city state it could not be the whole community. Most jurists agreed that it was the *ahl al-hall wa-l-'aqd*, literally, those who bind and loosen, that is to say the notables and powerful of the community. In practice, the *bay'a* became a ritual formality sanctioning dynastic or violent succession, but was maintained in juristic theory. This theory had to make further adjustments in dealing with the forceful imposition of military dynasties.

A succession of Persian and Turkish military dynasties ruled over Muslim lands, with the nominal suzerainty of the now puppet Abbasid caliph, starting with the Shi'i Buwayhids in 946. Throughout this period the rulers upheld Sunni Islam and fostered its institutions of education, the law and the *awqaf*. They built mosques and *madrasas*, appointed *qadis* and patronized jurists. Most affairs of state administration and security, however, largely bypassed these institutions, including taxation, which went far beyond what is prescribed by the *shari'a*. That is to say, a duality between religious law and institutions on the one hand and government and military establishments on the other was crystallized in this period. This duality was given theoretical justification by the Sunni jurists, notably in the work of the eminent Ghazzali, and that of the best known political theorist of Sunni Islam, Mawardi. The gist of their justification was that obedience was due to a Muslim ruler who protected and expanded the Muslim domains, fought heresy and error and fostered the conditions for Muslims to worship and apply the holy law in peace. Obedience was due even if such a ruler was impious in his personal and courtly conduct and oppressive in his rule. In Ghazzali's words:

> We consider that the function of the caliphate is contractually assumed by that person of the Abbasid house who is charged with it, and that the function of government in the various lands is carried out by means of sultans, who owe

allegiance to the caliphate. Government in these days is a consequence solely of military power, and whosoever he may be to whom the possessor of military power gives his allegiance, that person is the caliph. [Quoted in Gibb 1962a: 142–43]

Providing such a ruler did not command his subjects to disobey God's commands, then he must be obeyed, and Muslims should go to *jihad* on his side. Rebellion and insubordination were condemned as intrigue, *fitna*, which will divide the *umma*, the Muslim community, in mutual strife. This is a clear call for political quietism and acquiescence, and a mandate to any Muslim ruler for absolute and arbitrary rule. This line of reasoning postulates, implicitly or explicitly, two spheres of leadership and rule with different standards of legality: the community and the government. The community is ruled by the *shari'a*, maintained and operated by the *ulama*, but with the power of the ruler as its sanction. The government rules in accordance with its own reason and decrees, dictated military and fiscal exigencies, and the interest, *maslaha*, of the Muslims. Yet the jurists who ventured into formulations of public law, such as Mawardi, and the more outspoken Ibn Taimiya, never gave up on attempting to insert divine law and notions of righteousness and justice into the practice of government, but with little consequence for the latter. Many have argued that Muslim public law, based on *shari'a* principles and methods, can only fully apply to the utopian mode, since the actions of actually existing government do not conform to it. This has generated the fictional character of so much of public law in the *shari'a*, one that has been widely remarked, as in the following comment by Snouck-Hurgronje:

> The School continues to teach, with great seriousness, what functionaries there are in the theoretical Muslim state, which does not exist in reality, and what are their proper functions; it continues to describe the administration of imaginary revenues of this state, according to laws which were rarely applied, and then only in the earliest years of Islam. It continues to trace the paths which must be followed to bring the whole world under Muslim authority, and to determine the laws of war, the rights and obligations of conquered infidels…in one word, it continues to trace the rules of the law which should prevail if the world was other than it is in reality. [*Revue Histoire de Religion*, XXXII:21, quoted in Tyan 1960:9–10]

This view is largely correct, but needs important qualification. Prominent jurists, as we have seen, expanded divine law to include actual government practice. Such was the case with Mawardi, whose *Al-Ahkam al-Sultaniya*, the statutes of government, was a detailed manual of public law, a mixture of *shari'a* principles and actual practice.[14] In effect what this enterprise does is to extend *shari'a* concepts and vocabulary to cover existing practice. It gives religious legitimacy to government practice, and at the same time maintains the competence and authority of jurists in political and administrative matters. Such enterprises were particularly marked in the Ottoman period, as we have seen in Chapter 1 in the example of Hanafi law mutations to cover changing practices in land-holding taxes and rents (Johansen 1993), and as we shall see below in this chapter in the example of Ebussu'ud in relation to taxation and cash endowments.

Ibn Taimiya, unlike Mawardi and the later Ottomans, accompanied his juristic efforts with public stances which proved challenging to powerful quarters and authorities, thus making him, for subsequent activists, an emblematic figure of religious righteousness in politics.

IBN TAIMIYA AND THE MAMLUKES

Taqi Eddin Ahmad Ibn Taimiya (d. 1328) was a Hanbali *'alim*, born in Harran to a family of *ulama*, chased from there in his infancy by the Mongol invasion, the family settled in Damascus. Ibn Taimiya has a prominent place in the history of Muslim thought and politics. He was a militant *'alim* in the mould of Ibn Hanbal, jealous for orthodoxy and Sunnism, which at that point in time was at issue. His thought was distinguished by his attempt to bring politics and statecraft within the remit of the *shari'a*. As we have seen, there developed in the Sunni world a *de facto* acceptance of the restriction of the rule of the *shari'a* to the private affairs of the subjects, while the conduct of the rulers and the affairs of state escaped, for the most part, its jurisdiction. One of Ibn Taimiya's best-known treatises was entitled *Al-Siyasa al-Shar'iya*,[15] statecraft according to the *shari'a*, implicitly bringing the conduct of the ruler within the preview of the sacred law. It remained theoretical and did not change the existing practice. But its claims, and various other rulings by the shaykh, have been revived at various points of Islamic history, notably in the recent upsurge of political Islam, as support for religious advocacy in politics.[16] Ibn Taimiya's polemics, struggles, triumphs and defeats, revolved around his insistence to bring all practices in Muslim society within the rules of the *shari'a*. All social and individual practices, in daily and public life, had to be measured by the commands of the book and the *sunna* as to what was licit and what was forbidden. It is related that when imprisoned in Cairo in 1308 he found prisoners amusing themselves with games such as backgammon, and not observing the daily prayers (Memon 1976:55). His preaching, it is reported (by laudatory biographers), led them to abandon their error, and they became loyal followers of the shaykh. His primary targets were Sufi mystic orders, many presided over by leading jurists and judges and some enjoying the protection and patronage of Mamluke amirs, hence the trouble he courted. This zealous insistence on bringing social life within the rules of the holy law is another element in the Hanbali heritage bequeathed to subsequent generations, and revived in the Salafi and Wahhabi advocacy of recent history and the present.[17]

The situation during the thirteenth and fourteenth centuries in the Middle East was one of turbulence and war, in which Sunni Islam ultimately emerged victorious after dangerous challenges, some of which persisted. Salahuddin (Saladin; d. 1186) had defeated the Franks and retook Jerusalem for Islam. Lesser known is this chieftain's victorious struggles against Muslim heterodoxy. He first came to power by putting an end to the tottering Fatimid (Shi'i/ Isma'ili) caliphate in Egypt, establishing the rule of Sunni Islam there. His subsequent conquests included taking Shi'i Aleppo. The Mamluke regime in Egypt and Syria, heir to Ayubid rule, continued the championing of Sunnism and ortho-doxy, especially in the face of another enemy, that of the Mongol invaders.

The Seljukids (starting around 1040) ruled in the East, in Iraq (as protectors of the caliphate), Iran, central Asia and Anatolia at different points in time until the Mongol conquest in 1258, but surviving it in some territories. They faced the challenge of Isma'ili propaganda and revolts, and were the adversaries of the Fatimids. The collapse of the Fatimid state, and the control of Isma'ili movements constituted another triumph for Sunnism.

The Mongols swept through the Muslim world. Hulagu and the Golden Horde sacked Baghdad, the centre of the Abbasid caliphate, in 1258. They had occupied central Asia and Iran, and established the rule of their princes in these regions. Their advance was only halted by Mamluke armies at Aleppo. Campaigns, however, continued, and one Mongol army besieged Damascus, an occasion on which Ibn Taimiya is said to have played a part in saving the city (Laoust 1939:117–23). The Mongols, first as pagans, then as Muslims, had considerable influence in matters of religion. At first they favoured Christians and Jews as advisors and administrators. Subsequently they also raised Shi'ite jurists to pos-itions of prominence. As such, even after conversion to orthodox Islam, their religious credentials remained suspect to Sunni *ulama*. Ibn Taimiya issued a famous *fatwa* against them, on the grounds that they ruled according to the *yasa* (or *yasak* – the code of Genghis Khan) of the Mongols and not the *shari'a*, a ruling often cited in recent times against supposedly Muslim rulers who ruled by laws other than those of God.

This, then, was the political milieu in which Ibn Taimiya operated. Sunnism was triumphant, but continued to be challenged by various heterodoxies. Shi'ism flourished under the Mongols. Isma'ili propaganda continued. Pockets of frankish principalities survived along the Syrian coast. Most insidious for our shaykh, however, were particular brands of Sufism, that which followed the pantheistic monism (*wihdat al-wujud*, the oneness of being) of Ibn al-Arabi, which he considered most heretical. That and the related popular religious practices of saint worship exercised Ibn Taimiya greatly and were instrumental in the episodes of his persecution. Combating Shi'ism, Isma'ilism, Mongols and non-Muslims fitted in well with the policies of his masters, the Mamlukes. But attacking Sufis and the veneration of saints often brought him into conflict with powerful interests, with considerable influence in circles of power.

What of the Mamlukes themselves?[18] The Mamluke regime was highly factionalized. Amirs were warlords, with the sultan as their chieftain. Designation of amirs was at the discretion of the latter, but often hotly contested. There were no clear rules of succession: the original procedure was for succession to be kept within the ranks of military freedmen, but this was subverted, with sultans designating their sons as successors, ensuring that there was always a contest. A sharp rivalry, with conflicts and intrigues ruled among the amirs, over influence and, above all, revenue. Fiscal exaction, often extortion of the peasants and the urban classes was the bases for their revenues. Urban strata, including the *ulama*, were often recruited in the faction fights between amirs. Protection, patronage and advancement were the motives for factional attachments and solidarities, but these were always shifting.

The chief *ulama* came from notable families, often ones within which position and rank were hereditary. *Qadis*, muftis, teachers at the major mosques and the shaykhs of Sufi orders and the ashraf, descendants of the Prophet, constituted the religious elites. Their sources of revenue consisted of land-holding, including urban real estate, both as personal possession and as supervision of *awqaf* properties, as well as income from fees, grants and charities in their religious functions. They wielded considerable influence over networks of followers, students, protégés, and for the Sufi shaykhs, over the devout adherents of the order. Their relations with the Mamlukes were largely ones of subordination, but not without influence. The Mamlukes were barely Islamized foreign warlords. They claimed legitimacy primarily from the defence of the lands of Islam, and Ibn Taimiya valued these efforts with regards to the Mongols, and for their suppression of heresy. The Mamlukes set out to borrow some sanctity and legality from the *ulama*, and to that end patronized and rewarded their notables. Some also engaged in building mosques and *madrasas*, as well as Sufi *zawiyas* and *khangas*, and endowing them with *awqaf*. While sometimes soliciting advice and council from the notables, they were intolerant of criticism or censure. They did on occasion prohibit a particular jurist from pronouncing *fatwas*, as they did with Ibn Taimiya (Laoust 1939:144–45). Disobedience could lead to drastic punishment, such as the cutting of the tongue or execution (Laoust 1939:146). There was no question as to who had the final authority: the sword was immeasurably mightier than the pen. In fairness, it should be noted that Mamluke confrontation with a particular *'alim* was rare, largely because the *ulama* were careful not to offend. In the case of Ibn Taimiya, the confrontations were almost always at the instigation of rival *ulama* and shaykhs. That said, the elite *ulama* at the same time did have considerable power, partly as rich notables in control of resources, mostly as agents of legitimacy and social control, by virtue of their influence over the populace and control over networks of followers. Sufi shaykhs, some also jurists and *qadis*, were especially influential by virtue of their popular appeal and the sanctity of the sites and tombs that many of them superintended. In addition, we may speculate with Max Weber, there is a particular affinity of military men to ceremonial and mystical religion, of intercession and good omen. Mamluke sultans and amirs showed particular generosity in building and endowing Sufi monasteries. Both the sultans who were so influential in Ibn Taimiya's fate, Baibars al-Jashankir and Muhammad bin Qalawun, built sumptuous edifices for the Sufis. So did their Ayubid predecessors, including Salahuddin, the champion of orthodoxy (Memon 1976:48–49). When it was suggested to Salahuddin's contemporary Nur ad-Din Mahmud the Zangid Sultan that he should withhold his generosity to the Sufis and devote his resources to supplying his campaign against the Franks, he responded angrily: 'How possibly can I withhold the pensions of a people who, while I am peacefully asleep in my bed, fight on my behalf with arrows that never miss a target. You want me to spend their money on people whose arrows might miss?' (quoted in Memon 1976:49). We see here the warlord's faith in mystical armour.

The issues on which Ibn Taimiya quarrelled with his fellow divines were the classic issues of disagreement between Hanbali literalists, attached to the text and the *sunna*, against more speculative and philosophical tendencies. On another, and related, front, Ibn Taimiya took issue with the Sufis. While approving Sufi practices that added rigour and reflection to the observance of rituals and cults, such as prayer and fasting, he denounced the indulgence in music and dancing and the performance of 'miracles', such as walking into fire. These practices were not only illicit but they diverted the worshippers away from the prescribed observances. A related issue was that of the veneration of saints and the visitations of tombs, judged by the Hanbalis to be a form of *shirk*, the worship of other gods, one that had no Quranic sanction or *sunna* precedent. The popularity of Sufi affiliations and practices among the masses is shown by the frequency with which Ibn Taimiya was asked for opinions, *fatwas*, on these issues (Memon 1976:42).

Episodes of Confrontation

The first public confrontation occurred in Damascus in 1298 and related to a declaration of profession of faith, *'aqida*, made by Ibn Taimiya in response to a request from followers in Hama (Laoust 1939:111–17; Memon 1976:53). He was asked his view on the essence and attributes of God, a classic issue in Muslim theology. In the process of declaring his views, Ibn Taimiya took swipes at the scholastic theologians of his day, the Ash'arites, and those who followed the philosophical trends, denouncing them in insulting terms for their scholastic sophistry and departure from the true sources of knowledge. The theologians and Shafi'i *ulama* who were targeted naturally took offence. Both the Hanafi and the Shafi'i *qadis* took steps to bring the shaykh to account. Demonstrations erupted in the streets of Damascus, people brandishing the offending text and denouncing the author. The Hanafi *qadi* summoned Ibn Taimiya to defend his views, which the latter refused, questioning the *qadi*'s competence in matters of faith (Laoust 1939:116), at which the *qadi* sent the town crier to pronounce Ibn Taimiya a heretic.

The Attack on Sufism and Popular Religion

In 1305 Ibn Taimiya took on the Ahmadiya Rifa'ya Sufi order, well established in Damascus, under venerable and notable shaykhs. He launched a polemic against what he considered their heretical practices and departure from the law (Laoust 1939:125–31), such as walking into fire, swallowing snakes, wearing iron pendants and bracelets, iron chains on their necks and dressing their hair in a compact mass. The shaykh led a delegation of the pious to the governor, declaring that the mystics were introducing heretical practices, and abusing the credulity of the common people. The chiefs of the order, in their turn, went to the governor complaining of Ibn Taimiya's public denunciations. We are not told of a conclusion to this dispute.

More serious consequences followed from Ibn Taimiya's challenge to Shaykh al-Manbiji, a prominent Sufi of Cairo. Ibn Taimiya sent him a long dissertation refuting and denouncing the doctrines of Ibn al-Arabi which he held, regarding the mystical union with God (Laoust 1939:128; Memon 1976:51–52). This shaykh was influential, and had the ear of the Sultan Baibars al-Jashankir. He took his complaints to the Qadis of Cairo, and obtained a ruling from the Maliki *qadi* that Ibn Taimiya was heretical, an innovator and enemy of the pious. The *qadi* suggested that the amirs interrogate Ibn Taimiya on his faith (it is the amirs who must do it, not the *ulama*), and that he be brought to Cairo for the inquisition. Orders went to Damascus that the shaykh be tested on his faith. The governor and religious notables assembled to question Ibn Taimiya, who acquitted himself well during several seances, by his proclamation of faith and in answer to learned questioners. It appears that, at least in Damascus, his partisans were stronger than his detractors. Al-Manbiji in Cairo, however, did not give up, but obtained an order from the sultan that the shaykh was to be sent to Cairo for an inquisition, an order which the governor had to obey eventually. There he was subjected to a hostile inquisition, then imprisoned.

A *coup d'état* in the Mamluke state brought Muhammad bin Qalawun back to the throne, banishing then killing Baibars al-Jashankir and his entourage. Ibn Taimiya was released and honoured by the sultan, who sought his counsel and favour (Laoust 1939:139–43). He remained in Cairo till 1312, when he returned to his native Damascus. A physical assault by thugs in Cairo in 1311 may have precipitated his decision to leave that city (Laoust 1939:142).

In Damascus, after six years of calm study and writing, we find Ibn Taimiya resuming his polemics with adversaries, particularly against the cult of the saints. His adversaries succeeded in obtaining an order from the sultan in Cairo forbidding the shaykh from issuing any *fatwa*. Ibn Taimiya ignored this order and continued his activities. A council of *ulama* and notables, convened at the sultan's order, decreed his imprisonment. He remained in prison till 1321. He then returned to the fray, going to prison again, where he died in 1327.

A large crowd is reported to have gathered at the port of the citadel at the news of his death. Ironically, people were seeking relics of the holy man for blessing: some drank of the water used to wash his corpse, others quarrelled over the linen; one man paid 500 dirhems for his cloak (*taqiya*), another 150 for the camphor bag that he carried (Laoust 1939:149–50). He was buried in a Sufi cemetery, and his tomb became a shrine for visitations (Memon 1976:85). Clearly, in the eyes of the common people, Ibn Taimiya was another holy man from whose corpse and tomb sanctity and intercession could be hoped for. His theology and disputations passed them by. One is reminded of the turbulent scenes at the funeral of Ayatollah Khomeini in Teheran in 1989, in which the bier was mobbed by the crowd, people trying to snatch relics from the body, leading to the ugly scenes of the collapse of the bier dislodging the corpse. Another stern divine who disapproved of popular 'superstition' became, at his death, precisely an icon of common veneration.

IBN TAIMIYA'S *AL-SIYASA AL-SHAR'IYA* AND THE DILEMMAS OF ISLAMIC POLITICAL THOUGHT

Ibn Taimiya could not escape the duality of state and community, and of theory and practice, which we have noted above. He was, however, trying to find ways of overcoming or ameliorating it. This is related to the fact that much of his writing on the imama was directed as a polemic against his contemporary Shi'i theorists, notably Al-Hilli and his *Minhaj al-Karama*. Ibn Taimiya's *Minhaj al-Sunna*, the *Path of Sunna*, was a direct polemic, and the central issue is that of the imamate (Laoust 1939:279–302). As we have seen, the Shi'i theory depends on the legitimacy of lineage: an imama designated by those guided by God himself, and an imam made infallible by God's grace. It is also the most theoretical, with the neat escape from its necessity by its messianic postponement in the doctrine of occultation of the imam. Nor did Ibn Taimiya go along with the equally theoretical conventional Sunni doctrine of election, to which he advanced many practical objections (Laoust 1939:286–87). Both Sunni and Shi'i theorists have insisted on the qualifications of the imam, in terms of Qurayshi lineage, and in terms of personal qualities, of virtue, nobility and learning: the imam should present an example of perfection to the community as well as enforce the law and the religious life. Contrary to this elaboration of Utopia, Ibn Taimiya insisted on defining the imamate in terms of its functions. Any capable person, qualified to testify in a *shari'a* court could assume the function of the imama, a slave as well as a free man, a woman as well as a man (the rule of a woman is explicitly rejected in most doctrines) – even a child, providing that the prince is able to accomplish his tasks (Laoust 1939:295–96). The personal qualities required are no more than those of being responsible, to be able and free to formulate and follow a declaration, to be of good character and live according to his or her rank, to be able to control his or her personal impulses and preferences. These are the qualifications to act as a witness in court, and it should suffice for the ruler. This formulation has a Kharijite tinge to it: the person of the leader is not important, it is the leader's functions in upholding the law as formulated in the sacred sources. But whereas for the Kharijites this formulation constituted a doctrine of radical egalitarianism and 'anarchy', for Ibn Taimiya it served as an escape from the sterile theories of a utopian state, and directing attention to the tasks of the government in the real conditions.

As his public actions demonstrate, however, Ibn Taimiya, unlike many of his contemporaries, did not acquiesce in the arbitrary exercise of power by their Mamluke masters, but sought to bring the dictates of the *shari'a* into matters of state and the life of the community. His book *Al-Siyasa al-Shar'iya, Statecraft in Accordance with the Shari'a*, in its very title challenges the separation of *shari'a* from the conduct of government. He departs from the utopian stipulation of the Prophet and the Rashidun model as the ideal: Muslims at Ibn Taimiya's point of history could not go back to that model, but must seek realistic modes of government. What is required, in his view, is a regime of close collaboration between the two fundamental classes of the state: the amirs and the *ulama*, the sword and the book. 'When these two classes are healthy, everything is healthy within the community; their corruption leads to the corruption of the social body' (quoted in Laoust 1939:315–16). The state, however, needs the support and co-operation of the community: Muslims should not just be obedient subjects but active participants in the affairs of the community, commanding the good and forbidding the evil. State and community can unite on the basic requirements of Muslim life: recognizing the unique God and his Prophet, and submitting to the law.

The Mamlukes were an alien dynasty, and the one factor that tied them to indigenous society was religion, the common Islam of ruler and ruled. The *ulama* had the responsibility of using this tie in promoting co-operation between ruler and ruled. In his public actions Ibn Taimiya sought to bring about the fulfilment of his plans. He sought proximity to the princes to be able to counsel them on the application of the law for the health of the community and the life of the believers, with mixed results. He was outraged by what he saw as the profanity, laxness and corruption of many of the elite *ulama*, and their servility to the princes. His vociferous denunciations of fellow *ulama* and stern rebukes to their followers, led, as we have seen, to his persecution and imprisonment.

Did Ibn Taimiya's model of the state and community escape from the idealism and the dualism of mainstream Sunni theories? Laoust argued, with some justification, that Ibn Taimiya's prescriptions were more realistic in relation to the actually prevailing conditions. Yet, given the nature of Mamluke rule, its primary orientation to power and revenue, its fractious factionalism, its barbarity to its subjects, Ibn Taimiya's aspirations do seem rather unrealistic. Similarly, the material and spiritual orientation of both the *ulama* and the common people, could not possibly conform to the rigorous legalism of this zealot. In many ways, his model of the correct polity partakes in the utopianism of the classic theories: he still postulates an ideal organic unity between ruler and ruled, unified by religion and its law. Unlike his predecessors in political theory, however, Ibn Taimiya was an activist trying to bring ruler and ruled to the true path. Let us consider one more example of his advocacy, that in relation to fiscal matters and taxation. This is especially interesting for our concerns, because fiscality was such an important issue of variance between *shari'a* prescriptions and actual practice.

Al-Siyasa al-Shar'iya engages, like all books of *fiqh*, in the classification of sources of revenue, the forms of disbursement and the legal rules governing them. The model is that of the early Muslims and their treasury, *bayt al-mal*. This treasury is that of all Muslims, and the ruler is but its guardian and administrator. Sources of revenue are differentiated into alms taxes, *zakat* or *sadaqa*, levied on Muslims able to pay, to be disbursed to specific categories of the poor, the orphans and the destitute. Then there are the different taxes on land, *kharaj* and *fay'*, classified according to the type of land, the mode of its conquest, whether it is settled by Muslims or infidels, and so on (*kharaj* was, in the early days of Muslim conquests, confined to non-Muslims, but was soon generalized to all land-holding). In legal theory, land taxes are closely related to the laws of war, for the nature and amount of the tax relates to the mode of conquest and submission of the original inhabitants, and whether they convert to Islam or not. The laws of war also govern the types of booty obtained, their legality and their distribution: who is entitled and in what shares? How much discretion does the imam have in the distribution? and so on.

In the context of the military dynasties such as the Mamlukes, this legal discourse is purely theoretical. There was no such thing as the communal treasury of the Muslims, it was the royal treasury of sultan and amirs, and had been from the time of the Caliph Uthman, one of the venerated Rashidun, who dispensed largesse to his family, and justified it by the prophetic injunction of kindness to kin. By the time of the Umayyads and the Abbasids no apology was needed for the appropriation of the treasury by the caliph. All land was taxed, regardless of whether the cultivator was Muslim or not, and with little regard to the niceties of legal classifications. Non-Muslims paid more taxes and tributes, well beyond the legal specification of capitation tax. In addition, the Mamlukes were ever more inventive in avenues of taxation, their revenue hunger ever avid for further extortion. In this context, the legal classifications and prescriptions remained entirely theoretical, much as described by Snouck-Hurgronje (quoted earlier). Ibn Taimiya, however, did not stop at the legal niceties, but in typical campaigning spirit took up the issue of illegal taxation.

Taxes not specified in the Quran and *sunna* were justified by sultans and some jurists as contributions by Muslims to the *jihad* of a Muslim prince against the infidels. Another category of justification was that of *maslaha*, utility or interest of the community pursued by their prince. Ibn Taimiya was distrustful of this reasoning, and considered most of these impositions illegal (Laoust 1939:404). But what was the subject to do in the face of such impositions? To refuse would be rebellion, and exemplary punishment, which the shaykh did not advocate. His sense of illegality and injustice did not override his political loyalism. Subjects could only protest to the imam and point out the abuse of legality by their agents (Laoust 1939:405). Other practices he denounced were the appropriation by the authorities of legacy and inheritance. The right of succession to appropriate categories of kin was sanctified by the Prophet and enshrined in the law. The Mamlukes also procured revenue from illicit activities, such as the sale of alcoholic drink, taverns and brothels. All these should be forbidden by the prince as flagrant violations of the law and the injunction to command the good and forbid evil. To procure revenue from such activity would be doubly culpable (Laoust 1939:406).

The disbursement of revenues by the Mamlukes was equally in question. Ibn Taimiya outlined the different purposes of disbursement according to the *shari'a* and virtuous precedent: the affairs of the Muslims, *jihad* and the different categories of soldiers (none of this applied to the slave soldiers of the Mamlukes, who had no precedent in the sources), charities to the poor, the upkeep of roads and bridges, as well as mosques and schools, disbursements to religious personnel, and so on. Allocation should be based on services rendered and their utility for the community. The imam must not distribute in accordance with personal preference or sympathy, such as to kin or favourites. Imagine the shaykh's indignation, then, when confronted by actual practice. 'Is it not too frequent, he wrote, that in our days, the revenues of the state are disbursed to effeminate boys, free or slave, to courtesans and female singers, as far as buffoons, and even to sorcerers, magicians and astrologers?' (Laoust 1939:409)

Ibn Taimiya then denounces his fellow *ulama* who, faced with all these abuses, turn away from political involvement, arguing that the only way to stop them would entail rebellion and violence. He berates them for cowardice and corruption, and excessive concerns for their own material interests. It is incumbent upon the men of religion to set an example of public rectitude, concern for the community and its affairs, and the dignity of Islam, and by their good example to make a stand for what is right (Laoust 1939:412). Ibn Taimiya was true to his prescriptions, and did make a stand and set an example on many occasions, and suffered for his rectitude. He did not, by these actions, alter the nature of Mamluke rule or the society they ruled. His work, however, did leave significant traces in the history of Muslim thought. His ideas and rules were to be resurrected in many subsequent contexts, whenever zealous reformers invoked the *shari'a* against what they saw as corruption of their time. He was the major inspiration to the Wahhabis, and again his thought was a major inspiration for the Islamic advocacy of our own day.

The most influential trace of Ibn Taimiya's in modern times was to be his *fatwa* against the Mongols. Faced with adversaries who had professed Sunni Islam, he sought still to justify *jihad* against them on the part of his Mamluke masters, not merely as inter-Muslim war, but as war against infidels. To demonstrate their infidelity, the shaykh resorted to Quranic exegesis, citing Chapter V (the Table), which repeats the injunction to 'judge according to what God has sent down' (48 and subsequent verses), then: 'Is it the judgement of pagandom (*jahiliya*) then that they are seeking?' (55). The Mongols (in nearby Mardin) were not only breaking the rules and prescriptions of the *shari'a* (no more so in all probability than his Mamluke masters), but were judging by the *yasa* of the Mongols and not the *shari'a* (Sivan 1985:94–102). As such they were not real Muslims, but infidels, living in a *jahiliya*. This *fatwa*, as Sivan demonstrates, was to have many echoes in modern times, starting with Rashid Rida's accusation against the Muslim rulers of his time who adopted Western penal codes (Sivan 1985:101). The denunciation of supposedly Muslim rulers who rule in accordance with man-made laws and abandon what God has revealed as infidels and their realm as *jahiliya* was to become widespread among modern militant Islamists, as we shall see. As such, Ibn Taimiya became one of the few figures of historical *fiqh* to be revived and adulated in modern Islamism, the mainstream of *fiqh* being too subservient to rulers and tolerant of their foibles to serve radical directions.

LAW IN THE OTTOMAN STATE

Most of the modern states in the Middle East are heirs to the Ottoman Empire (1389–1922), and its official culture, including law, have left many traces. The reform movements of the nineteenth and twentieth centuries, as well as the reactions against them, developed within that polity. The genealogy of many of the issues and debates of the present can be traced to these reforms.

Centralization of state and formalization of rule were distinguishing elements of the Ottoman state from its inception. It featured an elaborate administrative apparatus with a formalized hierarchy of rank and detailed written regulations. This apparatus extended authority from the imperial court, to the administration of the provinces, from fiscal affairs to military provisions. It brought religion and law within this apparatus, with their own specialized institutions and personnel, formally bureaucratized, with hierarchies and regulations, ultimately subject to imperial authority. One might speculate that Ataturk's 'secularization' which meant, in effect, subordination of religion to the state and its bureaucratic administration, had a long Ottoman ancestry. This observation will appear odd in the context of the widely held view that religion was the cornerstone of the Ottoman state, the *shari'a* its law, with religious dignitaries enjoying the highest levels of power. This salience of religion and the sacred law was seen by many as the main factor in the conservatism of the empire and its resistance to progress and change. These issues will be elucidated in what follows.

The Ottomans started, in the early fourteenth century, as a dynasty of warlords carving a domain for themselves in the border regions of western Anatolia, shrewdly building up alliances and recruiting followers from the Islamized Turkish populations, but also among Christian neighbours, ultimately enlarging their territories, following booty and revenues to become major players in Anatolia. They conquered major cities and built up their courts and states in them, ultimately occupying Constantinople in 1453, to become the centre of their expanding empire.

Ottoman Religion: Between Orthodoxy and Sufism

Hand in hand with the centralization of the state and the imposition of bureaucratic controls went the process of increasing orthodoxy in religion and the control over it by the *ulama* and the schoolmen. At first, during the formative period, the Ottomans ruled over a frontier society, imbued with the mystical religious charisma of holy warriors (the *ghazis*) and diverse cults.[19] Haji Bektash Veli was the mythical figure who is attributed with miraculous deeds in assuring victory in battles, and who is the supposed founder of the janissaries, later to venerate him in the Sufi order of Bektashis. Heterodox and Sufi cults and associations were prevalent and tolerated. In the towns, some of the guilds were organized as religious brotherhoods, the *ahis* or *akhis*, imbued with Sufi mysticism and the *ghazu* (holy war) ideology, though in later times (seventeenth and eighteenth centuries) many guilds in Istanbul and Cairo were religiously mixed and included non-Muslims (Farooghi 1994:590–91). These brother-hoods played an important part in the process of the foundation and success of the empire. Yet, the imposition of scriptural orthodoxy seems to have been a correlate of 'routinization' of imperial power and the imposition of bureau-cratic control. Religious heterodoxy and diverse cults seem to have gone with social autonomies and political dissent. Dynasties that come to power on the back of religious enthusiasms seek to curb these forces once their power is established, not least because of the claims that these groups can make to credit for the foundation of power, and their consequent claims for position and influence. The Safavids came to power (in 1500) at the head of tribal confeder-acies fired with shamanic fervour believing in the divinity of the Safavid shah.[20] These were the Qizilbash (the red-heads, after the colour of their headgear), who were also to play a part in Anatolian religious and military organization. When the Safavids established their rule, however, they imported Shi'i *ulama* from Lebanon to bring orthodoxy and *shari'a* rule, and banished the charismatics and schismatics who brought them to power. The Ottomans preceded them on that path.

Centralization and bureaucratization of Ottoman power reached its peak in the sixteenth century under Suleiman (the Magnificent in western lore, Al-Qanuni, the Law-Maker, in Arabic or Turkish). This tightening and rationalizing of control extended to religion. Ebussu'ud, the grand mufti of Suleiman, embarked upon the task of rationalizing the laws of the empire to bring them into greater conformity with the *shari'a* (more *infra*). But this is only one side of the story, for the heterodox and mystical trends continued to flourish, as they did throughout the life of the empire. Orthodoxy versus heterodoxy, *shari'a* versus Sufism, the mosque versus the *tariqa* – these remained constant themes of tension, but also of co-existence and harmony throughout that history. These tensions provided issues and vocabularies of legitimation and of contest, which arose in political positions and struggles.

There were many Sufi orders in Ottoman cities. Qaderi (with the most numerous adherents), Mevlevis, Naqshbandis and Helvetis were among the prominent 'respectable' orders. To many of them (not so much the Naqshbandis) the philosophy of Ibn al-Arabi was constitutive, and the cult of Ali and his house and the passion of the Shiʿi martyrs were part of belief and ritual. The Mevlevis became a refined and aristocratic order: at various points members of the court, even the sultan, vizir and the *shaykhulislam* were members or patrons. The Bektashis, more heterodox and devoted to the cult of Ali and his descendants, were the order of the janissaries and the popular classes, but also of some of the high-ranking military. Many *ulama*, of various levels of status, participated in the orders. Sufism entered the fabric of economic and social life: the craft guilds and the markets were imbued with Sufi ritual and organization. Sufi culture, social networks and rituals, then, constituted a central element in the life of the urban classes of Ottoman cities.[21] How did this fit in with the orthodoxy of Ottoman religion, and how did it relate to the observance of *shariʿa* rules?

From a strictly orthodox point of view, such as that of Ibn Taimiya of an earlier age, many of the central activities and omissions of the Sufis were highly reprehensible. Music and dancing were central to most orders. Wine-drinking featured in Bektashi ritual, and perhaps also in Mevlevi circles. The doctrine of Ibn al-Arabi is heretical, and devalues the *shariʿa* and ritual observances as a superficial level of religious understanding. At various points, Bektashis and Mevlevis proclaimed the common truth of all religions and the unity of all belief. For the most part, these clear divergences were not spelled out, and *ulama*, judges and muftis, who upheld and practised the *shariʿa*, remained at the same time members of Sufi lodges. H.K.Birge, a British writer and traveller in the early years of the twentieth century, made the following observation in his book on the Bektashis:

> When the writer first visited Turkey in 1913 he went about under the impression that Turkey was...a Sunni country. He quickly found to his surprise that an enormous portion of the people not only were affiliated with dervish brotherhoods, but even the leaders who appeared on Friday prayers as Imams in the formal worship (*namaz*) in the mosque, were on other days to be found acting as *Seyhs* in dervish tekkes. During *Muharrem*, the month when Shiʿites especially remember the death of *Huseyin*...the writer visited tekke after tekke, and found in them dervishes passionately mourning the death of *Hasan* and *Huseyin*.

The writer questions 'one of Turkey's greatest scholars' about this phenomenon:

> The scholar replied that there is in Constantinople where the proportion was presumably less than in the rest of the country, probably sixty percent of the

people belonged directly or indirectly to dervish fraternities... in Muslim lands, he continued, the practice of *takiye*, dissimulation, has grown up to make possible a man continuing his standing as an orthodox member of the religious body while at the same time being a member of a mystic fraternity which emphasised an experiential rather than a traditional and formal approach to reality. [Birge 1937:13–14]

Only dissimulation was not always necessary, as many religious notabilities were open about their *tariqa* affiliations. This duality of religious practice would appear to have been a regular feature of Ottoman life over the centuries, as it was in the Mamluke period of Ibn Taimiya. This duality was not always peaceful: every now and again some strict *ulama* would wage a campaign against heterodoxy and moral laxity, and this would often have a political point in the struggle between factions. The reign of Suleiman was one of increasing orthodoxy and censure. In 1527, during the Qizilbash revolt in Anatolia, occurred the trial and eventual execution of an *'alim*, Molla Kabiz, accused of holding the view of the superiority of Jesus over Muhammad (Inalcik 1978:182). His prosecution was a sign of a clampdown in the name of orthodoxy against political challenges. The respectable Sufis were too cautious to provoke such reactions. At some points, orthodox *ulama* waged campaigns against 'innovations' in philosophy and the sciences. Astronomy and astrology were particular targets, seeming to intervene in the affairs of God in the cosmos. At the political level, court astrologers could wield great influence, arousing the jealousy and intrigue of court *ulama*. In 1577, on the order of Murad III, his astronomer cum astrologer established an observatory in Galata, with advanced instruments and astronomical clocks. A group of *ulama*, including the *shaykhulislam*, railed against this observatory as irreligious and an affront to God. The outbreak of a plague at that point seemed to vindicate their misgivings, and in 1580 the janissaries razed the observatory to the ground (Inalcik 1978:179). This was clearly part of court intrigue, to do with rivalry between different factions, and the triumph of the *shaykhulislam*, with janissary help, was clearly a reflection of the weakness of this particular sultan. Periodically, the call to orthodoxy and the censure of heresy came from some *ulama*, and found a response among their lower ranks of preachers and students. In the sixteenth and seventeenth centuries, such a movement of preachers, known as the *fakis*, waged periodic campaigns against heresy and innovation, calling for strict adherence to the *sunna*. Their call found a ready response among students and impoverished tradesmen. Because of their popular support and capacity to mobilize urban mobs, they were at times patronized and encouraged by court personalities, including Sultan Murad IV. In 1656 they planned an attack on all the *tekkes* (Sufi lodges) of Istanbul, and a massacre. This was prevented by the authorities and the group ultimately suppressed for endangering public order (Inalcik 1978:184–85).

The *ulama*, clearly, did not constitute a common body socially or ideologically. They were stratified, ranging in status from the senior court *ulama* to the common run of *qadis* and teachers, then down to mosque functionaries such as *muezzins* (those who call to prayer) and finally the religious students and the unemployed. At each level loyalties and interests were divided by social allegiances of family and patronage. Many of the religious functions and statuses were perpetuated within families, and social networks were the means of influence and advantage. Sufi orders were among the most important avenues of 'networking', patronage and mutual support.

To sum up, the religious field throughout Ottoman history was diverse. The sultan was always the defender of the faith, much like his European counterparts. The faith was Sunni, and successive sultans fought not only the Christian powers but the heretical Shi'a of Iran and persecuted those within the empire. Yet within this realm of Hanafi Sunnism flourished Sufi orders and cults imbued with mystical unitarianism (pantheism) and Alid passions. Their rituals included music, dancing and imbibing wine. They devalued the orthodox observances of prayer and fasting. The state, then, contained variety and heterodoxy within social frameworks, which ensured political loyalty. Insofar as these trends did not challenge the political order or constitute public scandals, they remained part of Ottoman court and society.

Elements of Sufism were only put at issue in the dynamics of political contest and intrigue, within and outside the court. Vocabularies of religious orthodoxy and the *shari'a* continued always to operate as media of legitimation and challenge, as we shall see presently in relation to the place of the *shari'a* in Ottoman institutions.

Shari'a, Qanun *and Ottoman Law*

The centralization and bureaucratization of the empire could only proceed with clear and detailed rules. These were provided for by sets of laws, covering administration, taxation and punishments, clearly inscribed and proclaimed. These were the *qanun-name* and *adalet-name* issued by each Ottoman sultan at his accession and augmented as new laws were proclaimed during his reign. These laws included some concepts and principles from the *shari'a*, such as the identification of certain taxes as *kharaj* and *jizya*. Later *qanun-name* made pious references to the *shari'a*. For the most part, however, they presented a different kind of legal discourse and principle to that of the sacred law.

Halil Inalcik, in a seminal paper,[22] examines the models of rule which lay behind Ottoman legislation. One was the traditional Turkish and Mongol tribal models which required the chief to proclaim a set of rules, based on tradition and custom, and to ensure their impartial implementation, avoiding arbitrary judgements. This is a kind of rule of law. Such was the *yasa* of Genghis Khan. The other model was that of the Persian kingdom, adopted by the Abbasid caliphs, in which the sovereign is omnipotent, for whom justice and law were but acts of grace. The institutions of *mazalim* tribunals and the *divans* of the Ottomans, presided over by the ruler or his agents, were an expression of this grace, in which the just sovereign heard directly the injustices claimed by his subjects and put them right (Inalcik 1978:107–8). Neither of these models assigns an intrinsic value to the *shari'a*. In Muslim practice, however, the *shari'a* is occasionally brought in for honorific sanction, pointing to it as the highest source of legislation. In Ottoman terminology, these laws issued by the ruler were known as *'urfi*.

The legends of origin of the Ottoman dynasty attribute to Osman, the founder, the first *qanun-name*, in line with Turkish tradition. It was Mehmed II, conqueror of Constantinople, who issued the first historically recorded *qanun-name*. His first book specified taxes to be paid by the *re'aya*, Muslim and Christian, his second promulgated administrative regulations for court and government. Neither makes any reference to the *shari'a* (Inalcik 1978:109). His successor, Bayazid II, attempted to remedy that omission by appealing to the *shari'a* and restoring the religious sciences. It is not clear, however, whether this went beyond rhetoric and piety, inspired by political strategies to gain support against his brother Cem Sultan's challenge for the throne. Once Bayazid was securely established on the throne, he restored most of the decrees of his predecessor, and the principle of the independence of *'urfi* law and executive power were maintained (Inalcik 1978:109–10).

Suleiman, though known as *qanuni*, the law-giver, did not, according to Inalcik, actually innovate in legislation, but followed his predecessors: 'I think it is no exaggeration to assert that *one Ottoman law-book existed which evolved throughout Ottoman history*. The new *kanun-hukms*, issued according to new conditions and needs, were incorporated later into the body of this *kanun-name*' (Inalcik 1978:125, original emphasis). Within this framework, Suleiman did issue a number of *'urfi* laws, enlarging and elaborating preceding legislation, especially with respect to the newly conquered territories. Inalcik classifies his laws into three categories: the *qanun-name* issued for each *sanjaq*, province, the *hukms*, decrees containing laws pertaining to specific issues and situations, and thirdly a general *qanun-name* systematically combining the body of legislation (Inalcik 1978:111–17). These *qanun-name*, drafted by specialized palace scribes and administrators, were distributed to the governors of each province, with copies deposited in the *qadi* courts. In Ottoman practice, the *qadi* was expected to rule in *'urfi* as well as in *shar'i* cases, and he had to rule in accordance with the ruler's decrees. The *hukms* issued by the sultan in relation to matters arising were then inscribed in the margins of these copies, then incorporated in subsequent editions. The *qadi* was also required to seek clarification from the sultan in any *'urfi* case for which he can find no covering rule. The sultan's ruling must then be inscribed in the court register and henceforth used as precedent.

Issues covered by these law texts were primarily fiscal, specifying taxes as they applied to different provinces and different categories of persons and communities. These were primarily in the context of the feudal structure of land-holding and military organization, which differed from province to province. In addition to the general taxes, such as tithes, and their applicability in different categories, they specified taxes on building plots, tithes on cotton, flax, madder and saffron, privileges of timariots, prebendaly land-holders, in selling the revenues of wine in kind, marriage dues and hog tax. One central concern of the legislation was to regulate the relationships between the government and timariots, regarding the definition of rights and privileges of land grants, and between those latter and their peasants, aimed at protecting the peasants from excessive dues, as well as securing revenues for the imperial treasury. The fundamental principle of Ottoman government was that '*re'aya* [subjects] and land belonged to the sultan' (Inalcik 1978:129). With this absolute sovereignty the sultan would protect the subjects from excessive and unjust exaction, by officials or timariots, at the same time ensuring their loyalty and ability to sustain state revenues (Kafadar 1995:131).

EBUSSU'UD AND THE RECONCILIATION OF *'URF* TO *SHARI'A*

The reputation of Suleiman as *qanuni* is closely tied up with the efforts of his *shaykhulislam*, Ebussu'ud Efendi, in systematization of the law and lending it religious legitimacy. The life and career of this figure also illustrates the nature and standing of the clerical profession at that point. He was born in 1490 to a prominent clerical family. His father Muhiyyudin was a prominent scholar as well as a mystic, credited with charisma and miracles (Imber 1997:8–20). It was in this capacity that he became a close protege and associate of Sultan Bayazid. Ebussu'ud studied with his father and associated scholars, and from his youth enjoyed the patronage of the court and the notabilities. At an early age he received a stipend from Bayazid, continued under his successor Selim I. His career proceeded with teaching appointments in leading medresses, culminating in a professorship at one of Istanbul's eight colleges, the top of the teaching hierarchy. From there he moved to the judgeship of Bursa, one of the most senior in the empire, then promoted, under Selim, to the Qadiaskar of Rumelia, in which he distinguished himself as an able administrator and organizer. In 1545, at the age of 55, Ebussu'ud was appointed to the muftiship of Istanbul, as *shaykhulislam*, a post he was to occupy till his death in 1574. In this position, Ebussu'ud acted as a conduit for patronage for his sons, his son-in-law (who became *shaykhul-islam* at a subsequent date), and many of his associates. His sons assumed senior professorships in their young years, in their teens and twenties, which illustrates the role of nepotism and patronage, even for one so distinguished.

Ebussu'ud's output as mufti was prodigious: he issued thousands of *fatwas*, as responses to questions from the public, each week. He devised a system by which a bureau of clerks received the questions and reformulated them in legal terms amenable to brief and direct answers. The *fatwas* that were to be of lasting importance were those concerning public administration, in particular land-holding and taxation, to which we shall turn presently. His great life's work, however, was a commentary on the Quran, which occupied him for 30 years, and for which he was showered with honours and wealth from Sultan Suleiman. In addition, he left many legal commentaries, as well as anthologies of poetry, in Turkish, Persian and Arabic.

I shall illustrate Ebussu'ud's innovations in reconciling secular law and practice to the *shari'a* with two examples: cash *waqf* and land taxation. Immovable property or real estate is the 'orthodox' form of endowment, and endowing movable property was controversial in legal discourse. By the time of Ebussu'ud, endowing movable property such as animals to rural dervish lodges became quite common. Endowing cash, however, was particularly problematic, the revenues being interest on the capital endowed. Yet, this was an important source for smaller charitable endowments, and these were widespread in prac-tice. In his capacity as judge, Ebussu'ud had validated many such endowments (Imber 1997:144). The practice, however, was challenged by more conventional Hanafi scholars, notably one Birgi (d.1573), known for his 'fundamentalist' positions. More seriously, Chivizade who preceded Ebussu'ud as Qadiaskar of Rumelia, issued a *fatwa* against the practice. Ebussu'ud's *fatwa* legalizing cash endowments, and therefore interest payments, came as a relief to the authorities and the foundations, for to interdict them would have led to serious disruption in economic and religious life. Ebussu'ud's reasoning was a fairly common device in the class of *hiyal* or stratagems, by which interest is formulated in terms of a fictional circle of sales between three agents (Imber 1997:145). In practice no-one bothered to go through this rigmarole, but lent and borrowed with specified rates of interest. Ottoman law, however, from the time of Bayazid, was concerned to protect borrowers from extortionate rates, and the maximum was fixed in law at 15 percent. Ebussu'ud confirmed this maximum in a *fatwa* (Imber 1997:145–46). Ebussu'ud's endorsement of this common practice was motivated by his pragmatic attitude in favour of the interest of the people and the needs of the time. In his view, the only factor determining what may or may not be endowed in a *waqf* was contemporary custom and practice. Yet this pragmatism served the purpose of enlarging the inclusiveness and authority of the *shari'a* by extending its concepts and terms to comprise existing legal practice.

Regarding the issue of land taxes, Inalcik gives an illuminating account in his essay 'Islamization of Ottoman laws on land and land tax' (Inalcik 1998:155–72). Ebussu'ud's main concern, it would seem, was to classify existing Ottoman taxes in accordance with *shari'a* terms. He classified all agricultural land in the empire as *kharaj* land, as it was taken by force, whether cultivated by Muslims or *dhimmis*. As such, it was subject to *'ushr*. This had the effect of justifying state control over the lands and preventing them from being converted into freeholds. The *'ushr*, literally 'tenth', was liberally interpreted to include both a portion of produce (ranging, however, from eighth to fifth) as well as a lump-sum payment related to the area under cultivation. Contrary to *shari'a* rules on succession, Ebussu'ud justified the rule that prohibited the division of the peasant's standard farm between the heirs. He justified this ruling in terms of practical necessity, for if the land is distributed among the heirs in the usual manner, then it would be impossible to determine the share each heir was to pay for *kharaj* (Inalcik 1998:163). Such exception to the *shari'a* were usually justified under the rule of *ijma'*, widely used in Hanafi jurisprudence. Ebussu'ud also classified timar-holders' taxes on peasants: the sheep tax is classified as *zekat*. The swine tax is not religiously lawful, but 'it has been collected for a long time, so it would be inappropriate to change it' (quoted in Inalcik 1998:167). Only personal taxes imposed on landless peasants are ruled inadmissible (but not abolished in practice). The efforts of Ebussu'ud, then, were to Islamize the law, not so much by transforming it into conformity with the *shari'a*, as in classifying existing practice in *shari'a* terms, and when that is not possible, to justify existing practice in terms of *ijma'* and necessity. Inalcik concludes:

> While in the sixteenth century *nisancis* [heads of chancellery] ... continued the old Ottoman tradition of *'urfi*-state rulings on landholding problems now seyhulislams' fetvas became prevalent on such problems in the 'new and valid' law codes of the sultans. The curious thing is, however, that seyhulislams followed, though using Islamic terminology, the well-established Ottoman notions in landholding, so that no basic change occurred in the Ottoman *miri* [state land] system until 1700 ... [Inalcik 1998:167]

And the changes after 1700 were not *shari'a* bound. However, Ebussu'ud's formulations, which were to persist until the nineteenth-century reforms, served the purpose of including the provisions of *qanun* within the ambit of the *shari'a*, in terms of concepts and vocabularies, and consequently within the sphere of competence and authority of the *ulama*. Thus pragmatism, in accommodating to existing practices, was at the same time a means of maintaining the overall legal authority of the jurists.

QANUN, SHARI'A AND PENAL LAW

Other sections of the *qanun-name* covered penal law. This is an interesting area of interface between *qanun* and *shari'a*. Uriel Heyd, in his *Studies in Old Ottoman Criminal Law*, introduces the book with the following passage:

> The criminal law of the *shari'a*, as is well known, never had much practical importance in the lands of Islam. Its substantive law is rather deficient: fixed penalties are prescribed for a limited number of crimes only, many are not dealt with at all. Moreover, its rules of evidence are so strict that a number of offences cannot be punished adequately. Since the very first centuries of Islam, therefore, criminal justice remained largely outside the jurisdiction of the cadis. [Heyd 1973:1]

He goes on to list the different forms of courts and tribunals used at different times. It is important to note, however, that in Ottoman practice *qadi* courts did deal with penal cases, alongside other tribunals, but these courts were required to apply *qanun* regulations alongside the *shari'a*.

The chapters on criminal law in the *qanun-name* have a revenue focus: practically all clauses specify fines, graded according to the wealth of the offender (Heyd 1973:91–131), and many assume that the *qadi* or the official will impose corporal punishments, typically strokes, and specify a fine to be imposed on the offender for each stroke. Clauses regarding theft prescribe chastisement (unspecified) and a fine, if the offender's hand is not cut off. For example: 'If a person steals a purse or a turban or towels - unless his hand is to be cut off, the cadi shall chastise him, and a fine of one *akce* shall be collected for every two strokes...' (Heyd 1973:112). The option of cutting off the hand is left open, though not required, and the conditions for the *qadi* to determine amputation as against chastisement and a fine are not specified. As we have seen, there was general reluctance to apply limb-amputation penalties, and the combination of strokes and fines became predominant. Fines are alien to the *shari'a* tradition, and early jurists prohibited them explicitly: criminals should not have been able to avoid divinely prescribed punishments by paying fines, and a few early Ottoman *ulama* and muftis recognized this principle, though few pressed it (Heyd 1973:280–82). In effect, the Ottoman penal system was geared to fines. Fines became important sources of revenues for state treasury and for a whole body of officialdom throughout the empire. In some instances the collection of fines was farmed like taxes.

This is not to say that Ottoman legislators and officers were indifferent to the *shari'a*. *Qanun-names* were generally seen as complementing the *shari'a* and not supplanting it, and legislators were anxious to assert that their provisions did not contradict the holy law. On occasions, particular *qanun* clauses would be struck out for clear incompatibility (for examples, see Heyd 1973:127). Clear incompatibilities such as those of fines were classified as *ta'zir*, which were at the discretion of the judge.

There remains the question of capital punishment. The *shari'a* specified a choice for the heirs of murder victims: death to the murderer or monetary compensation (*diya*).[23] This matter was largely left to the *shari'a* court, though sentences of death had to be confirmed by the sultan or his agents. If monetary compensation was accepted, then the *qanun* added a specified fine to be paid by the offender to the state. The death penalty, however, was not confined to *shari'a* provisions, and the sultan and his officers could issue death sentences for many offences, sometimes quite arbitrarily. On occasion, the sultan or a governor would ask a *qadi* to investigate a particular charge in accordance with *shari'a* rules of evidence, and if proven would pronounce a death sentence, even when the offence, such as wounding, did not call for it in the *shari'a* (Heyd 1973:107).

A whole range of punishments and fines were specified in the *qanun-name* which were classified as *siyaset*, administration, as distinct from *shari'a*. In this regard, the *shari'a*, often mentioned with reverence in the *qanun-name*, was nevertheless subordinated and marginalized in the actual substance of the law.

Finally, chapters of the *qanun-name* specified and regulated the hierarchy of the military and officials of the court and the state, their duties, privileges, remuneration and revenues, and punishments of offences they may commit.

THE IDEOLOGICAL RESONANCE OF THE *SHARI'A* IN THE OTTOMAN WORLD

The official discourse of the Ottoman state venerated the *shari'a*. The sultan as defender of the faith always declared his steadfast adherence to the holy law. The Ottoman court included religious offices of high rank: the *shaykhulislam* enjoyed a status equivalent to that of the grand vizir, and the two Qadiaskars of Rumelia and Anatolia were powerful offices (see Chapter 2). Ottoman bureaucracy included a vast section of religious institutions of justice and education, with a hierarchy of graded posts and remuneration. The position of the chief *qadi* in each provincial centre was equivalent to that of the governor, and had an elaborate bureaucracy, revenues and powers under his control. On the other side, popular movements of discontent, protests and uprisings denounced the authorities and the upper classes for their deviance from the dictates of the holy law, clamouring for its proper application, especially in matters fiscal. The rule of 'good' sultans, especially Suleiman, was celebrated as a golden age precisely because he was supposed to have upheld religion and applied holy law, hence his title of '*qanuni*'. Subsequent decline was often blamed by critics on departure from this virtuous norm. From the beginning of the seventeenth century,

Ottoman law books became ever more religious in appearance, comprising numerous *fatwas* from *shaykhulislams* (Inalcik 1978:136). Ebussu'ud's treatise on taxes was one such exercise in 'Islamizing' law. In addition, so much of social life, urban space, economic functions and popular culture revolved around religious practices, institutions and personnel. The major mosques were nuclei of a set of buildings and *madrasas*, of *awqaf* of welfare and services such as *imarat* or soup-kitchens for travellers, guests and the needy. The Suleimaniya complex in Istanbul is a well preserved example of this mosque complex. Some Sufi *zawiyas* or *tekkes* played similar roles, notably the Mevlevi complex in Konya. Markets were regulated by the *muhtasib* and his men, this being a religiously defined function. Craft guilds were, at times, organized as religious brotherhoods, with ceremonies and rituals. The *qadi* had wide powers in monitoring public conduct and enforcing morality and religious observance in domains under his control.

We should note in passing that this deep penetration of religion into society and institutions side by side with a pragmatic adaptation of its teaching was also a feature of much of European society till the seventeenth century. Princes and emperors were 'protectors of the faith' and champions of the church, fighting its enemies and uprooting heresy. The churches and their personnel enjoyed great authority, backed by law, and entered into all aspects of social organization and everyday life. The Reformation only reinforced these religious preoccupations and added factional zeal. Guilds and corporations were religious brotherhoods with their own cults and chapels.[24] Of course, the mode of institutionalization of religion, especially the separation of church and state, constitute crucial differences, which played a part in the different trajectories of development in Europe and the Ottoman world.

It would seem, then, that Ottoman state and society were thoroughly imbued by religion, and, in particular, with devotion to the holy law. Indeed, historians have remarked on the centrality of Islam to the empire, and many orientalists blamed this 'fanatical' religious adherence for the backwardness and decline of the empire when confronted by a Europe committed to (secular) science and progress. Paradoxically, Gibb and Bowen, who entitled their seminal book on the Ottoman Empire *Islamic Society and the West* (1950/1957), at one point appear to be searching for this 'Islamic society' and finding it mainly in the religious institutions. The first chapter in the section on religion opens with the following passage:

> The term 'Islamic Society' applied to the social organization which we are analysing implies that its distinguishing features are related in some way or another to the religion of Islam. Yet those groups and activities which have been considered up to this point [aspects of government, social and economic life] there is little which can be regarded as specifically Islamic; on the contrary, the organization

of village and industrial life belongs rather to a stage of social evolution which finds close parallels in many non-Islamic regions of Europe and Asia; and that of the Court and the army, though of a more peculiar type, is based upon principles to which such Islamic elements as they display appear to be purely incidental. [Gibb and Bowen II 1957:70]

They go on to ask, apart from the specifically ecclesiastical and legal side, in what manner Islam stamped its imprint on society. They answer in terms of the idea of the community of the faithful and the place of religious institutions and personnel in social life and sentiment, as we have outlined.

How far did the practice of government and of religion itself conform to the official discourse? The foregoing exposition has demonstrated the large degree of pragmatism and *raison d'etat* thinking and practice in Ottoman government, throughout its history. The *qanun-name* largely bypassed the *shari'a*, and while treating it with reverence, assigned it to the margins of government practice. *Qadis* were figures of power and influence, and legal judgements delivered by sultans and viziers had to be formally ratified by a *qadi*. At the same time, *qadis* were required to rule in accordance with *'urfi* laws side by side with the *shari'a*, as well as administering government regulations in their domains That is to say, *qadis* were treated as state functionaries administering state law, and not as purely religious judges following the books of *fiqh*. Fiscal and administrative matters were largely covered by *'urfi* law, in spite of the existence of *shari'a* provisions to cover some of them. Many of the practices central to Ottoman rule were clearly at variance with *shari'a* principle. The institution of *devshirme*, the levy of boys from Christian families, so crucial for military might and administrative efficiency till the late seventeenth century, was clearly at variance with *shari'a* provisions for the protection of *dhimmis*, non-Muslims living peacefully and obediently in the lands of Islam and paying the poll-tax due from them. Add to this the forcible conversion of the boys to Islam, explicitly prohibited. State *ulama* devised ingenious arguments for justifying the practice (Inalcik 1998:237–38). The prohibition on interest payments was disregarded and the *qanun-name* specified maximum rates. It was breached in the very religious sphere of *awqaf* by allowing cash endowments, as we have seen. Another area of variance from Hanafi prescriptions was that of price-fixing by the government. Administered prices, often enforced and regulated by religious functionaries such as the *qadi* and the *muhtasib*, were an essential part of Ottoman policy, especially with respect to the provisioning of cities. Hanafi law favoured free-market determination of prices and opposed price-fixing. Some *ulama*, including one learned grand vizir in the seventeenth century, voiced their reserve on this matter. However, dominant *ulama* opinion justified the practice. 'It was frequently claimed that the moral fiber of mankind had deteriorated since the time of the Prophet and the early legists, so that measures of control unnecessary and even blameworthy in those times had become allowed and necessary' (Faroqhi 1997:546). In fiscal matters, Ottoman practice, in line with all other Muslim states, imposed taxes over and above those specified in the *shari'a*, as we have seen. The fiscal focus to Ottoman penal law, with its emphasis on fines, was clearly contrary to *shari'a* provisions. Although it did not exclude these provisions, it left their application open, to be decided by the particular courts or tribunals, while the fiscal element, often in addition to *shari'a* punishments, was rigorously enforced. In any case, much of penal law was in the province of *'urf* rather than *shari'a*. The increasing religious content of law books from the beginning of the seventeenth century, with *fatwas* and legal opinions from religious authority, while framing *'urfi* law within the concepts and vocabularies of the *shari'a*, nevertheless preserved the content and thrust of that law, giving it religious legitimacy.

Some *ulama* and other elements raised their voices on occasion against these violations of the *shari'a*, and now and again a sultan, from piety or to shore up a weakness in his position or enhance his reputation for piety, would respond positively. Such was the case with Bayazid II, who made great pretence to restore the *shari'a* after its neglect in his predecessor's law book, as we have seen. Sultans whose rule was faltering and whose enemies had gained the advantage, could be deposed in the name of the *shari'a*, and a *fatwa* from the *shaykhul-islam* secured to confirm the legitimacy of the act. Such was the case with Selim III, deposed and killed in 1807 by a janissary revolt against his plans for military reform. None of these episodes, however, have led to drastic changes in the legal system. The system was elaborated and expanded, following the greater complexity of government, and sometimes reflecting shifts in power positions, but the combination of *shari'a* and *'urf* and the salience of pragmatic considerations prevailed.

The *shari'a*, as we have noted, is not only 'law', but also contains a set of rules regarding ritual observance, and specifying what is licit, disapproved and illicit in a whole range of everyday activities. We saw that, in many respects, the religious and cultural practices of most Sufi orders and the popular classes did not always conform to these rules. In particular, the mystic philosophy of Ibn al-Arabi, common to many of the Sufis, devalued the *shari'a* as a preliminary and superficial phase of religious knowledge and practice. The true initiates could dispense, many assumed, with its rules and rituals. Music, dancing and drink were regular features of Sufi cults, while regular prayer was not.[25] Alid sympathies and the cult of mourning for the martyrs of Shi'ism were also common, and mostly tolerated, despite their variance with Sunni adherence. We saw that these practices were common at all levels of society, including the court, and that religious dignitaries, such as the *shaykhulislam* and prominent *qadis* were, on occasion, active members of Sufi orders. Wine-drinking, and drinking culture and poetry, were common at all levels of Ottoman society, and certainly at its apex in the court and the elite circles. Drink was common to the janissaries, and formed part of their rituals. The humorous stereotype of the drinking *qadi*, common to many Muslim epochs, was equally prevalent in the Ottoman. In the reign of Suleiman, one Nihali was the Qadi of Galata, a cosmopolitan part of Istanbul, known for his drinking and frequenting of taverns. He was also a poet, with a *nom de plume* of Ja'far of Galata. Commenting on Suleiman's order to one of his border commanders to refrain from raids on Habsburg territories, with whom he had concluded a peace treaty, Nihali wrote: 'To give Ali Beg [a commander's position in] an uc (border area) and forbid him to operate is like giving me the judgeship of Galata and telling me not to drink' (quoted in Kafadar 1995:150).

The heterodox and ecstatic elements of religious practice were periodically denounced by oppositional elements, and the denunciation would be taken up by figures of authority, including the sultan or a vizir or *qadi*, often in efforts to court popularity and to mobilize opinion in their favour in political contests. We have seen that Murad IV in the seventeenth century embarked on such a course, taking the side of a mob led by low-ranking preachers, cracked down on Sufi lodges. He also forbade wine-drinking and ordered the closure of taverns, though he himself was known for excessive drinking. These were mostly political manoeuvres, though no doubt motivated for some by religious convictions. In any event, Sufi cults continued to flourish and to enjoy favour and respectability, some richly endowed by sultans and nobility. Wine-drinking and drinking cultures similarly continued, now open, now discreet, throughout that history. At some point in the nineteenth century, wine gave way to *raki*, a distilled spirit which found favour with Bektashis, and with many other sectors of urban society until the present time.

The high-ranking *ulama* were fully members of the Ottoman elite and the *askari*, military class. They participated in the life and culture of this elite, and were often major players in political contests. Their religious culture, for the most part followed the tastes and inclinations of their society. But some, at particular critical conjunctures, could adopt orthodox and pious positions – in some cases, no doubt, out of conviction, but always with political consequences.

CONCLUSION: STATE AND SOCIETY

I shall here try to focus on some of the questions raised in this chapter regarding the relationships between rulers and ruled, or state and society. For the Muslim scholars, rule was conceived in personalized terms, as that of the sovereign and his dynasty (and these conceptions were not unique to Muslims). The word *dawla* (*devlet*), now translated as 'state', was used in previous periods to refer to dynasty, conceived as the property or patrimony of a family, hence Weber's concept of 'patrimonial' authority. In juristic discourses, as discussed in this chapter, authority was always conceived in personal terms as that of the ruler. Discussion of authority came under the heading of *imama*, and pertained to the person and attributes of the imam or the caliph. Sultans or amirs come onto the scene as princes without the religious connotations of the other titles. The term came into use to designate the military usurpers who became the masters and patrons of the caliphate, then replaced at the end of the Abbasids in the Mongol sack of Baghdad in 1258.

Juristic discourse, then, conceived all authority as emanating from the sovereign power of the prince, with the exception, that is, of the law, which emanated from a divine source, making it, as we have seen, the province of the scholar as the specialist in sacred sources and texts. Institutions of rule and of law, then, were conceived as deriving their authority from the ruler or from God, in some instances combining the two, as in the earlier conceptions of the caliph as God's deputy. It is only in the early nineteenth century, with the reforms introduced by Mahmud II (see Chapter 4) that the idea emerges of authority residing in impersonal institutions of state which are neither sultan nor God, as we shall see.

We have seen that the law of God, presided over by the *ulama*, has tended to accommodate itself to the practices of the prince and his servants their rules and ordinances. On many occasions the *ulama* extended the concepts and vocabularies of the *shari'a* to accommodate the practices of state, thus maintaining their own authority and competence in these areas. This tendency has been called 'Sunni realism'. The question arises, however, as to what extent has this realism separated ethics, righteousness and religious legitimacy from the sphere of rule? Gibb concludes his essay on Mawardi: 'Necessity and expediency may indeed be respectable principles, but only when they are not invoked to justify disregard of the law' (Gibb 1962a:164). This led to the collapse of the juristic theory of the caliphate.

Patricia Crone, then Ernest Gellner have elaborated a theory of Muslim society over the whole of its history in which this tension between realism and legitimacy is given a central role, giving a kind of essence to Muslim polity, in the case of Gellner to the present time. Let us examine the arguments.

Patricia Crone[26] has pointed out that the political theorizing of Sunni realism is neutral on questions of morality and justice in government. The argument is pragmatic: security and unity of the community, the enforcement of orthodoxy on the subjects is all that is required from the ruler. There are no specifications of what constitutes justice other than the *shari'a*, which the ruler is free to bypass. At the same time, the jurists had a clear idea of what constituted justice and correct Muslim rule in the *sunna* and practice of Muhammad and the first caliphs. This is the model of the idealized Madinan community, of leaders ruling in accordance with divine commands and the divinely inspired example of the Prophet. Following these commands, they ruled in consultation (*shura*) with their community. They were meticulous in handling the treasury of the Muslims, to the extent that they traded in the markets to cover their own needs rather than take a penny from the communal treasury for their personal use. This utopian model was clearly impossible in the medieval polity, ruled by dynasties and sultans, whose *raison d'être* was the accumulation of personal wealth. For the medieval jurist, then, the Madinan Utopia becomes a messianic dream, perhaps to be re-enacted in millennial time. In the meantime, standards of justice with regard to government are suspended.

Crone argues that juristic ideal harked back to the desert and the tribe, which gave their stamp to the Madinan model. As such, the logic of the jurist's theory could not grant religious legitimacy to urban government. They placed it in a moral vacuum, withholding any form of legitimacy except the pragmatic. This ideal, she argues, was embedded in the logic of the politico-legal discourse of the *ulama*, even when those in subsequent generations became active participants in government, court dignitaries and protégés and beneficiaries of the rulers, as well as always having themselves constituted a part of the urban bourgeoisie. Gellner[27] takes up this theme, attributing great significance to the *ulama*'s withholding of legitimacy to political rule and their control over the affairs and allegiances of the urban community. This characterization of the Muslim polity is in contrast to a presumed European model, in which claims to legitimacy and standards of justice were not confined to religious sources. The church recognized state law and political legitimacy deriving from pre-Christian as well as extra-religious sources, though always divinely inspired reason. Gellner then advances a model of Muslim society which is bifurcated into the sphere of the community of believers, presided over by the *ulama* and their law, separated from and often hostile to the state and the ruler. The community is strong in its cohesion and leadership, while the state is weak, suffering from a deficit of legitimacy, as well as the threat of tribal confederations, often armed with religious zeal, waiting at the gates for the moment of weakness to pounce and install their own dynasty. Gellner considered this process to be a cyclical feature of Muslim society, with the possible exception of the Ottomans. Modernity, goes the argument, has brought the former tribes and religious zeal into the city to pose their challenges in the name of the *shari'a* to the nation-state superimposed on them. Muslim society, concluded Gellner, is uniquely resistant to secularization (Gellner 1992:5–22).

Like all essentialist arguments, Gellner's is ahistorical. It downgrades important differences between the various societies and polities of Islamic history, as well as those between the different societies of 'the West'. We have seen, and will see further, many different examples of state–society and ruler–*ulama* relations, from accommodations to conflicts. Juristic theory of the state did not end with Mawardi. Ibn Taimiya produced his own synthesis, and the Ottomans went further in integrating religion into the state. Patterns of state–society relations have varied greatly in medieval polities and were not always compartmentalized in separate spheres. The segmentarity of Mamluke power, for instance, divided as it were into rival households of warlords, also segmented urban society in vertical alliances including *ulama*, merchants, city quarters and guilds. Istanbul in later Ottoman history saw an interpenetration of janissaries into the urban fabric of trade and guilds, between *ulama*, the court and the commoners through *awqaf* and Sufi orders. Albert Hourani, in a famous essay, 'Ottoman Reforms and the Politics of Notables' (Hourani 1968) demonstrated another kind of interpenetration in the cities of the Arab provinces, in which the notables of merchants, landlords and *ulama* played central roles in the rule and the economy of the city, and were as such indispensable for the Ottoman authorities. Religion in its official institutions of the law, supervision of *awqaf* and the organization of Sufi orders, entered into the economic and political fabric of urban life.

The arguments advanced by Crone and Gellner seem to suppose that features of Muslim society and polity inaugurated in their formative period continue throughout their subsequent history.[28] This would exempt Muslim societies from the processes of socio-economic and political transformations, or at least subordinate these processes to the essential elements of origin. There is no intrinsic justification for this argument. I have tried to demonstrate in this chapter the patterns of relationship between rulers and *ulama* and the mutations of the themes and concepts of the law in these contexts. In the next chapter we consider the crucial transformations of the state, the law and religion in the processes of modernity and the eventual incorporation of the law in the state.

4   THE AGE OF REFORM:
THE ETATIZATION OF LAW

This chapter will consider the processes and ideas of reform in the nineteenth and earlier parts of the twentieth centuries, and their impact on the development of law and its institutions. It will concentrate on the Ottoman lands, with references to Egypt, as these were the main loci of reforms which eventually affected the whole region. Modern developments in Iran came later and proceeded at a slower pace, only really taking effect in the twentieth century. They also occurred in different political and religious landscapes. Occasional references to Iran shall be made here, but shall discuss it more fully in Chapter 6, as a background to the recent developments in the Islamic Republic. The chapter is concluded with examples of the institutionalization of reform in the legal systems of the nation-states succeeding the Ottoman Empire with respect to family law. We shall see that the overall direction of the reforms was to make law into standard codified state law, taking what remained of legal authority away from the religious establishments, and ending the legal pluralism of the historical *shari'a* tradition.

THE OTTOMAN REFORMS

The ascendancy of European power, military and economic, forced some radical rethinking among rulers and elites in the Muslim world, notably in Ottoman lands. Military defeats in wars with European powers, and increasing subordination to France, Britain and Russia in the eighteenth century, weakened the firm belief in the inevitable superiority of Islam and the traditional institutions and practices. The decadence and impotence of the main military forces in the empire were evident to all. The janissaries had long ceased to be an effective fighting force, most of its members settling down to urban trades and crafts, until their regiments (*ocaks*) coincided with trade guilds. Certificates of inscription in the force, entitling the holder to draw military pay, were traded between equally unmilitary buyers and sellers. Moves to modernize the military by circumventing the janissaries continued through the eighteenth century, with the foundation of schools and units of military engineers, for instance. At the end of that century, under the sultanate of Selim III, such moves culminated in an attempt to found a new army, along modern European lines, named the *Nizam-I Jedid*, or New Order. This step was strongly opposed by the janissaries, now dominant in the urban landscape of Istanbul, in alliance with sectors of the *ulama*, the *derebeys* and the *a'yan* (provincial notables), that is all the power elites of the old order. All innovation, especially that emulating European methods, was deemed contrary to religion and a betrayal of the *shari'a*. Resistance to the reforms ended in a revolt which unseated Selim and led to his execution, as well as a massacre of his followers and supporters in 1807. His successor, Mahmud II continued the project of reform, but with more subtle planning and realignmenting of forces, leading to the defeat and massacre of the janissaries in 1826. This was the beginning of the era of reform and the formation of a modern state in the Ottoman lands.[1]

Mahmud's reforms coincided, and were in part stimulated, by the success of Muhammad Ali in Egypt. This military adventurer established his dynasty in Egypt, which was in most respects independent from Ottoman power, and superior to it in military might. He combined traditional dynastic objectives of accumulating wealth, and through it, military prowess, with increasingly modern methods of economic exploitation and military organization, aided by European technique and personnel (Marsot 1984). These reforms, in Egypt and the Ottoman lands, constituted the framework for administrative, fiscal and legal reforms in the direction of modern forms of the state and new conceptions of politics.

The history of Ottoman reform in the nineteenth century can be broadly divided into three periods: the early reforms under Mahmud, with the sultan and his supporters grappling with new notions of government, institutions and law; the Tanzimat era of administrative, legal and fiscal reforms, often under European pressure; finally, the adaptation and adoption of elements of European legal codes and procedures. This was the decisive period in the etatization of law, including the codification of elements of the *shari'a* into state law. The constitution of 1876 was the culmination of the Tanzimat period, and the setting for the following phase, that of the reaction against reform and consti-tutionalism fostered by the Sultan Abdul-Hamid in favour of an ideological pan-Islamism, directed against European domination. This ideological and political reaction, however, did not reverse the reforms, which continued apace, driven by the momentum of socio-economic and cultural transformation, as well as the continuing centralization and bureaucratization of government power set in motion by the earlier development and the penetration of world markets and processes.

Reforms in Egypt under Muhammad Ali, no less momentous at first, followed a different logic of dynastic interest. After 1840, European penetration and domination played similar roles in that country, eventually leading to virtual colonization by Britain in 1882, and the control of European powers over finance and administration, with concomitant legal innovations.

The economic thrust of the Tanzimat was to open up the Ottoman lands to European trade, with little hindrance or restriction (bureaucratic attempts to reimpose protectionist measures after 1860 had little success: Quataert 1994:763). The old protective measures of monopolies, tolls, taxes and tariffs were largely swept away, giving European merchants wide access (Quataert part IV 1994: 759–944). An increasingly indebted government became ever more dependent and susceptible to European finance. The growth of the infrastructure of transport and communications facilitated this opening: the steamship, then the railways, and crucially the telegraph lines, establishing communications between Istanbul and London in 1860 and continuing to expand for the rest of the century. The consequences of these developments for the native Muslim populations of the empire were often disastrous. Certain areas of agriculture benefited, but at the cost of ever-greater dependence on external markets. Industries, crafts and guilds of the provinces and countryside were often devastated by this free trade and easy access, in which the Europeans and their non-Muslim Ottoman associates and agents held the upper hand. The rout of the janissaries in 1826 deprived guild and craftsmen of their protection and corroded their monopolies. Impoverished peasants sought relief in the cities, which could ill absorb them. Many sectors of the popular classes, then, had little reason to celebrate the Tanzimat and the European influences and models they brought, despite the seemingly liberationist thrust of their political rhetoric. Much resentment and ammunition for reaction were stored at the popular level in these developments.

The overall political and administrative thrust of the Tanzimat was for increasing centralization of government and control, and a concomitant expansion in the size, reach and power of the bureaucracy. By the end of the century, it is estimated that there were 500,000 civil servants (Quataert 1994:765) who, in addition to mainstream government administration and finance, also administered hospitals, secular schools, agricultural schools and model farms, highways, telegraph and railroads. Crucially, these were 'modern' functionaries, with institutional positions and powers (as distinct from the personalistic networks which characterized earlier administrations). They, together with professionals, army officers and some sectors of business, constituted the modern middle class, and the cadres of modernization and secularization. They supplied the leadership and personnel of the Young Turks movement. During the Tanzimat era, this central administration gained in power and control over other power elites. The military reforms, though not a brilliant success in external wars, were instrumental in imposing the central power on the provinces and their elites. The *a'yan* and *derbeys*, with extensive autonomies till the middle of the eighteenth century, came firmly under government control and its centrally appointed functionaries, although many maintained their local power bases as power-brokers and tax-farmers – a practice that the central government did not succeed in breaking (Quataert 1994:769). In the Kurdish and Arab provinces the nomadic tribes were firmly subordinated by the new military forces and the extension of transport and communications. This was an important step in pacifying these provinces and enhancing the security and productivity of the settled agricultural populations.

On the international and regional levels, the empire sustained great territorial and fiscal losses in the course of the century and till its demise in World War I. The loss of Egypt at the start of the century was followed by the losses of European territories: Serbia in 1817, Greece in 1828, Romania and most of the remaining Balkan provinces in 1856 and 1878, and so on (Quaetert 1994:767). These were economically the most advanced and productive provinces and a major source of tax revenues. Muslim refugees from these provinces were resettled in Anatolia and some in Arab lands. These constituted and fomented a reservoir of Islamic nationalism and resentment of European influences and models.

With so many sectors of the populace suffering economic decline, Abdul-Hamid's appeal to pan-Islamic sentiments against constitutionalism and European models found a ready response at a popular level, with so many sectors of the populace suffering economic decline. Loss of territory and the swarms of refugees exacerbated anti-European and anti-Christian feelings, and made appeals to Islamic nationalism and tradition ever more potent. Abdul-Hamid's Islamic appeal, however, was largely confined to the ideological level. Government reforms proceeded apace, and the powers and controls of the central government were a central plank of Hamidian autocracy. This phase, in contrast to that of the Tanzimat, saw the firm subordination of prominent administrators and statesmen to sultanic power, buttressed by a traditional claim to the legitimacy of the Muslim ruler.[2]

POLITICAL AND LEGAL CONCEPTS

The course of the reforms of the nineteenth century brought new concepts and practices of political authority, government and law. These were in the nature of the transformation of the dynastic empire, ruled over by a sultan-caliph with religious and worldly authority, into a proto-nation-state. The elements of this emergence included the following conceptual shifts.[3]

First was the separation of government from the absolute sovereignty and will of the sultan, as well as from the religious authority of the *shari'a* and its personnel. This process started under Mahmud when the concept of *adalet*, justice, emerged, as a form of justice outside the will of the ruler and the jurisdiction of the *shari'a*, and part of a process of law-making by institutions, in accordance with rational considerations of utility (Berkes 1964:94–99). The institution which fostered this concept was the Divan-i Ahkam-i Adliye, the Council for Juridical/Justice Enactments/Ordinances, which was to play an important part in legal reforms. This was a crucial conceptual and institutional step, because it located legislative authority in a formal institution that was distinct from the sacred sources on the one hand and the will of the sovereign on the other. Indeed, the sovereign undertook to be bound by the law. Subsequent development under the Tanzimat located this authority in a Supreme Council of State, and the elaboration of state institutions later spawned the said Divan-i Ahkam-i Adliya as part of a Ministry of Justice, whose very concept asserted state responsibility for the law. Another step was to abolish the office of Sadr-i Azam (chief vizir), as absolute vicar of the sultan, in favour of a *bashwakil*, a chief minister, co-ordinating a number of ministers with clearly specified departmental functions. The title was later restored, but within the context of the new conception of cabinet government. A consultative council was established with the title of Meclis-i Umur-u Nafia, Board of Useful Affairs (Berkes 1964:98), clearly orientated to the concept of utility.

The second shift was the gradual separation of religion from government by the identification of religious functions and institutions as distinct from state functions. Under Mahmud, the office of *shaykhulislam* underwent transformation from that of a chief mufti and court notable with diverse powers and functions to that of the head of a religious institution, with responsibility for *shari'a* courts (Berkes 1964:98). Religious courts and their law were thus given a separate institutional setting, apparently insulated from the process of reform, but in the process explicitly recognizing that there was a sphere of government, legislation and law outside this sphere of religion (Mardin 1989:105–10).

Third was the emergence of the notion of 'citizenship': the new notion of *adalet* included the idea of the equality of all subjects before the law. This clearly contradicted the *shari'a* doctrine of the inferior status and legal disabilities of non-Muslims, as well as the traditional Ottoman legal particularism in relation to different statuses of corporate groups. In fact, in general Ottoman practice over the centuries, corporate status overrode individual status. In terms of taxation, legal liabilities, family law, and even, in some cases, collective punishment, the individual had a legal personality largely by virtue of his or her membership of a corporate group, be that a religious millet, a guild, a village or a tribe. In addition, there was the special distinction and privilege of the *'askari* class of military and civil servants of the sultan, as distinct from the general body of the subjects, *re'aya*, and the distinction between (Sunni) Muslim and non-Muslim, and between the *ulama* class and the 'lay' population. The idea, and subsequently the decrees, of equality before the law, threatened all these distinctions and privileges. These ideas and some steps to implementation started under Mahmud, but were fully developed in the edicts of the Tanzimat.

There were two edicts which declared and defined the Tanzimat reforms: the Hatt-i Serif of 1839, then and the Hatt-i Humayun of 1856. Both took the form of royal decrees delineating administrative, military and fiscal reforms, but also making general declarations of principle regarding the rights and protection of subjects. The formulation and the implementation of these decrees was the work of the new men of government and bureaucracy, starting with Resid Pasha, followed by his disciples Ali Pasha and Fuad Pasha.[4] These decrees were issued partly under pressure from the European powers, and many of their clauses were aimed at mollifying these powers to stop their interference in the internal affairs of the empire by showing that they were dealing with the issues of their concern. One issue was the treatment of Christian subjects, and the declaration of equality before the law. The more elaborate 1856 edict declared equality in matters of military service, in the administration of justice, in taxation, in admission to educational institutions, in public employment and in social respect. Insulting or derogatory references to persons on grounds of religion, class or race were forbidden (Davison 1973:55–56). While seeming to declare common citizenship (though the term used was still 'subject' and not citizen, but these were to be equal children of the sultan), the edict did not abolish the millet organization of Christian and Jewish communities,[5] but sought to reform it. The millet authorities, especially the ecclesiastical hierarchy, were resistant to abolition of the system, and they were backed by the European powers, who paradoxically called for equality but wished to maintain separate identity and autonomy. The reform of the millets involved the establishment of representative councils, to include lay elements, thus limiting the arbitrary authority of the clerics. The fiscal privileges of the clerics were also limited, with the change of their remuneration to fixed salaries as against revenues and benefices at the expense of their subjects. Conversions of Christians from the Orthodox and Catholic rites to the Protestantism through the European and especially American missions were in some instances recognized in the formation of separate millets in some instances: there were both Armenian and Greek Catholic millets, and the Armenian Protestants subsequently established their own organization.

Reactions to these edicts of equality were predominantly hostile from the majority Muslim population, and mixed from the non-Muslims. Muslims, and many of their *ulama*, strongly resented what they saw as a breach in *shari'a* rules which relegated non-Muslims to inferior status, and affirmed the superiority and privilege of Muslims in a Muslim state. Their resentment was fuelled by the fact that the decrees were made under Christian/European pressure – these were precisely the agents behind the decline of the empire and the immiseration of its Muslim population. In practice, throughout most of the Ottoman lands this declaration of equality was a 'dead letter'. As for the non-Muslims, the clerics and the traditional leaders strongly resented the limitations on their powers and privileges, and the weakening of their authority over their members. Further:

> The Greek hierarchy, fearing the loss of their primacy among the non-Muslims, disliked not only this invasion of traditional prerogative, but also the general emphasis on equality. 'The state puts us together with the Jews', some of the Greeks were reported to have said [...] It is quite probable that the Greek metropolitan of Izmit uttered the wish attributed to him as the Hatt-i Humayun was put back into its red satin pouch after the ceremonial reading at the Porte: 'Insallah – God grant that it not be taken out of this bag again'. [Davison 1973:59]

The element of 'equality' most disliked by the general run of non-Muslims was military service. There was, however, provision for buying out of this obligation with a monetary payment. In practice, with the exception of some Greek sailors, few non-Muslims served in the armed forces until the early twentieth century.

One important corollary of these declarations of equality was the development of a concept of common Ottoman nationality, over and above the particular identities of religion and community. This was an essential element in the conceptual transition from dynastic empire to nation-state.

The fourth change was the emergence of public law: part of the process of bureaucratization of the state was the increasing formalization and writing of regulations defining public office, rules of governance and the concept of public service. From the time of Mahmud II, regulations were printed and appointments announced in the official gazette, the first Turkish newspaper. Traditional positions, including palace sinecures, were abolished. Officials were given legal security and guarantees against the arbitrary power of the sultan, who had held the power of life and death over them. This included the abolition of the practice of confiscation of an official's property at his death. Mahmud tried unsuccessfully to abolish bribery by paying salaries regularly. The hierarchy of civilian officials was reclassified. As we have seen, ministries were reorganized in line with the European model of functional ministries and a cabinet system

(Davison 1973:27–28). Later developments under the Tanzimat furthered these processes of formalization, and brought in some principles of representation. The Hatt-i Humayun specified representative provincial and communal councils, to include Muslim and non-Muslim delegates, and guaranteed them freedom of discussion. The Supreme Council of Judicial Ordinances was to include non-Muslim representatives, and the millet councils were to include lay delegates (Davison 1973:57).

New conceptions accompanied these changes. There emerged the concept of a public law, which was distinct from the *shari'a*, from custom and tradition, and while enacted by the ruler, had a *raison d'être* other than the emanation of the will of the ruler: namely it followed a logic of utility, of social improvement, of progress (Berkes 1964:132–35). These were the beginnings of modern notions of 'governmentality', that is of a government with the object of managing a population, to further its welfare and productivity. Education, industry, and economic policy, all these were emerging as matters of state concern, to be implemented and regulated by bureaucracy and law. The conception behind these developments is, perhaps, best expressed in the title of the Board of Useful Affairs, already noted, embodying the concept of utility. Mahmud's reign, then, set the stage for the Tanzimat to come. This is not to say that the traditional idea of a just ruler did not include the welfare of the subjects: indeed this was always part of the pious formulae of the virtue of the just prince. However, this was always premised on the will and virtue of the ruler, with rudimentary institutional expression, such as the *mazalim* tribunals discussed in Chapter 2, exemplifying the personal power and justice of the prince.

The fifth shift was proto-nationalism – the idea of the peoples of the empire constituting an Ottoman nation ruled over by a nation-state. This, as we saw, was the implication of equality before the law. Loss of territory at the hands of nationalist movements of Christian populations, backed by Christian powers, aroused a kind of popular Islamic nationalism. Rulers and bureaucrats increasingly felt the need to mobilize popular sentiment behind state legitimacy and action: 'At some point after the turn of the nineteenth century Ottoman power holders began increasingly to feel the need to address an appeal to those elements in society who were hitherto only commanded to obey' (Deringil 1998:45). This was not easy, for the Tanzimat state operated by the logic of reform and modernization, which went against the Islamic nationalism of the populace. In this tension, the *shari'a* acquired added ideological resonance, as the symbol of what is correct and legitimate for a Muslim people and government. The rulers, while gradually departing from or insulating the idea of the *shari'a* and its institutions, at the same time felt compelled to glorify it in rhetoric and assert the compatibility of their reforms with its dictates. The proto-nationalism of the Tanzimat period consisted of a dynastic state imposing a nationalism from above, much like the Russian czar and the Habsburgs in Austria-Hungary (Hobsbawm 1992:73), thus reconceptualizing their domain as a nation-state, with loyalty due from citizens to a common fatherland (*vatan* or *watan*). For the 'citizens', this appeal was successful insofar as it addressed their grievances, often conceived in terms of transgressions against Muslims. Abdul-Hamid's success at the popular level was precisely because he tackled this tension by adopting Islamic nationalism as state ideology, and used it as an instrument of state centralization and control, as well as one of appeal to Muslims outside the empire. I shall return to these issues presently.

THE LEGAL REFORMS OF THE TANZIMAT

The Hatt-i Humayun of 1856 repeated, elaborated and enlarged the promises and principles declared in the earlier Tanzimat decree, the Hatt-i Serif of 1839. They both promised much more than they could accomplish, notably the abolition of tax-farming and the abolition of bribery. Given that these edicts were promulgated under European pressure (but not without native roots in the court and bureaucracy: Deringil 1998:45–46), many of their provisions were addressed to European concerns, prominent among them the affairs of the Christian communities, equality before the law, equal liability to military service, equality in taxation and the administration of justice, admission to schools and public employment. A special anti-defamation clause forbade the use of derogatory epithets by officials or private persons against any class or religion (the epithet *gavur*, infidel, was favourite). A note annexed to the edict addressed the touchy question of apostasy from Islam: this was not to be punished by death (Davison 1973:55) – presumably not punished at all. It affirmed the establishment of mixed tribunals to hear cases involving Muslims and non-Muslims, before which witnesses of all religions were to have equal status (with the implication that they did not in other courts). On other matters, the second decree promised administrative and fiscal reforms and rationalization: observance of annual budgets, the establishment of banks and, crucially, the codification of penal and commercial law.

An interesting difference between the two edicts was that the earlier one was steeped in honorific references to the *shari'a* and the glorious traditions of the empire, whereas the later edict was almost free from any such reference. This omission reflected, perhaps, the greater influence and confidence of the secular statesmen, but also the fact that the edict was promulgated under immediate pressure from the Paris Conference sitting at that time (Davison 1973:54–56).

The commitment of the Tanzimat to legal reforms, including the codification of law, implied a crucial conceptual shift. As we have seen, from the time of

Mahmud the idea was established of an impersonal, institutional and non-religious legislative body, in the form of the Supreme Council for Judicial Enactments, and this was an important departure from the principles of both *shari'a* as divine law and *qanun* as the will of each ruler. Indeed, the implication of the language and principle of legal reform was that the ruler himself was bound by the law. Although the 1839 edict and many subsequent pronouncements affirmed loyalty to the *shari'a*, the process of reform consisted in gradual departures from the *shari'a*. The emphasis on equality before the law also went in the direction of codification and rationalization, beyond arbitrary edicts, and towards the idea of a superior law governing the process of legislation. This, logically, would lead to the notion of a constitution, which was to be a controversial demand by some sectors of the political and intellectual elites, and one which, as we shall see, was to have a chequered career into the twentieth century.

Reform of Judicial Institutions and Procedures

The first step in codification and institutional innovation was that of the introduction of a commercial law, following the Commercial Treaty of 1838, which also spawned commercial tribunals, at first informal and organized by merchants, ruling in accordance with European practice, but formalized in 1847 into the mixed tribunals (Berkes 1964:161–62). This was by agreement with the European powers holding capitulatory privileges.[6] The tribunal consisted of 10 Muslim Ottomans, 10 non-Muslim Ottomans and 10 foreigners. These were progressively formalized and codified in steps: the Commercial Code was enacted in 1850, drawn from the French code of 1807, further codes and procedures were added in 1861 and 1863, when the tribunals became regular courts responsible to a Ministry of Commerce. These were the first courts to operate outside the remit of *shari'a* and *qanun*. As we have seen, they were the first to admit the testimony of non-Muslims on a basis of equality. This was justified in terms of precedent in the *shari'a* admissibility of traders regulating their own affairs. But once established, modern court systems expanded and eventually spilled over into *shari'a* areas, including the codification of the *shari'a* itself.

The next area of law to undergo modernization of sorts was penal law. As we have seen, in traditional Ottoman practice the penal provisions of the *shari'a* were largely bypassed in favour of the *qanun*, and penal cases were often dealt with by the police and administrative bodies. When it came to modernizing penal law, however, the reformers had to deal with the theoretical claims of the *shari'a* to jurisdiction over this area. The first attempt at a penal code was made by Mahmud II, but that was largely confined to penal provisions for state officials. The Supreme Council drew up a penal code in 1840. This contained elements of modern penal codes side by side with *shari'a* provisions of *qisas* and *diya* (compensation for death or injury). It confirmed the principle of equality, and of a fair and impartial trial, and of no punishment being inflicted without due process of law. According to Berkes, this code, despite the modernity of its concept, maintained the character of medieval law books, in being 'a collection of percepts rather than a precise digest of acts, punishments and procedures' (Berkes 1964:163). The code of 1851 was similar. In 1858, after the second reform edict, an entirely new penal code was enacted, which was an adaptation of the French code of 1810. Although this was much more modern in form and content, its first article stated that it did not abrogate the penal provisions of the *shari'a*, and that its provisions were merely a formalization of *ta'zir* and of the rights of the ruler. The code, therefore, retained articles to the effect of maintaining *qisas* and *diya* provisions. This dual nature of the code created many confusions and rival claims. The new code was applied in the secular *nizamiya* or *adliye* courts, instituted by the Tanzimat, but its inclusion of *shari'a* provisions made it possible for litigants to take their cases to *shari'a* courts. These anomalies were only removed with the partial unification of the court system under the Divan-i Ahkam-i Adliye, which, in 1868, became the highest court of the new *nizami* system under the jurisdiction of the Ministry of Justice and outside the control of the *shaykhulislam* (Berkes 1964:165). Among the innovations that came with the *nizami* courts was the office of prosecutor general, 'whose function was such a novelty that it caused much confusion and many amusing court-room scenes' (Berkes 1964:166). As we have seen, the *shari'a* conceived of litigation as a claim by one private party against another. A prosecutor general assumes a public function, on behalf of the state, with the implicit concept of the 'public interest'. As such, the creation of this post constitutes an important step in the etatization of the law.

The main engineer of these developments was Ahmed Cevdet Pasha, who played a crucial role in legal reforms, and in finding justification for them from Islamic precedent and principle. Cevdet Pasha (Jawdat Pasha) (1822–95) was a member of the *ulama*, who formally renounced his status as an *'alim* in 1866 to become a secular minister (Berkes 1964/1998:165; Davison 1973:251). He was a protege of Resid Pasha, the main initiator of the Tanzimat, and as part of his modern outlook, he was one of the few *ulama* to learn French. He was to become the main figure in the committee which drafted the Mecelle (Majalla), the statute which codified part of the 'civil' provisions of the *shari'a* in its Hanafi form. As such Cevdet was a Tanzimat statesman eminently suited to legitimize the etatization of law with an Islamic reference. He searched out a medieval authority – Jalal al-Din Dawwani's *Diwan-i Daf'i Mazalim* (the title suggesting a reference to *mazalim* courts) – arguing the compatibility of secular courts with Islam, and indeed their necessity (Berkes 1964:165).

Civil law was a crucial area for the reformers, especially on the economic front and with the increased commercial contact with Europe. One option, advocated by Ali Pasha, the then prime minister in 1867, was the adoption of the French civil code (the so-called *Code Napoleon*) of 1804 (Davison 1973:252), at least in the mixed courts, where French commercial law was already in operation. The code had already been translated into Arabic in Egypt and partly applied there, and Ali had it translated into Turkish. This proposal was ulti-mately debated in the council of ministers, opposed by Cevdet and others, and defeated. It was judged that the adoption of European codes in such a sensitive area, in which the *shari'a* had strong claims, was to invite potent opposition. Cevdet argued for the necessity of civil courts judging according to a clear law, which had the confidence of foreigners (with ever-wider presence on the commercial scene) and Ottoman non-Muslims. These were reluctant to face *shari'a* courts, which devalued their testimony against Muslim litigants:

> Thus, certain persons took up the idea of translating French [civil] codes into Turkish for judgement in the *nizami* courts. This idea was not acceptable because changing the basic laws of a nation would entail its destruction. The *ulama* believed that those who had gone astray to hold such Frankish ideas were unbelievers. The Franks, on the other hand, used to say 'bring forth your code; let us see it and make it known to our subjects.' [Quoted from Cevdet Pasha, *Tezakir* (*Memoirs*), in Berkes 1964:167]

Clear codes, but based on the *shari'a*, would seemed to fit the bill in coping with this dilemma. The codes, to be applied in the *nizami* courts, would be *shari'a* to the Muslims and *qanun* to the non-Muslims, whose testimony would be equally valued in these courts.

A commission of Muslim jurists, presided over by Cevdet, was created in 1868 to undertake the task of codification. The commission sat until 1876, during which time it was affected by the vagaries of Ottoman politics, and its president moved about to various other jobs. By 1876, the commission had produced 16 books of the law of transactions, known as *Mecelle-i Ahkam-i Adliye* (Davison 1973:253). The work of the commission was ended in that year, at the accession of Sultan Abdul-Hamid, who was swayed by the conservative opposition to its work, as we shall see presently. The whole sensitive area of personal status was left out, and remained the province of traditional *shari'a* courts until Ataturk's reforms in the following century.

The rationale of the *Mecelle* was that it would present Hanafi law in a clear and systematic order. It would render reference to the older books of *fiqh*, with their arguments and disputations, unnecessary. The judge would instead rule in accordance of with clear legal statutes. Part of the *Mecelle* was also concerned with civil procedure. Commentators and critics remarked on the coincidence between some of its provisions and the French civil code. Davison (1973:254) cites the view that the coincidence is fortuitous, or 'the result of some far older influence of Roman on Islamic law'. This is an interesting point, which, as we shall see, features in the modern debate on the application of the *shari'a*.

Predictably, traditional Islamic opinion disapproved of the *Mecelle* project. The *shaykhulislam* at the time, Hasan Fehmi, argued that any such project was the province of his office and not that of the Ministry of Justice. He contended that codification was tantamount to an act of *ifta'*, which was his function as mufti. The *ulama* had very good reason to oppose these acts of codification: they saw clearly that this was a takeover by the state and the sovereign of their authority as the enunciators and guardians of the law. Berkes puts the issue clearly in the following passage:

> Although by no means a legislative act of parliament, the enactment of the Mecelle was the first instance of legislation within the field of Seriat [*shari'a*] exclusively by the sovereign and his government in their temporal capacity. Although no one could find any religiously legitimate grounds for declaring the Mecelle unacceptable from the viewpoint of the Seriat, there was no precedent for it in tradition. As the matter involved a new encroachment upon the religious or traditional realm and, ultimately, the jurisdiction of the Seyhul-Islam, the latter consistently strove to reassert the right of his office to promulgate the provisions of the Seriat and to interpret the disputed issues submitted for ratification by the ruler. [Berkes 1964:171]

The overt Islamism of the Hamidian era favoured the reaction of religious authority against further etatization of law, but did not reverse progress to date. It stopped the deliberations of the Cevdet's commission on codification (though Cevdet himself was to enjoy great favour with Abdul-Hamid). The result was the continuing duality of *shari'a* and *nizamiya* courts, the latter judging in accordance with the commercial, civil and penal codes produced by the reforms, while the former was concerned with personal status and family law. Conflicts over jurisdiction could arise because cases could spill over the boundaries, and the question of *qisas* and *diya* could still be raised in accordance with the *shari'a*. This situation continued till reforms were resumed under the Young Turk regime from 1908, but even then the duality prevailed till the total secularization was effected by Ataturk.

THE SIGNIFICANCE OF CODIFICATION

Codification is an interesting enterprise in relation to the present discussion. The object was to preserve an Islamic or a national authenticity in law, but to cast it in a 'modern', that is, European form. The *Mecelle* was written in accordance with a French methodology and format, but draws its substance and its initial axioms from the *shari'a*: the 'form' is European, the 'content' Muslim. We may ask, however, to what extent does the content survive the form? The *Mecelle* resembles European codes much more than it does Muslim *fiqh*. While starting from some general maxims derived from canonical sources (such as the *hadith*: 'al-Umur bi-maqasidiha', matters are to be understood by intentions or objectives), the actual content is ordinary and profane. The difference from European rules of transaction seems arbitrary, and in many respects there is none. For instance, the principle of contractual liberty upheld in Roman law as *pacta sunt servanda*, has its parallel in the *shari'a* principle, derived from the *hadith*: Al-Muslimun 'ala shurutihim, the Muslims are bound by the conditions they stipulate (Botiveau 1993a:289). The sacred ancestry of codified elements of the *shari'a* is nowhere evident. It may be argued that the *fiqh* and historical forms of the *shari'a* also dealt with mundane and profane matters for the most part and have little intimation of the sacred, and that is largely true. However, the separation of *mu'amalat*, transactions, from *'ibadat*, ritual, intricately bound up in the historical *shari'a*, goes some way to further abstraction from the religious. Most important, however, codification in a modern legal system cuts the *shari'a* off from its traditional locus which gave it its specific character. As we have seen, in theory, the *qadi* arrived at a judgement with reference to principles and interpretations rather to generalized codes. His judgement was final and not subject to appeal. It is accepted, of course, that he may have been in error. But as long as he had honestly striven to arrive at a judgement to the best of his ability, then he was not ruled to have departed from the path of virtue.

The Islamic nature of the *shar'ia* is surely closely related to the forms of practice of the legal craft, and the location and personnel of this practice: al-Azhar and other *madrasas*, the books, the forms of argument and disputation, the institutions and procedures of judgement, the location of *qadi* courts, often in mosques, and above all the designation and qualification of the practitioner. All these institutional props and their relation to the sacred and to worship are what make the law religious. Codification as civil law practised in civil courts denudes the *shari'a* of all its institutional religious garb, it is 'dis-embedded' and de-ritualized. The content in the new form is a different and entirely profane creature. Crucially, codified law in its modern form is the law of the state, and the judge is a functionary of the state who has to arrive at a judgement from the codes and procedures determined by it, rather than by autonomous judgement through reference to sacred sources and the principles derived from them by authoritative ancestors.

Court procedures and rules of evidence were also brought into line with European models: the employment of lawyers and systematic advocacy, for instance, were unknown in *qadi* courts (Botiveau 1993a:160–65). Legal education for *shari'a* lawyers was gradually brought into line with European models. In

Egypt the Azhar was bypassed with the establishment of *shariʿa* faculties at the modern universities; such as Cairo and Damascus; then, from 1961, the Azhar itself was reformed as a modern university (Botiveau 1993a:48–74).[7] The survival of elements of *fiqh* and *shariʿa* in modern legal systems, then, was at the cost of transforming these elements into positive state law, and of its practice into modern (European-style) court and juridical systems.

These reforms, and others which were to follow, could only satisfy a secular modernist nationalism by pretence to national or Islamic authenticity as against foreign legal systems. In reality they represent a triumph of European models. That is to say, the parts of the *shariʿa* on civil transactions, once codified in European forms, shows no intrinsic or fundamental differences from its European equivalents.

CONSTITUTIONS

In the politics of reform, the call for a constitution became a crucial issue, in Iran as well as the Ottoman Empire in the closing decades of the nineteenth century and the turn of the twentieth. A constitution was promulgated in Ottoman lands in 1876, only to lay dormant under Hamidian absolutism until revived in 1908 by the Young Turks. In Iran agitation culminated in the Constitutional Revolution of 1906, after which the constitution and the parliament it inaugurated underwent a chequered career. In this section the political and ideological conflicts surrounding the idea of the constitution shall be explored, with particular attention to the Islamic dimension and the relation to the idea of the *shariʿa*.

From the outset it is important to note that the reformers of the nineteenth century were, for the most part, no democrats. Reforms were conceived as top-down affairs. Their effect in terms of the distribution of power was, initially, to empower the bureaucracy of the Porte at the expense of the (theoretical) absolute power of the sultan and the court. The early legal enactments gave the top bureaucrats immunity from the arbitrary displeasure of the sovereign and his entourage, of execution and the sequestration of property. It also gave them institutional niches, with rules and regulations which they could manipulate to their advantage. With the architects of the Tanzimat, notably Resid Pasha, then his disciples Ali and Fuad, their connections and influence with the European powers were also levers of dominance and control. The Hamidian reaction put a stop to this process by restoring the absolutism of the sultan's power, shorn by revivals of medieval theories of divine rights and the vice-regency of the caliph over worldly affairs. The bureaucracy grew and decayed during this period, but in firm subordination to the sultan.

The constitutional demand emanated from modernist critics of the reform, first in the voices of the Young Ottomans, Namik Kemal, Ziya, and Mustapha Fazil. Namik, perhaps, was the most prominent and consistent voice.[8] He denounced the reforms on the grounds that they were poor copies of European models, dictated by dominant foreigners, and alien to the people and traditions of Islam and Ottomanism. He was not, however, a traditionalist: the Young Ottomans were modern intellectuals, many coming through the Translation Bureau, well-versed in European languages: Namik was a translator of major works of European political thought. They were, however, engaged in the modern exercise, which was to become common, of finding modern ideas and institutions in Islamic origins. Namik attempted to find in these sources and in the Islamic *shari'a* the philosophical concepts of natural right. By the same token, notions of liberty, right, consultation and representation, the contract of government and the consent of the governed, were found in these original sources. The Young Ottomans were among the earliest advocates, of the now-familiar translation of *shura* (consultation) and *bay'a* (oath of allegiance) into modern political concepts of participation, representation and consent. These were the founding concepts behind Namik's project for a constitution and a parliament.

The most effective advocate of the constitution was Midhat Pasha, an energetic and effective reformer who assumed many influential posts in provincial government, and was the ultimate architect of the 1876 constitution. Midhat was in touch with Namik and the Young Ottomans, and they shared the objective of founding a constitution, involving a legislative parliament and a cabinet government responsible to this parliament, all constituting legal conditions for the power of the sovereign. Namik, in fact, drafted a text for such a document in 1875. Midhat utilized a conjuncture of events and intrigues to bring up the issue of the constitution. On the international stage, Russia was once again manoeuvring to gain territorial and political advantage in Ottoman lands, and one of its arguments in international forums was the old one of the rights of Christian subjects. Midhat, with encouragement from the British ambassador, was pushing for a constitution as a step to undermine Russian claims by showing the advance of the Ottoman state in liberalizing its laws, establishing the equality and rights of all citizens and the rule of law, in contrast to the absolutist Russian state. This was, of course, a naive argument, ignoring the real political motives of the great powers, including Britain (Berkes 1964:224–26). On the domestic front, Midhat was involved in the successful intrigues to depose Abdul-Aziz in favour of Murad, believed to be favourable to the constitution. Murad prevaricated, was judged mentally disturbed and was deposed in favour of Abdul-Hamid, who was waiting in the wings. All this in the year of 1876, which Davison termed 'the year of the three sultans' (Davison

1973:311–57). Meetings to discuss the constitution started under Murad. Ministers and men of state were convened, including the *sadrazam* (prime minister), the *shaykhulislam* and the *qadiaskar*, as well as various ministers. These included Cevdet, who sided with the *sadrazam* and the *shaykhulislam* in opposition to a constitution – a position that was in line with the dominant ideology of Tanzimat reformers, who were no democrats: they believed in reforms from above and under absolutist rule. The *sadrazam* argued that the affairs of the empire could not be entrusted to ignorant and illiterate Turks. The *shaykhulislam* objected to the representation of non-Muslims in a legislative assembly making laws for Muslims without regard for the *shari'a*. One *'alim*, however, the Qadiaskar Seyfeddin, consistently supported the constitution, citing verses from the Quran and prophetic *hadith* in favour (Berkes 1964:228).

Abdul-Hamid declared himself favourable to a constitution, and encouraged Midhat to proceed with his project. The project then went through various committees and councils, with many hostile members, which eventually whittled down the constitutional provisions limiting the power of the sovereign, while enhancing the elements of religious and caliphal grounds for the powers of the sultan. In effect, Abdul-Hamid did not oppose a constitution, but he welcomed one fashioned according to his own design, not to limit but to enhance his powers (Berkes 1964:228–41). While these committees sat, many of the *ulama* instigated campaigns and protests against the purportedly anti-Islamic thrust of the constitution, which would depart from the *shari'a* and empower infidels over Muslims. Medieval political theories were resurrected and paraded, emphasizing the bases of the Islamic state in the religious sources, the absolute power of *amir al-mu'minin*, the commander of the faithful, that is the ruler, and the respect for status and rank, all incompatible with democracy (Berkes 1964:236–41). In the final committee drafting the constitution, presided over by Midhat, many compromises had to be made by the constitutionalists, who were anxious to reach a conclusion at any cost. It would appear that the draft finally submitted to the sultan was based on a combination of European autocratic charters, including the French Constitutional Charter of 1814, the Belgian of 1831, and that of the German Reich of 1871, all of which granted extensive rights and powers to the king. Even this draft, however, was rejected by the ministers and the *sadrazam*, who objected to the specification of the power of the sovereign, who did not need to be empowered by a constitution, since his powers were unconditional. They also insisted that the appointment of ministers was to be made by the sultan, and that they should be responsible only to him and not to an assembly. Clauses to the effect that Islam was the religion of the state, and that the *shari'a* was the basis of the state, were also inserted. The final insult was the addition of an article giving the sultan the power to banish from the country, without trial, any person of whom he had doubts. This last clause proved to be a sticking point with the constitutionalists, but Midhat, now appointed *sadrazam* himself, was pressured into accepting a compromise by making the banishment of suspected subversives subject to police reports. The constitution, which was signed by Abdul-Hamid on 23 December 1876, gave the sultan and his government absolute powers and created a national assembly with few powers, always subject to the ruler's will and which could be dismissed at any time (and soon was). The episode served to emphasize and formalize the Islamic nature of the state, and its base in the *shari'a*, and the character of the sultan as the caliph with all the sanctity of religious rule. This step endorsed and encouraged the Islamic nationalism, coinciding with a centralized state, which were to be the hallmark of Hamidian rule (Berkes 1964:226–50).

The Russian declaration of war in 1876, with the neutrality of the other powers, followed by defeat and a highly unfavourable settlement, all seemed to expose the errors of Midhat's policy, and gave the sultan the pretext to arrest him. Midhat was tried, banished and ultimately killed in 1884 in exile in Taif (Arabia). The other constitutionalists, including Namik Kemal, suffered similar persecution and banishment. A parliament was convened, comprising Christians, Jews, Turks and Arabs, elected on the basis of the population composition of constituencies; the lines of alignment were not religious or racial. However, this parliament was dissolved by Abdul-Hamid in accordance with his constitutional powers in February 1878, on the grounds of compelling crises. It was never recalled, and Abdul-Hamid ruled as an absolute sultan-caliph until the Young Turks' constitutional *coup d'état* in 1908.

Abdul-Hamid and the Nationalization of Islam

The modern instrumentalization of religion as nation-state ideology and its use as a weapon against internal and external opponents had their systematic beginnings in the reign of Sultan Abdul-Hamid. Selim Deringil's book on this period includes a chapter entitled 'The Ottomanization of the Seriat [*shari'a*]' (Deringil 1998:44–67), which sums up the Hamidian project. Hamid continued with the Tanzimat project of centralizing and reinforcing state controls. He also reinforced the trappings of the nation-state as a model of the empire. He did this within the framework of Islamic legitimation, in which he assumed the pivotal position of the sultan-caliph (but also retained the ancient titles of Persian kingdom, the Padishah, and of Turko-Mongol chieftancy as Abdul-Hamid Khan). He surrounded himself with religious scholars and mystics who propagated the medieval models of the Islamic caliphate as God's vicar on earth, commanding the loyalty and obedience of all subjects. This was the principal instrument against all claims of democracy and representation.

This project of religiously sanctioned absolute rule was facilitated by the catastrophes which beset the empire over the preceding and the current decades, in which it lost most of its European and Christian provinces to the nationalisms of Christian nations aided by Russia, Austria and other European powers. The remaining population was predominantly Muslim, with Turks, Arabs and Kurds, all susceptible to the concept of an Islamic nation under the righteous Muslim rule of the caliph. Islamic nationalism was reinforced with the perception of a Christian alliance against Islam and the presence in many areas of resettled Muslim refugees, displaced from the many areas in the Balkans, the Caucasus and the Crimea lost to the empire.

Abdul-Hamid's Islamic call went further in addressing the Muslim peoples outside the empire – those under British and Russian rule. His claim to the caliphate included all Muslims in his spiritual domain. Hamidian propaganda imitated the Christian concern for their co-religionists under Muslim rule by speaking for Muslims under Christian rule (Deringil 1998:132–34). Many Indian Muslims responded favourably to this propaganda, and considered the caliphate as a symbol of religious identity against British domination.

In the context of the etatization and nationalization of Islam, religious conformity became an essential component of loyalty to the ruler and the state, and religious dissent came to be seen as subversion. The Shi'a and the Yezidis of Iraq and the Alevis of Anatolia were, thus, considered a potential source of dissidence. Various strategies were formulated for dealing with them. Education and conversion to the true faith was the main strategy. To that end, special imams and missionaries were trained and sent to these peoples to guide them to the true path of Sunni Islam. Modern schools were established in their areas for the same purpose. Conscription and military service were also considered to be means by which the young men of these dissidents could be socialized in the ranks of the faithful. Some, such as the Yezidis were naturally resistant to these measures, especially to conscription, and military expeditions were (unsuccessfully) sent to punish them (Deringil 1998:68–92).

In relation to law and the *shari'a*, Hamid halted, as we have seen, the process of codifying the *shari'a*, but did not reverse the reforms already effected. Indeed, he saw the expansion of the *nizamiya* court system to remote provinces such as Yemen as a means of reinforcing state centralization and control. Another important step in ensuring conformity was the enforcement of the Hanafi *madhhab* in all the courts, departing from the Ottoman tradition of recognizing Sunni courts of other orthodox schools following the allegiance of local populations. This policy encountered particular difficulties in Hijaz and Yemen, where the local elites and people objected to the substitution of state *nizamiya* courts for their own *shari'a* courts, ruling in accordance with their doctrines (Deringil 1998:50–63). Abdul-Hamid's constant worry on this front was the idea of the Arab caliphate, developing in Egypt and the Hijaz and encouraged by some British personalities (Berkes 1964:268–70). This constituted an alternative pan-Islamism, one based on Arab separation and historical legitimacy of the Qurayshi caliphate, and as such a considerable threat to the unity of the empire he was trying to foster. Abdul-Hamid's jealousy of any alternative source of religious authority or legitimacy, such as alternative schools of law or sectarian Muslims may have constituted, can be understood within this political framework.

The religious personnel and institutions fostered and enlarged by Abdul-Hamid's patronage tended to be those inclined to mysticism and piety as well as ideologues of past Islamic glories presided over by great caliphs, including the medieval theories of the absolute authority of the Muslim ruler. Sufi *turuq* flourished, and many Arab and African orders (such as the Tijaniya) established successful lodges in the capital (Berkes 1964:259). The sultan's closest religious associate was Abul-Huda al-Sayyadi, an Arab mystic shaykh from Aleppo, 'whose alleged supernatural powers gave him a position in the imperial court which was sometimes likened to that of his contemporary Rasputin' (Berkes 1964:258). In these religious directions, the *shari'a* had honorific status, frequently invoked but with little development or enhancement. A pertinent consideration in this respect was the Wahhabi challenge in Arabia, which was literalist, legalist and strongly anti-mystical, which posed a military as well as a doctrinal challenge to the caliphate.

The regime also generalized and expanded the network of state schools, establishing an education system with a national and correct Islamic syllabus, supervised by a Ministry of Education, but with the aid of the *shaykhulislam*. These were considered instruments of state control and ideological purity, especially in areas of dissidence and religious heterodoxy.

We see, then, that the Hamidian regime expanded and reinforced many elements of the Tanzimat project of centralization and state control, under a government approximating ever more to a modern nation-state model, with its education, legal and military systems. Its Islamic adherence and enforcement were integrated into this project as instruments of legitimacy and control.

THE SECULARIZATION OF CULTURE

Side by side with the state enforced Islamic conformity and control, the socio-economic and cultural processes of modernization, including secularization, proceeded apace. As Berkes points out, 'while Abdul-Hamid's reign was boasting of the superiority of the Arab civilization over that of Europe, the economy of Turkey was settling more firmly into the hands of European bankers' (Berkes

1964:271). In a decree of 1882, Ottoman finances were put under European control by the establishment of the administration of the Ottoman public debt. Subsequent investments ranged widely over the infrastructure of transport and communications, notably with extensions of the railways, utilities, agriculture and trade. In particular, the project of the Berlin–Baghdad railway opened up the interior hinterland of Anatolia, previously insulated from reforms, and integrated it into this emerging network of markets, leading to wider rural–urban migrations.

The expansion of government service, employment in the expanding private sectors of commerce, transport and communication, the growth of educational institutions and the professions – all these developments led to a large expansion in the numbers and significance of the modern educated middle classes, as well as the beginnings of a modern working class. These literate strata constituted a market for print products: newspapers, magazines, novels and plays (many translated from the French, with a special fascination for Jules Verne and other science fiction: Berkes 1964:278), and books on science and discovery. Government censorship and control precluded political news and analyses, or discourses on European government, parliaments or revolutions. But newspapers and magazines filled their pages with news of scientific discoveries, biographies of prominent men, travel, practical tips on health and domestic organization, and so on (Berkes 1964:277). Many people read, and the illiterate listened to others reading aloud. The effect of these interests on the secularization of culture was in the way they presented an alternative universe to that of traditional limited horizons and ranges of interest. These were sources of knowledge and models of living quite outside the world of religion, custom and authority. It also had a profound political effect: Juan Cole points out (in relation to contemporary Egypt) that the accessibility of news of government and politics and evaluations of events and actions in the press engender a frame of mind of a participant in events, with opinions and interests, as against a passive subject to the decisions and policies of rulers and *ulama*, the traditional *ahlu al-hall wal-aqd*, those who bind and loosen (Cole 1993:115–26).

The emergent literate classes of bureaucrats, officers, teachers and professionals, constituted a 'public', nourished by print, and espousing political and social ideas outside the framework enforced by Hamidian censorship and religious conformity (Mardin 1989:136–38). They nurtured the ideologies and ideals of liberty and constitution, and were the milieu of support for the revolutionary movements to follow, the Young Turk *coup d'état* and subsequently the Republic.

To sum up the processes of nineteenth-century reforms, their overall direction was the creation of a centralized modern state, in which the institutions and practices of law were formalized and integrated within state bureaucracy, thus withdrawing them from the control of the scholars and their locations. This state presented itself increasingly as a nation-state, with the fiction of common citizenship and equality before the law, but the moves towards a constitution which would actualize these claims were consistently resisted. The Hamidian period did not reverse these trends, but continued and reinforced them, while injecting the language and controls of Islamic legitimacy, and superimposing a religious dimension on the nation-state model, in the direction of a new Islamic nationalism. The socio-economic and cultural processes of modernity, however, continued the underlying trends of secularization of state and society.

THE INTELLECTUAL FRAMEWORKS OF LEGAL REFORM

The Tanzimat, as well as the Egyptian reforms, were ad hoc, pragmatic affairs, enacted in response to political pressures and legitimized by whatever came to hand, but often with a good measure of religious rhetoric and glorification of the *shari'a*. The traditional resistance to the reforms was in predictable terms. What was interesting was the modernist opposition, typically from the Young Ottomans, couched in the romantic language of authenticity and celebrating the emancipatory justice they found in a construction of early Islam. Their discourses, however, did not constitute contributions to a systematic juristic or theological theory, but attempts to find Islamic formulations for natural law doctrines derived from European thought.

It was a later generation of Islamic reformers, in the latter part of the nineteenth century and into the twentieth, who undertook the task of providing a theoretical framework for the reforms. The names of Afghani (1839–97) and Abduh (1849–1905) were closely associated with this theorizing. Afghani was, by all accounts, an inspiring and charismatic figure who influenced modern intellectuals in Egypt, Iran and Turkey, but was also an opportunist in politics and eclectic and polemical in philosophy. It was Abduh, his erstwhile disciple, who engaged in systematic theorizing on religion, law and philosophy. He assumed positions of authority and influence, including that, in his last years, of Mufti of Egypt, and was thus in a position to implement some of his ideas, though he encountered determined resistance from many *ulama* and politicians.

Like the other reformers and modernists, including the Young Ottomans, Abduh was primarily exercised by what he saw as the weakness and decadence of Islam in relation to Europe, and the problem of how to revive the Islamic nations and set them on the path to progress. Science, reason and education, as well as social and political reform, were to be the tools of a renaissance. These, however, were not merely in imitation of European models, but to be brought about by reviving the principles and models of original Islam, discarding the foreign accretions and corruption that had befallen religion and society (Hourani 1983:130–60). In this respect, Abduh was influenced by a strand of contemporary French thought, that of Auguste Comte. Comte developed sociology as the positive science of the social order and a rational source of morality, to replace religion, which constituted the source of knowledge and morality of a previous age. Abduh favoured the idea of a rational source of order, knowledge and morality, but argued that Islam, properly understood, and unlike Christianity, provided precisely such a source. Interestingly, soon after Abduh, Zia Gokalp was to find inspiration in a similar but later strand in French thought, that of Emile Durkheim, to construct his ideas of the Turkish nation and the place of Islam within it (Davison 1995; Mardin 1989:144–45).

We are here particularly concerned with the thrust of Abduh's ideas in relation to law and *shari'a*. By Abduh's time, legal reforms, in Egypt and in Ottoman lands, had introduced law codes, partly adopted from European laws, partly a codification of the *shari'a*. Modern courts and procedures, the *nizamiya* (in Egypt *ahliya*, civil) were instituted, and operated side by side with *shari'a* courts. Abduh was not opposed to the codification and unification of law as state law, but considered it desirable. He deplored, however, this duality of spheres, between the religious and the secular, with the latter ever expanding at the expense of the former. Such a bifurcated society, increasingly divorced from its roots, could not be a happy or harmonious one (Hourani 1983:136). Abduh embarked, instead, upon the creation of a unified and modern system of Islamic law.

The steps Abduh followed in this enterprise, were to become paradigmatic for reformers to the present time. In effect, it involved a rejection of the major part of the historical *fiqh* tradition. *Taqlid*, blind imitation and following of the consensus of predecessors and authorities led to a rigid and backward attitude to a law frozen in time, and irrelevant to the functions and needs of modern life. *Ijtihad* was the only way out: Islam does not prohibit but enjoins the resort to reason. In this respect, Abduh rejects the Ash'arite theology, so dominant in Islamic thought over the centuries, in favour of a Mu'tazilite rationalism (Hallaq 1997:212–14). Ash'arites, as we have seen, maintained that human reason could not fathom the divine will, and that God's commands were the only guide to correct conduct, and therefore to law. Rational argument as to the intentions and objectives of law in terms of a God's concern for justice and human happiness, advocated by Mu'tazilites and various philosophers, were generally regarded heretical by the orthodox. Abduh's rejection of *taqlid* went together with his emphasis on reason in the derivation of law. But how was reason to be articulated to revelation? How is the holy text to be approached in the formulation of what is licit and illicit?

The Quran and the *hadith* (to be sifted carefully for Abduh, and only well-attested elements admitted) contained elements which were clear and binding, and others that were in the nature of general principles, apart from elements that were ambiguous or contradictory. Reason entered Abduh's deliberations, first to attest the basics of religion, the existence of God, his attributes and the prophecy of Muhammad (Hourani 1983:145–50). Abduh felt there were elements of revelation which were not open to human reason, and must be accepted and followed. The divine essence, for instance, was such an imponderable. In terms of rules, it was, for Abduh, principally the rules of ritual and worship, the *'ibadat*, which were excluded from reason: God dictated to men what was acceptable and pleasing to him and what was not. On the rules which regulate the relations between men and the principles of social organization, what in the *shari'a* tradition is known as *mu'amalat*, Abduh declared that the revealed text mostly enunciated general principles, open to elaboration and deduction in terms of reason, and in relation to their own circumstances and needs (Hourani 1983:148; Hallaq 1997:211–12). It was, therefore, incumbent upon every generation of Muslims to embark on *ijtihad*, to interpret rationally God's commands in the light of general welfare, and then to live in accordance with them. This would lead to a happy, prosperous and solidaristic society. In this formulation, past consensus and imitation of the historical traditions of the *fiqh* schools is abandoned or radically limited. Indeed, Abduh and his disciples relegated the principle of *ijma'* in favour of ongoing *ijtihad*.

How, then, is reason to be exercised? What are the concepts and methodologies of deduction to be? Hallaq divides the reformers into two broad categories: the utilitarians and the literalists. The first advocated the concept of *maslaha*, as public interest, derived from some of the medieval jurists, as we have seen, but employed with much greater licence in the modern context. The second were the true rationalists, discarding all historical methodologies in favour of a fresh approach to revelation and prophecy. Hallaq attributes the roots of both these trends to Abduh (Hallaq 1997:214). The utilitarian strand was developed by Abduh's principal disciple, Rashid Rida (d. 1935). Rida followed his teacher in attacking the scholasticism and complexity of traditional legal theory, presenting the believer with bewildering and baffling obstacles to following the divine law. He proposed to simplify matters in only drawing upon the revealed text, prophetic tradition, insofar as this could be reliably corroborated, and the consensus of the first generation of Muslims, that is, the Prophet and his companions. All other sources were open to question. The sacred sources were clear on *'ibadat*, but postulated general principles on matters of human relations, and certainly on political organization. Rida, however, did draw upon particular medieval authorities who resorted to the principles of *maslaha*, notably Shatibi (see above). These were the theorists of *maslaha* and of *maqasid al-shari'a*, the intentions of the *shari'a*, leading to the public interest, justice and human needs. Necessity, *darura*, was another concept that came into play, and became almost synonymous with *maslaha*. A crucial question is how to resolve the issue when the canonical source contradicts conclusions on the bases of these principles of utility. It seems that Rida and those who followed him have glossed over these questions, ultimately pleading a reasoning in terms of the general tenor of the *shari'a* overriding particular texts and commands. Hallaq argues that this line of argument amounts to a general licence and arbitrariness of legal theory. The careful hermeneutics of the *fiqh* tradition are discarded in favour of the (marginal) concept of *maslaha*, but without the careful textual evidence which the early authors of this concept required. In short, all the rigours of legal theory are abandoned, resulting in a pragmatic subjectivism. Human needs become the paramount principle for creating new rules. Hallaq quotes Kerr approvingly: '…this equation of interest and necessity, put forth in such a manner as to make formal deductions from the revealed sources only a secondary confirmation of what the law should be, amounts to an affirmation of natural law' (Kerr 1966:201–2). Hallaq traces the development of this strand of religio-legal thought into recent contributions by Hasan al-Turabi, considered a leading thinker of modern Islamism. He finds similar fault with all of them, namely the failure to enunciate a legal methodology that can govern the formulation of rules in relation to the sources on the one hand, and the concepts of interest and necessity on the other. He concludes that the theories espoused by religious utilitarians 'amounts to nothing short of subjectivism' (Hallaq 1997:231).

Religious liberalism for Hallaq consists in the arguments of the relativity of religious knowledge to time and place (Hallaq 1997:231–53). One of his main examples of liberalism is the Egyptian judge Muhammad Sa'id Ashmawi, who distinguishes between religion as a pure idea and religious thought as an elaboration of that idea. The Quran and the *sunna* of the Prophet embody that idea, but all exegesis, commentary and deduction are human understanding determined by the social context of the production of that knowledge. Yet Ashmawi seems to extend this relativism to revelation itself. Like most modernists, he rejects the medieval doctrine of the eternity of the Quran, that is, that the book is eternal in God's knowledge, then revealed to humans through the Prophet. He argues that the verses of the Quran have to be understood in the context of their revelation, in relation to contemporary social conditions and events; only then can we understand their real meaning and implications for our own time and conditions. The *shari'a*, then, is not a set of fixed rules, but a *Weltanschauung*, a world view from which men have to deduce rules in relation to their conditions and understanding. Here again we have a permissive charter, with little in the way of a systematic methodology.[9] We shall return to Ashmawi and other liberal theorists in the next chapter.

Some reflections on the ideology of reform: Abduh and his disciples aimed for a radical reform of the law. Abduh was content with the passing of legal authority to the modern state and away from its traditional centres in religious establishments. The modern *'alim* and *mujtahid*, however, were to be incorporated into the process of law-making. Law could not be made piecemeal from diverse sources: a nation could only be rightly governed by its own laws and traditions, and that was where the *mujtahid* was needed. We have here the quest for authenticity which has persisted till the present day: a nation, to be happy and prosperous, must develop its own roots, and the law is an intimate part of its organic unity. Implicit in these ideas is the Comtean model of a historically constituted and evolved society governed in accordance with scientific knowledge and rational norms by an executive of scientists and philosophers. This model was to be developed explicitly by Rida in his plan for the caliphate. After Ataturk's abolition of the Ottoman caliphate in 1924, there was a search for a new caliphate in many Islamic quarters. Rida came up with the idea of a pope-like caliph: a supreme *mujtahid* presiding over the diverse nations, each with its own government and political authority, but all deferring to the spiritual and moral authority of the caliph (Hourani 1983:239–44; Enayat 1982:69–83).

In terms of the substance of law, as we have seen, the employment of the *maslaha* and *darura* principle favoured by Abduh and Rida allowed the *mujtahid* considerable licence in innovation with respect to the historical body of law. In practice there would be few theoretical constraints of legal methodology on Abduh's *mujtahid* or Rida's caliph. Legal authority was shifted to a centre with an Islamic title, but few religious constraints. Its Islamicity, and therefore authenticity, was guaranteed by the personnel in authority and the language of the law. The content of the law, however, could be dictated by considerations of public interest and the common good, as defined, presumably, by the reformer.

This model was, of course, utopian, and no element of it was ever realized. The legal concepts, however, were widely used in the legislative vocabulary of the modern states which succeeded the Ottoman Empire. Many of these states continued in the adaptation of European codes, but with occasional attempts at incorporating elements of the *shari'a*. Such adaptations of the *shari'a* were dominant in the field of personal status and family law practically everywhere, but always with modifications to accommodate modern sensibilities and social attitudes. Let us turn to a consideration of these directions in actual legislation.

SHARI'A REFORMS IN FAMILY LAW

In the modern state legal systems which succeeded the Ottoman Empire personal status and family law remained for the most part within the sphere of the *shari'a*. Initially, with the establishment of civil state courts in many countries, special *shari'a* courts co-existed with these to deal with family matters. In Egypt, for instance, these specialist *shari'a* courts continued until their abolition in 1955, when personal status matters were transferred to the jurisdiction of normal courts, but ruling according to codes derived from the *shari'a*. Authorities, it seems, did not dare – or did not want – to take this area outside the aura of religion, at least not until Ataturk's daring reforms, which even so remained unique in the region. That is not to say that family law was not reformed. Many changes were introduced, the most important and radical of which was the codification of selected *shari'a* provisions into state law, taking it out of the sphere of discretion of the *qadi* and the legal school Ataturk followed. In most instances this codification privileged the most 'liberal' interpretations of *shari'a* provisions, and as such was eclectic between the different schools of law. It is important to note, however, that liberalization of this sphere, touching as it did people's most intimate relations, would be the most resisted and resented by conservative and patriarchal interests at all levels of society. People who were liberal on politics and social policy would react much more conservatively in the family sphere. It is interesting to note that in Europe, long after the law and its institutions were secularized and separated from the church, family issues such as marriage, divorce, contraception and abortion continued, and still continue, to be politicized in religious terms.

There are a number of *shari'a* rules on marriage and family matters which have posed problems for modern sensibilities and were dealt with in various ways by legislators. Polygamy, the right of the husband to unilateral renunciation, the limits on the wife's ability to initiate divorce and rules of custody, as well as the complex problems of inheritance, are all issues which the legislators grappled with in various ways. Since the early decades of the twentieth century, both the Ottoman Empire and Egypt have seen the enactment of laws on family rights, ostensibly based on the *shari'a*, but codified, and introducing elements which eased the plight of women. These were often eclectic borrowings from the different Sunni schools, and later, in the case of Iraq, from Shi'i jurisprudence, to arrive at formulae more favourable to wives and children. This enterprise was to continue throughout the twentieth century, with legislators imposing various restrictions on polygamy, right of divorce, and custody, sometimes clearly in breach of the *shari'a*. Let us look at examples of legislation on the main issues.

Since the nineteenth century, modernists and reformers have grappled with the issue of polygamy, which they have regarded as an essential element of the backwardness of society, and its abolition a mark of progress. The first prominent statement on this issue came in 1900 from the Egyptian Qasim Amin in his book *Tahrir al-Mar'a* (*The Liberation of Women*), which, as the title indicates, proposed to elevate the position of women in family and society, and in that context found polygamy abhorrent.[10] Amin appealed to the Quran for support: the verse on polygamy allows a man four wives but stipulates that he should only embark on multiple marriages if he is able to be just in the equal treatment of all his wives (Women IV:3). Since such justice is impossible, it is argued, no more than one wife should be allowed. Other reformers have added that the verse in question comes in the context of caring for orphans, and multiple marriages related specifically to widows and orphans. But, ask the conservatives, why should the Quran not be direct and clear if this was the intention? The answer given by the modernists is that in Arabia of the time, men could take many wives and concubines, and that these customs could not be abolished at one stroke, so the holy book compromised with the times, but reluctantly. This would also explain, for the reformers, the legitimacy in the Quran of concubinage with female slaves, unlimited in number (What your right hands own IV:3), as being too widespread and accepted at the time to forbid. Conservatives argued – and continue to argue – that revelations in the text are not time-bound, and that the allowance of four wives is confirmed by the *sunna* of the Prophet, his house and his companions, and the fact that the Prophet allowed polygamy in his time. So the stipulation of justice between the wives, argue the conservatives, must be interpreted as an injunction to the husband to do his best, within the limits of human weaknesses, to be just (Anderson 1976:62 n. 32).

From the early decades of the twentieth century the reformers have contrived to limit the *shari'a*-given right for a man to marry four wives. One way was to allow marriage contracts stipulating that the husband would contract no further marriages, and if he did for the first marriage to be dissolved, sometimes with financial penalties. We shall see that this kind of use of marriage contracts has been widespread throughout the region, and notably in Islamic Iran, as a way around illiberal *shari'a* conditions. There has also been, however, an imposition of limits by direct legislation. This was first attempted by an Egyptian committee set up in 1926 to recommend reforms in family law (Anderson 1976:62), which advocated that a man proposing to contract a second marriage must obtain court permission by showing that he had the means to maintain a second marriage, and the character to be just in equal treatment of his wives. This was vetoed by King Fuad in 1929, at the time concerned to establish his religious credentials against constitutionalist and liberal opponents, and to make a covert claim for the now-vacant caliphate. Such reforms were not subsequently introduced in Egypt until the controversial so-called Jihan amendments under

Sadat in 1979 (more below). Other countries in the region, however, introduced more or less drastic reforms: from the Syrian case in which the husband had to prove his financial capability for a second marriage to a court, to the Iraqi case in which he had also to demonstrate justice in equal treatment in addition to establishing a 'lawful benefit' in the polygamous marriage, such as the sterility of the first wife (Anderson 1976:63), to the Tunisian case in which polygamy was simply forbidden. All these reforms were justified with reference to the Quran and maintained within a *shariʻa* framework.

The *shariʻa* position on divorce or renunciation, with minor variations between the schools, allows the husband the right of unilateral renunciation of the marriage by verbal declaration, with the provision that the divorce becomes final with the third such declaration. He then has the obligation to maintain the divorced wife for only a brief waiting period of *ʻidda* (around three months), during which she is not allowed to remarry. The husband and his family also have the right to ultimate custody of the children, once they reach a certain age (between 3 and 9 years for boys; up to 13 years for girls, depending on the school). Only the Maliki school (mostly North Africa, and parts of black Africa) gave the wife the right to petition a court for ending the marriage on grounds of inability of husband to consummate the marriage, or his being afflicted by some debilitating or shameful illness or disability.

Divorce and renunciation pose a number of issues for the reformers. The right of the husband to renounce his marriage verbally, without any legal procedure, puts divorce outside the powers and regulations of the state and its courts. Once the renunciation is uttered in front of witnesses, all the husband has to do is to register the divorce with the appropriate authorities. This is clearly anomalous in the context of a modern legal system and of the social policies of centralized modern states. Another issue is the housing and support of the divorced wife and her possible claims on a share in the matrimonial home. The only provision in the *shariʻa* is for support for the wife during the period of *ʻidda*. After that, the husband's only obligation is for the support of any dependent children in the custody of the wife. Typically in the past, a divorced wife went to live in her father's or brother's or other kin's households. Under modern urban conditions these options are increasingly restricted, and with the scarcity and costs of urban housing, a divorced wife can be destitute. Finally, there is the question of the wife's ability herself to divorce, called *khulʻ*, literally 'removal', heavily restricted in the *shariʻa*, and in some schools almost impossible, until formalized in the Egyptian legislation of 2000 (see *infra*). It is to these issues that modern reforms have addressed themselves, with various degrees of success. In Egypt, and many other Arab countries, the man continued until recently to enjoy the right of unilateral renunciation without reference to the courts, a right to be qualified but not ended by recent legislation. In Iran, the Family Protection Law of 1967 and 1976 required the husband to petition the court for divorce and to present a case. It also provided for a degree of support for the divorced wife. These provisions were to be repealed under the Islamic Republic, ostensibly in favour of a return to traditional *fiqh* provisions, but later arrangements of legislation and an official marriage contract have restored some of the previous reformed measures and modified others, as we shall see in Chapter 6.

In practice, a financial disincentive to renunciation was the customary stipulation in many marriage contracts of arrears of the dower, which the husband would have to pay in the case of the dissolution. Other conditions favourable to the wife may have been written into the contract to override powers of the husband given in law. Stipulations allowing the wife herself to divorce under certain conditions, precluding further marriages by the husband, establishing the freedom of the wife to practise her work or profession and so on, could be written into the contract in many countries. In Jordan, middle- and upper-class wives frequently resorted to such contracts, and provisions of this kind were allowed by the Iraqi Law of 1959. Recent provisions in Islamic Iran have included a standard government-issued marriage contract containing some of these stipulations. Yet in Egypt there is currently a wide debate about the legitimacy of such contracts. Conservatives of most schools have always maintained that contracts cannot alter the basic rights and obligations given by the *shari'a*, such as the husband's rights to multiple marriages or unilateral renunciation. Only contract items which stipulated conditions compatible with *shari'a* rules were acceptable by conservative opinion (Anderson 1976:115). The Hanbali school approved such stipulations, arguing that polygamy, for instance, was allowed but not compulsory, and that a contractual stipulation precluding it did not affect the essence of a Muslim marriage (Anderson 1976:49, 115). The legal systems of many Muslim countries have, in practice, accepted this Hanbali flexibility.

Inheritance is subject to complex rules in the various law schools. A common principle is that a legacy must be distributed among beneficiaries in accordance with the legal rules, and not the will and testament of the legatee. Some legal opinion allows the legatee the disposal of no more than one-third of their estate by will, the rest to be distributed in accordance with legal rules. These divide the legacy into 'shares', normally of one-eighth or one-sixteenth, to be allocated to the various categories of kinship. For instance, a son inherits twice the shares of a daughter, and a wife is usually allocated a share of one-eighth. The Sunni schools tend to favour agnatic male relatives, such as father, brothers and even in some cases uncles and cousins, at the expense of the nuclear family, especially wives and daughters. This reflects the Arab background of tribal and kin solidarities revolving around male agnatic relations. Shi'i jurisprudence, by contrast, favours the nuclear family, including daughters, against the wider male kin. This may, in turn, reflect the historical roots of Shi'ism in urban and non-Arab milieus.

Modern reforms were primarily concerned with the establishment of rules to favour succession within the nuclear family and the exclusion or subordination of wider kinship claims. Some countries, notably Iraq, with a considerable Shi'i population, adopted, at one point, the Shi'i provisions to that end (Anderson 1976:146–62).

Finally, regarding reforms of family law, we should note that legal provisions making life easier for women and children do not necessarily reach the whole population of a country. Resort to the law and the benefits of its provisions are often restricted, as in most societies, to those in possession of adequate social powers and capacities, such as material resources, literacy and social knowledge, and connections. In practice, this largely excludes rural and poor women from the benefits of the law.

THE LEGISLATOR BETWEEN *FIQH* AND SOCIAL REFORM

The impulse behind personal status legislation since the beginning of the twentieth century has been twofold: social reform, to provide security and some liberty to women and children under modern conditions; and the subsumption of family affairs under the legislative powers and controls of the modern state and its administration (part of social governance). Politicians and legislators, however, were (and continue to be) constrained by their declared respect for the provisions of the *shari'a* and the pressures of its advocates and protectors in conservative social forces and agencies. We have seen some of the strategies employed by reformers to negotiate these difficulties. The Egyptian case is particularly instructive in this respect: the most 'advanced' of the Arab countries, chronologically and politically, yet the one in which conservative religious forces are most effective, especially in recent decades.

In Egypt, the personal status legislation of 1920 and 1929 tried its best to bring family matters under state law and administration, while declaring the conformity of this sphere to the *shari'a*. Marriage contracts and unilateral renunciation by the husband, for instance, had to be registered in order to be legally recognized. The *ma'dhun* or notary was made into a state functionary, the post subject to training and qualifications and governed by law and its sanctions. For a unilateral renunciation to take effect, for instance, the notary had to ensure that the divorced wife, if not present at the registration, was informed in writing. These steps ensured the administrative recording of divorces, and also some degree of protection for the wife, who sometimes only discovered that she was divorced when it came to transactions such as inheritance (Botiveau 1993a:197–204). Crucially, the law introduced the idea and practice of judicial divorce, allowing judges some control over the process, especially in situations where doubt could be cast on the condition or state of mind of the husband (such as drunkenness or constraint) when pronouncing the repudiation (Botiveau 1993a:198).

Judicial divorce, crucially, became open to the initiative of the married woman. Three conditions were specified for such action: the absence or disappearance of the husband, his failure to support his wife (the payment of *nafaqa*) and the serious illness of the husband. The imprisonment of the husband was added as grounds for divorce in 1929, as was the rather vague condition of 'incompatibility', which gave the judge wide discretion, but at the same time introduced the principle of *al-talaq li-l-darar*, or divorce on the grounds of causing harm (Botiveau 1993a:227). The husband continued to enjoy the privilege of unilateral renunciation.

The 1920 and 1929 laws continued to operate in Egypt till the so-called Jihan law of 1979. Jihan was the wife of the then President Sadat, and had been a leading figure in feminist programmes for the reform of personal status laws which were seen to cause great suffering to women and children. These were actually promulgated as law in 1979 by presidential decree, without reference to the National Assembly, which was not in session at the time, and under emergency procedures. The laws were referred to a commission of *ulama* for judgement regarding their consistency with the *shari'a*, and their judgement authorized the legislation. After Sadat's death, strong opposition was expressed to the law from religious and conservative quarters, on the grounds that it oppressed the husband with respect to rights given him in God's law. In 1985 a lower court referred the law in question to the Constitutional Court to adjudicate its constitutionality, and the law was judged by that court to be unconstitutional, on the grounds that it was promulgated by presidential decree and not ratified by parliament. Amid public controversy and conflicting pressures from Islamists, feminists and secularists, new legislation was passed by the assembly which incorporated most but not all of the 1979 provisions. The controversies and debates regarding the Jihan law and its repeal will be taken up in Chapter 5.

Finally, in the year 2000, after much pressure and lobbying by liberal and feminist quarters, the issue of a woman's capacity to initiate divorce was raised, and new legislation used the category of *khul'* to enable a wife herself to divorce, even against her husband's wishes. She can now do so by returning all money and gifts given by the husband and giving up all financial rights (Law No. 1, 2000). The category of *khul'*, allowing a wife herself to divorce in certain limited circumstances, while known in *fiqh*, was rarely used. Its resurrection in this law has been highly controversial and strongly opposed by many *ulama* and conservative quarters. We shall consider the debates over family matters in the *shari'a* in Egypt in the next chapter, and in Iran in Chapter 6.

Islamic advocacy and the political struggles it has entailed in the years since the 1970s have led to legal formulations designed as compromises between modern legal principles and social commitments on the one hand and deference to *shari'a* principles on the other. This struggle and its effects will be discussed in the next chapter. In the context of the present discussion it will suffice to quote article 11 of the 1980 constitution (in which Sadat inserted the provision that the *shari'a* was the source for all legislation) regarding women's rights: 'The State guarantees the compatibility of the woman's duties to her family and her activity within society. Equally, it guarantees her equality to man in the domains of political, social, cultural and economic life, without transgressing the legal statutes of the Islamic *shari'a*.' (Botiveau 1993a:222). The qualification at the end opens wide and indeterminate fields of interpretation and disputation inside and outside legal processes. In effect it leaves the area outside specific and codified legal provisions.

A NOTE ON THE SAUDI EXCEPTION

The kingdom of Saudi Arabia is the one major country in the region which has not followed the general pattern of the codification and etatization of law. Saudi courts and *qadis* rule in accordance with Hanbali *fiqh*, which is not codified as state law but formally left largely to the discretion and *ijtihad* of the *qadi*. In theory, senior *ulama*, in their capacities as *qadis*, muftis and religious functionaries, remain the guardians of the law and the sources of new *ijtihad* as required in relation to new cases and situations. Insofar as the divine law-giver allows any scope for legislation, the *ulama* remain the main legislators. However, this realm of *ulama* authority is qualified by the power of the king, as *wali-amr* (guardian), to legislate on matters of policy and administration, as well as the areas of penal law under *ta'zir*. In effect, the formal picture of law in the kingdom is that of the historical dynastic state, in which *shari'a* law is in the hands of the *ulama* and their institutions, but operating side by side with the ruler's policies and edicts on a range of matters, often at the ruler's discretion. In practice, this partnership comes under the strains of modernity and the exigencies of modern society, as well as the global interrelations of the Saudi economy and society with external institutions and forces. Before turning to these strains, let us survey the factors that make this Saudi exceptionalism possible.

The parts of Arabia which were to become the Saudi kingdom in the twentieth century were, for the most part, backwaters, with little connection to the outside world. Though nominally under Ottoman suzerainty, this was largely theoretical except for the holy shrine cities of Mecca and Madina, and by extension parts of the Hijaz. Modernity came to these parts, mostly in the second half of the twentieth century, in the form of petrolic wealth, largely a patrimony of the royal house, distributed in accordance with a political calculus of legitimacy and support. These resources resulted in the importation of a vast labour force from various countries, who were not Saudi subjects, had few rights or entitlements and were subject to dismissal and deportation at short notice. These foreign workers performed functions in the occupational structure both at the manual and the professional or technocratic levels. As such, the scope of expansion for a native working class as well as an educated middle class was restricted. It is significant, for instance, that so many of the literate young men of the kingdom followed courses of religious study at the numerous *madrasa* catering for these subjects.

Wealth also exempts the kingdom from many of the social pressures of a modern economy. For instance, strict rules remain which restrict the movements of women and their public visibility. Authoritative conservative quarters in countries such as Egypt and Iran would strongly favour similar measures, but socio-economic pressures make that unrealistic. Most households in those countries, for instance, cannot function without the income from the wife's wages. In addition, social developments from the nineteenth century have led to certain cultural expectations which can only be denied with considerable repression. These considerations, while pertinent, operate to a much lesser extent in Saudi Arabia, at least until recent times. The contraction of petrolic resources in relation to a rapidly expanding population are squeezing the distributive largesse of the kingdom, and economic pressures similar to the other countries in the region are fast mounting. These developments are exacerbating the strains emanating from the contradictions between the requirements of a modern state and society and the legal system, to which we now turn.

A fundamental feature of Saudi exceptionalism is the peculiar history of the kingdom, built upon a close alliance between a revivalist religious movement, that of the eighteenth-century reformer, Muhammad bin Abdul-Wahhab (commonly known as Wahhabism) and the ancestors of the Saudi dynasty in Najd. A central historical inspiration for bin Abdul-Wahhab and his successors has been the doctrine of Ibn Taimiya considered in Chapter 2, his notion of *siyasa shar'iya* and its implication of a partnership between *ulama* and rulers (Vogel 2000:Chapter 2, especially 70–76). The fortunes of the dynasty and the doctrines were intertwined, from their rise in the eighteenth century and expansion in Arabia, to defeat at the hands of the Ottomans and their Egyptian vassals in the early nineteenth century, to their rise in the twentieth century under Abdul-Aziz al-Saud, founder of the modern kingdom. Hanbali Islam in its Wahhabi form has been the ideological and institutional cornerstone of legitimacy and control for the absolute patrimonial powers of the Saudi dynasty to the present day. This religious legitimacy and its agents have been crucial for the defence of the dynasty against modernist political opposition of nationalism, constitutionalism and democracy, as well as against the Islamic opposition from various quarters, mainly centred on the dependence of the dynasty on US power, as well as the perceived hypocrisy and corruption of the royal house and its circles. This latter outlook overlaps with the sentiments of many influential *ulama* at the present time, and as such presents a serious challenge the power of the rulers, as we see in the support accorded to Osama bin Laden and his appeal to the very founding ideals of Wahhabism.

This dependence of the rulers on the Islamic legitimacy operated by the *ulama* gives the latter considerable leverage in preserving and defending their privileges as custodians of the law. Successive Saudi rulers have attempted measures of reform and modernization in legislation, in standardization of law and in the administration of justice, but many of these have been ad hoc measures, some qualified, reversed or made redundant by *ulama* opposition. One central element in the concern of the authorities has been the area of commercial and financial transactions (Vogel 2000:Chapter 7, 279–308). We have seen in the Ottoman case that reforms were often forced by the pressures of relations with foreigners and the exigencies of modern trade and finance: the objective was to make the law standardized, predictable and compatible with modern practices. These latter clashed with elements of *fiqh* law in the centrality of interest calculations in their operation, as well as in elements of contracts which are conditional on uncertain outcomes (especially insurance), much disapproved by traditional *fiqh* formulations as forms of gambling. In the Ottoman state and its successors, commercial codes were the first to be adapted from European models. These pressures apply equally in the Saudi case, especially with the vast expansion of modern transactions in recent decades. Commercial codes and tribunals were introduced from the earliest foundation of the kingdom initially restricted to Hijaz, the most modern and Ottomanized part, but then spread to the rest of the kingdom (Vogel 2000:302–3). These always came up against *ulama* opposition and obstruction. Overall, the kingdom has continuously featured legislation (by the king) and tribunals dealing with specialized matters of commercial, labour and traffic regulations. These came under the heading of *nizam*, order or regulation, distinguished from *shari'a*, though theoretically compatible with it. Under *ulama* pressures there were attempts in the 1980s to unify these tribunals in one system under a specialized *shari'a* bench (Vogel 2000:304–8). *Qadis*, however, refused to apply rules contravening the *shari'a*, leading to serious problems, especially when plaintiffs renounced obligations to pay bank interest. To cope with these cases, complex procedures of sanctions against these defaulters were instituted, not by the courts but by various ministries and authorities, such as blacklisting from government contracts and bank loans (Vogel 2000:306–7). This has made transactions complicated, unpredictable, and more costly for the government, in that contracts have to factor in the costs of unpredictability.

The Saudi government includes many of the features of modernity, such as specialized ministries, including a Ministry of Justice, as well as the usual bureaucracies and procedures. The administration of justice, while in the hands of *shari'a* courts operating with traditional *fiqh*, now also include many modern features, such as a hierarchy of courts dealing with matters of increasing seriousness and complexity. The higher courts include three judges rather than the traditional single judge. Some areas of litigation include lawyers in their modern functions. There are various appeal procedures and tribunals. All these are features of modern, bureaucratized legal systems. Yet, these co-exist with a traditional *fiqh* operation of the law as judges' and jurists' law, which gives the *ulama* functions and powers denied to their counterparts in neighbouring countries. The pressures towards codification mount, and are the subject of an ongoing debate between different parties of opinion in the kingdom. Contending arguments are surveyed by Vogel (2000:Chapter 8, 309–62). The outcome will no doubt be determined by the balance of powers and pressures, between the *ulama* as custodians of religious legitimacy, especially under current circumstances when the dynasty suffers from a serious deficit, and the demands of a modern economy and society.

CONCLUSION

The twentieth century witnessed the progressive etatization of the law started by the Ottoman reforms in the previous century. A few countries, such as Saudi Arabia and some of the Gulf states, maintained *shari'a* courts and procedures, with judges' and jurists' law. They had, however, to exclude vital economic functions from their jurisdiction and into special 'commercial tribunals'. Reference to the *shari'a* and codification of some of its provisions continued to play varying parts in the modern state legal systems. Some countries, such as Jordan and Iraq, retained the Ottoman Majalla well into the twentieth century, to be replaced in Iraq by a later codification of the civil provisions of the *shari'a*, as they were in Egypt. These existed side by side with adaptations from European codes, especially with respect to penal law and commercial codes, in which the provisions of the *shari'a* were deemed inadequate or at variance with modern sensibilities. Religious authorities and schools largely acquiesced in this over of law by the state for much of the twentieth century. The bifurcation of the spheres of the religious and the secular, feared by Abduh, progressed apace, with the secularization of so much of social, political and cultural life in most of the countries of the Middle East. Religious authorities reacted, for the most part, when secular or dissident elements intruded into their proper sphere, such as the Abdul-Raziq episode in Egypt in the 1920s. Abdul-Raziq (d. 1966), an *'alim* and a shaykh, published a book arguing that Islam did not provide for a system of rule and that the historical caliphate was not a properly religious institution (Hourani 1983:183–91). This coincided with King Fuad's aspiration to the then empty caliphate, with the support of some of the leading *ulama*, no doubt aspiring to another Abdul-Hamid-style Islamization. Fuad's ambitions were not realized, but the vehement campaign against Abdul-Raziq led to his resignation from religious functions, the Muslim equivalent to a 'defrocking'. A similar campaign was waged against Taha Hussain, the prominent man of letters, who published a book on pre-Islamic poetry in which he implicitly challenged some of the orthodox narrations of early Islam (Hourani 1983:327–33). Otherwise, for much of the twentieth century the religious centres raised few objections to the growing spheres of secular culture, including a thriving and popular film industry, with songs, dances and love scenes, or to secular education, the media, literature, art and politics. The Muslim Brotherhood, founded in 1928, and some religious scholars, resisted and protested against some of these manifestations, but were not followed or supported by the mainstream religious establishment. In Turkey, too, the secular republic elicited some initial opposition, ruthlessly suppressed, then settled down to enjoy the acquiescence of a religious establishment, segregated from other functions and firmly subordinated to the state. It was in the closing decades of the twentieth century that the rise of political Islamic advocacy revived the call to Islamization of state and society, the pillar of which was to be the application of the *shari'a*. We turn to these issues in the next two chapters.

5   THE *SHARI'A* IN MODERN DEBATES AND INSTITUTIONS: EGYPT

By the second half of the twentieth century, most of the countries of the Middle East and North Africa, as indeed most of the Muslim majority countries, had instituted modern legal systems, embracing a unitary state law (the major exception being Saudi Arabia, discussed in the previous chapter). These legal systems comprised varying elements of *shari'a*-derived positive law. Only the Turkish Republic rejected the *shari'a* outright and declared an entirely secular legal system. Even advocating the application of the *shari'a* became an offence in Turkish law. Most of the other countries included a reference to Islam as the official state religion in their constitutions, and some gestured towards the Islamic *shari'a*. In the case of Tunisia, such reference was minimal, and the personal status laws of that country included radical reforms of the *shari'a* traditions, to the point of outlawing polygamy outright. Other countries, as we have seen, included more or less reformed and modified elements from the *shari'a* in their personal status codes, and some also included elements of codified civil law, mainly survivals from the Ottoman Majalla, or subsequent codification, such as that of Sanhouri in Egypt.[1] The major part of positive law in most countries, including penal law, was predominantly adapted from European models.

The last decades of the twentieth century, from the 1970s onwards, saw various reactions against the reforms and against the marginalization of the *shari'a*. These came from oppositional Islamic political movements which came to prominence in the 1970s, notably the Muslim Brotherhood in Egypt (after the fluctuations in its fortunes since its foundation in 1928), but also various others in that country and elsewhere. At the same time, in some countries, notably Pakistan and Sudan, military rulers tried to buttress their legitimacy and reinforce state and social controls by declaring the application of the *shari'a* in their legal systems. Zia' ul-Haqq in Pakistan and Numeiry, then the current military regime, in Sudan insisted on applying all those elements of Muslim law that were distinctive and contrary to the reformist spirit: *hudud* penal specification of amputation and corporal penalties, the banning of alcohol and the interdiction of dealing in interest, as well the patriarchal elements of family law. The most dramatic transformation, however, came in Iran with the 1979 Revolution and the formation of the Islamic Republic, the central pillar of which was the application of the law of God as interpreted by the ruling *faqih* (the subject of the following chapter).

These issues, of the ideas, contests and institutions regarding the *shari'a* in the contemporary period will be the subject of this chapter. It will proceed in the following order: religious institutions of law and education: religious authority and the state; state responses and compromises to the Islamist call for the application of the *shari'a* in Egypt; political and ideological debates on the application of the *shari'a*. Much of the material for this chapter will be on Egypt, where the question of the *shari'a* has been so prominent in the social and political fields, and where the debates have been so well documented.

RELIGIOUS AUTHORITY, INSTITUTIONS AND THE STATE

The modern period has seen the increasing etatization of both religion and the law, while differentiating and separating the two. This process is seen at its most extreme in the Turkish Republic, where 'secularism' has meant not so much the separation of religion from the state as its incorporation in the state and subordination to political authority. Religion is bureaucratized as a department of state, the Religious Affairs Directorate, in charge of mosques and their establishments of imams, preachers and other functionaries, of schools to train this personnel (so-called *imam-hatip* schools), of religious *awqaf*, and of religious missions abroad. The traditional connection to the law is severed. It is only with the flourishing of social and political pluralism in Turkey since the 1980s and the prominence of the formations of 'civil society' that non-state religious associations and foundations have emerged from semi-clandestinity and onto the public stage.[2] The other states in the region, while not declaring a secularist constitution and many instituting Islam as state religion, still proceeded on similar paths of etatization and bureaucratization of religious institutions and authorities. The *awqaf*, their administration and personnel were from the early stages of political modernity entrusted to government ministries in most countries. Al-Azhar, the great mosque-*madrasa* and the Sunni world's most important centre of higher education, was modernized and reformed in stages from the late nineteenth century. In 1961, under Nasir, the educational component was converted into a modern university, offering curricula in the religious sciences alongside modern faculties of science, arts and technology, and under its own rectorship. The Shaykh of al-Azhar, now appointed by the president, and not, as previously, chosen by his peers, presided over the religious institution. In effect, religious personnel were largely converted into state functionaries, and official religious authority firmly subordinated to the political directorate. Only Shi'i Iran represented a partial exception to this trend, which will be discussed in the next chapter.

In politics, ever since the beginnings of the processes of modernity, including inevitable secularization, and accompanied by Western dominance, there have always been elements of Islamic opposition, both traditional/ reactionary and modern/romantic, in search of authenticity. The general tendency is for rulers to combat this opposition in the name of keeping religion out of politics, while at the same time seeking to appropriate religious symbols and rhetoric for their own legitimacy. Often, rulers from Abdul-Hamid to Sadat and many of the present chiefs, have utilized what they perceived as conservative and pliable religious forces as allies against liberal or leftist challenges. The objective was always to eliminate political opposition and incorporate religious forces, in so far as possible, into state authority. In the heyday of nationalist ascendancy, such as Nasir's rule before 1967, the official religious institutions and personnel, such as those of al-Azhar, were firmly subordinated to state policy, and issued *fatwas* as required to suit the occasion, while the oppositional Muslim Brotherhood and its offshoots were firmly suppressed. It was the subsequent rise of Islamic advocacy in the 1970s, aided by Sadat, then boosted by the Iranian Revolution, which emboldened the official religious establishment into a more confident and challenging stance, while still remaining state institutions. Increasingly, official religion was called upon to denounce radical manifestations and to buttress the rulers' legitimacy, and more concessions and powers were given to its personnel in social and cultural affairs and the official media. Conservative Islam in present-day Egypt spans government and opposition, official institutions and political parties, and is emboldened to embark upon extensive censorship of cultural products and attempts to moralize public life and space (Skovgaard-Petersen 1997:208–14; Botiveau 1993a:25–56).

RELIGION AND LAW

In the development of modern legal systems, law, even when referred to religious sources, is ultimately divorced from religious institutions and traditions. The judge in a modern court rules in accordance with codified state law, whatever its origin, and not by reference to the books of *fiqh* or the opinions and disputes between jurists of whatever school. Legal procedure and rules of evidence proceed in accordance with modern (European-derived) principles, and not in accordance with historical *shari'a* court requirements. Prosecutors and lawyers, absent from the historical courts, are features of the modern, the former asserting the public nature of prosecution, by the state and not merely private parties. Even when the law is ostensibly derived from *shari'a* sources, all these aspects pull it away from any religious institutional anchors.

The training of legal personnel, lawyers and judges, is now the function of law schools with a wide curriculum, in which Islamic jurisprudence is one subject among others. Where Islamic *madrasas* continue to train modern lawyers, they have been transformed into modern universities with law faculties, in which *fiqh* has been assimilated into positive law. At the University of al-Azhar, the Faculty of Law became, at the time of the 1961 reforms, the Faculty of Shari'a and Law (Botiveau 1993a:266). This has to be viewed against the historical background, in which training in the crafts of the law were the main *raison d'être* of these institutions. In effect, these developments undermine a considerable element of the authority of the religious institutions. They also divorce the profession of the law from piety and religious discipline. The insistence of the modernizers on the separation of *'ibadat* (ritual) from *mu'amalat* (transactions), and subjecting the two to different rationales of application removes an important implicit element in the training and qualification of the judge, that of righteousness, acquired through a regime of religious practice in sacred locations (Asad 2001:13). It also follows that lawyers and judges trained in the modern system acquire a vested interest in maintaining it. Even those who are Islamist by conviction, and advocate the progressive Islamization of the law and the full application of the *shari'a*, are reluctant to follow that path as far as the restoration of *shari'a* courts and procedures, and of jurists' law in place of state law, as that would render them redundant.

Botiveau (1993b) distinguishes a number of different positions among Arab jurists on the question of the *shari'a*. A majority of jurists favour the status quo: the maintenance of positive law, in which they are professionally trained, and its courts and institutions. They respond to the popular demand for Islamization by asserting that the present laws respect the Muslim tradition and no longer depend on borrowings from Europe. A second view favours a gradual Islamization of existing law codes, through new legislation and amendments. They want to guard against rapid transformations that would bring instability and incoherence to the system, but aim, nevertheless, at increasing the Islamic input and content of the law. This approach characterizes the programme of influential government and political circles in Egypt, and indeed can be seen in operation in that country. This is a view held more or less strongly by most of the political currents in Egypt, including elements within the ruling National Democratic Party (NDP), and the traditionally liberal neo-Wafd. For the different strands of the Islamic current, the Islamization of law takes precedence over consideration of legal continuity and coherence. The existing legal system, they argue, is based on foreign imports, alien to Islam. Any true project of Islamization will have to break up and reform existing laws and legal institutions. These are matters of ideological advocacy and political contest. Yet the legal professionals within this current are uneasy at the prospect of a return to traditional legal institutions and practices which would render them redundant. It is significant that when the Muslim Brotherhood secured control of the Lawyers Syndicate in Egypt in 1992, the elected leaders made it clear that their first objective was the defence of the profession. Islamization of the law, while desired, was not the issue for the time being, and would certainly not involve the return to traditional legal and court procedures, which, as we have seen have no place for advocacy or lawyers (Botiveau 1993a:274).

Religious authority is further undermined by the dominant trends in religious and political thinking, both Islamist and liberal. Both these trends have insisted on the separation of *shari‘a*, understood as divine legislation in the sacred sources, from *fiqh*, understood as human interpretations and formulations, bound by tradition, the accumulation of the *ijma‘* of dead generations and of blind and rigid *taqlid*. *Fiqh*, the central pillar of traditional religious authority, is thus undermined in favour of new *ijtihad*, which is to be open to philosophers, intellectuals and activists, and certainly not confined to *ulama*.

It is not surprising, then, that in Egypt, Iran, Iraq and elsewhere, there has been a considerable decline in the numbers of students pursuing the religious sciences over the course of the twentieth century. It is notable that the cadres of the Islamic political movements, whose main advocacy is the application of the *shari‘a*, are drawn primarily from students and graduates in the natural and technical sciences, with few from religious studies.

The area of religious authority retained by the religious institutions is that of *ifta’*, the issuing of *fatwas*. It is this area which has expanded in recent decades, especially in Egypt. It is also in this sphere that religious institutions and personnel have sought to expand and assert their authority over public morality, space and cultural production. At the same time, it has become the area of contested authority. The modern media of communication have facilitated the diffusion of *fatwas* and other proclamations by a variety of individuals and centres that claim competence in the field. Official centres of authority, such as the state mufti and al-Azhar bodies, are challenged by radical and oppositional Islamists, and taunted for their perceived subservience to the state. International heroes of Islamic combat, notably Osama bin Laden and his associates, issue *fatwas* and calls to *jihad*, which many consider binding. Internet *mujtahids* are free to propagate their arguments and conclusions. In this field of dispersion it is increasingly hard to establish the overriding authority of the official centres. One result in Egypt has been for the official *ulama* and al-Azhar to attempt the extension of their authority over the public sphere, and to compete with conservative and radical forces in the zealous application of Islamic norms.

Al-Azhar is the foremost institution of Sunni Islam, and its recent history is instructive. As we have seen, Nasir's reforms of 1961 placed the institution firmly under state control. The Shaykh of al-Azhar and the Grand Mufti of Egypt remained state appointments, and were increasingly subordinate to political direction (Skovgaard-Petersen 1997:182–98). One of al-Azhar's essential functions was, and remains, to provide religious legitimacy to state policies: it endorsed Abdul-Nasir's socialism, then Sadat's *infitah* ('opening up'; economic liberalization) policies in the 1970s. Crucially, *fatwas* were forthcoming in legitimizing Sadat's peace with Israel in 1977, then also in favour of Egypt's participation in the coalition against Iraq in the Gulf War of 1991 (Botiveau 1993a:267). In the confrontation with radical Islamists, al-Azhar always offered rulings and interpretations of Islam which supported authority against religious challenges. It is this continuing confrontation between the state and the militants which led the political directorate to try to incorporate Islamic orthodoxy into its own apparatus of legitimacy; in this endeavour, al-Azhar and the official *ulama* had a crucial role to play. This process empowered official Islam vis-à-vis the state and the public sphere, and opened the way for co-operation between religious bodies and government agencies in attempting to enforce orthodoxy in public life.

In line with the bureaucratization of the institution, al-Azhar has developed different centres and functions. The grand shaykh presides over the Supreme Council, which, in turn oversees the Islamic Research Academy, the Administration of Islamic Culture, the University of al-Azhar and al-Azhar's primary and secondary schools (Abdo 2000:51).

Side by side with al-Azhar is Dar al-Ifta', the office of the state mufti, formed in 1895 and expanded into a large establishment. Its function has been to respond to questions posed by private individuals, as well as public bodies and the state. Skovgaard-Petersen (1997:101–3) traces the history of this institution. From the nineteenth century, the mufti becomes a public servant appointed by the head of state, acquiring the title of Mufti al-Diyar al-Misriya, the mufti of Egyptian territories, later Mufti al-Jamhuriya, of the Republic. A whole hierarchy of muftis were then established, attached to courts and government departments, until the full codification and rationalization of the legal process made them redundant in the courts. The function of *ifta'* became increasingly one of public pronouncements. This was facilitated by printing and the press: from the early days, the *fatwas* were systematically recorded and classified, then printed in collections. The press extended the exposure of *fatwas* on social and political issues of concern, and *fatwas* became orientated to this public dissemination.

Muhammad Abduh, in the role of mufti, made extensive use of the press, including his own journals, in his campaigns for reform and education (Skovgaard-Petersen 1997:126–27). Under modern conditions of the extension of the public sphere through media and communications, *ifta'* could not be monopolized by the one centre, and was bound to become an issue of contested authorities. In the official domain, as we have seen, al-Azhar bodies also entered the field of *ifta'* and public declarations. Oppositional bodies, notably the Muslim Brotherhood and its leaders, also issued their own *fatwas*, and contested the authority of the official *ulama*, denounced as state functionaries (Skovgaard-Petersen 1997:155–57). This was more recently extended to the radical Islamic groups, such as al-Jama'a al-Islamiya, which followed the *fatwas* of its own Shaykh, Umar Abdul-Rahman, now languishing in a US jail for his part in violent projects. These groups were even more vociferous in their denunciation of the official *ulama* (Skovgaard-Petersen 1997:214–20).

These contests and denunciations were made plausible by the firm subordination of the *ulama* in the Nasir and Sadat era, and the issuing of *fatwas* to order. The later empowerment of the *ulama*, from the 1980s to the present, already noted, by the attempt of the political directorate to outdo the Islamist opposition in religious devotion and legitimacy, has led to a much more strident stance of the state mufti and the official *ulama*, first signalled in the incumbency of Jadd al-Haqq (1978–82), and continued by his more liberal successor, Tantawi. Note here that there is a duality of official authority of *ifta'*: the state mufti, with the institutions of *ifta'* under him, and the Shaykh of al-Azhar, presiding over the various bodies and committees of the institution. Those latter, in turn, do not always follow the shaykh, as we shall see.

It was under Shaykh Jad al-Haqq Ali Jad al-Haqq (d. 1996; state mufti 1978–82, then Shaykh of al-Azhar) that al-Azhar extended its authority into advocacy of Islamic orthodoxy in the public sphere and the moralization of public space. This shaykh attacked writers and intellectuals whose work he judged to be contrary to orthodoxy, and his rulings over social issues were controversially conservative, going as far as endorsing the practice of female circumcision, a view that outraged reformist opinion, which always held that this practice is 'backward' and non-Islamic (Abdo 2000:59). The present shaykh, Muhammad Sayyid Tantawi, is more liberal and as such not often in agreement with the conservative bodies of the institution, notably the Committee for Research and Publication. Since the 1980s this body, the Majma', has claimed the power of censoring all works judged to be at variance with Islamic orthodoxy or morality. It also charged some authors, such as Ala Hamid, author of *A Distance in a Man's Mind*, which makes reference to prophets, with apostasy. It has various relations, not always clear, with state-censorship authorities. In some instances, judges and censors refer published works to this committee for adjudication. In

1994, a decree from the Department of Fatwa and Legislation in the Council of State (written by Tariq Al-Bishry, a senior state councillor with Islamist affiliations) gave al-Azhar a wide authority of censorship over cultural products. It ruled that the Islamic Research Academy must protect public order and morality in general. This gave it authority beyond the bounds of religious pertinence and into the wider cultural field, with a moralizing mandate. Al-Azhar's ruling on these matters was to be binding, and could not be overturned by the Ministry of Culture (Abdo 2000:66–67). Censorship according to criteria of security remains in the hands of state censors. There have been instances of some conflict over drawing the line between the two spheres of competence.

An important aspect of this extension of religious authority and censorship is the activity of groups of Islamist lawyers bringing court cases against authors, intellectuals and artists, utilizing loopholes, ambiguities and gaps in Egyptian legislation to indict what they see as blasphemy or moral failures. The claim of *hisba*, religious accountability, in these cases is especially interesting, and will be considered below.

THE *SHARIʻA* AND POLITICAL CONTEST IN EGYPT

The *shariʻa* has always been central to Islamic political advocacy. The Muslim Brotherhood held the application of the *shariʻa* at the centre of its political programmes. The failure of the free officers' regime in 1952, then of Nasir's regime from 1954, to adopt this objective was a central plank of opposition. Subsequently, Nasir's socialism and generally secular stance alienated Islamists further. We can divide Islamic opposition at this point into two broad strands, that of the conservative mainstream of the brotherhood and the radical strand adhering to Sayyid Qutb's ideas. During Nasir's rule, which ended in 1970, the first strand found refuge and succour in Saudi Arabia, and came ever closer to conservative Wahhabism, especially in its opposition to Nasir's brand of state socialism and radical nationalism. The second was uncompromising with all existing governments, precisely because they did not rule in accordance with what God has decreed (*bima anzaluhu allah*). As such, all supposed Muslim countries and their governments were, in the radicals' view, not truly Muslim, as they ruled in accordance with man-made law, and were as such godless tyrannies, in a state of barbarism and ignorance – termed *jahiliya*, a term used for pre-Islamic idolatry which Muhammad confronted and defeated, a task to be accomplished again by a new Islamic generation, a vanguard (Qutb 1980; Zubaida 1993:51–55).

Sadat, in his attempt to displace and reverse Nasirist doctrines and its associations with socialism, the political left and the Soviet Union in the 1970s, entered into alliances with the mainstream Islamists of the brotherhood. While not licensing it as a political party, he allowed it a wide range of organization, publication and propaganda, especially in the universities which had been the centres of leftist activism and dissent. This accommodation also accorded with Sadat's new found alliances and rapprochement with Saudi Arabia and the US. Sadat's regime was subsequently involved in a number of balancing acts. He encouraged religious forces against the left, while at the same time resisting and repressing challenges from Islamic opposition; he tried to appropriate Islamic symbols and establish himself as a religious figure (*al-ra'is al-mu'min*, the believing president, was one of his appellations), while at the same time declaring his liberal and democratic credentials to his Western friends and world public opinion. These balancing acts included his legislative programme: on the one hand writing the *shari'a* into the constitution (more below), and on the other introducing significant reforms in family law, the so-called Jihan law of 1979, representing a move away from the *shari'a*. His religious posturing did not save him from assassination at the hands of Islamic Jihad, animated by Qutbic ideology and considering him an apostate and a pharaoh, confirmed by his peace treaty with Israel.

THE *SHARI'A* IN THE CONSTITUTION OF EGYPT

Two constitutional amendments were enacted, one in 1971 and the second in 1980. The first inserted a clause (Clause 2) in the constitution stating that 'Islam is the religion of the state; Arabic is the official language; and the principles (*mabadi'*) of *shari'a* are a principal source of legislation'. The second amendment in 1980 strengthened this provision by making such principles *the* principal source. Given that much of Egypt's civil and penal code were adoptions and adaptations of European positive law, a contradiction (or *izdiwajiyya*, duality, to put it in the terms of Egyptian lawyers) was created, which has become a rich source of contests and debates, and attempts at constructive syntheses. Some of these debates were conducted in parliament over legislative programmes, others came up as challenges in courts and legal tribunals, and many of the campaigns were fought in the public media.

Since the mid-1970s, Egypt has had a formally plural political field, with licensed parties fielding candidates for the People's Assembly. This 'democracy', however, is severely restricted. The licensing of parties is entrusted to particular tribunals, who have rejected applications from disapproved quarters, and have not, for instance, allowed applications from any Islamic group as such. It also took many years and political manoeuvres to get licences for leftist and Nasirist parties (granted in 1992, some think as a measure to limit Islamist influence).

These parties, in any case, are often organizational skeletons, centred around prominent personalities as leaders, and, crucially, the editor of the party newspaper. Government and security organs are vigilant in preventing parties from recruiting popular constituencies, even if they could do so. This is what gives the Islamic organizations such great advantage over rivals: while not licensed as parties, they have access to popular constituencies through mosques, religious associations and charities. The NDP is the party of the president and the government, acting as a vehicle of loyalty and patronage. It is the only party with any real power or influence, and one that always has the lion's share of parliamentary seats. Elections are normally 'managed' by the authorities, which ensure a few seats for the main opposition parties.[3] Through this system, the Muslim Brotherhood, though not licensed as a party, has managed to have deputies in practically every parliament since the 1980s, mostly through alliances with other, licensed parties, or, more recently, as independent candidates. Its voice in parliament has, predictably, been in campaigns for the application of the *shari'a*.

It is interesting to note that in this broad project the Muslim Brotherhood seems to have no opposition. A measure of the Islamization of Egyptian society has been the near unanimity on the desirability of conforming to the *shari'a*. Some gesture in this direction has been part of the programme of every party in successive elections. The NDP reiterated the constitutional formula that the *shari'a* is the principal source of legislation, and even the leftist Tagammu', generally secularist in outlook, made some ambiguous reference to 'drawing inspiration from the principles of the *shari'a*' (Abdul-Fattah 1997:36). Only the Muslim Brotherhood and its allies (especially the Socialist Labour Party in the 1990s) made the application of the *shari'a* a central plank of their advocacy (Abdul-Fattah 1997:34–44).

We may ask, if there is such general agreement, then why the contests and why is the *shari'a* not legislated forthwith? All parties, including the Muslim Brotherhood, recognize that the process of legal transformation must be gradual and measured, and especially that with many issues *ijtihad* and deliberation are necessary. However, while the brotherhood and its allies want to take immediate steps in this process, the government and the NDP stall, with procedures and committees. Clearly, a wholesale application of the *shari'a* would bring about disruptions and embarrassments. In particular, the application of penal *hudud* and the interdiction of bank transactions specifying interest payments would lead to strong opposition and disruption, not least in sensitive Western quarters. As such, the government is seen by all the Islamic groups as an obstacle to the application of the *shari'a*.

All these debates were conducted in the framework of the constitutional amendments apparently enshrining the *shari'a* as the principal source of law.

Political agitations and parliamentary debates, as well as court challenges referred to this framework, which set the agenda. In the 1970s and 1980s, after the respective amendments, a number of attempts were made at the codification of the *shari'a*, against opposition to the project of codification by traditionalists who argued for the *shari'a* in its traditional location in *fiqh* (Skovgaard-Petersen 1997:200). In 1972, the Academy of Islamic Studies completed codes based upon the four Sunni schools regarding contracts of sale and penal law (Botiveau 1993a:31, 283). This codification project was not taken up by the People's Assembly when it established its own committees to pursue the question. A parliamentary commission, headed by the then speaker Sufi abu-Talib, established specialist committees which sat in 1978–82 and prepared *shari'a*-based codes in their specialist fields of law. These, however, were only considered as working documents (Skovgaard-Petersen 1997:201). Significantly, while the *ulama* of the academy maintained the separation of the four schools, the parliamentary commission sought a unified state law. The report of this commission was approved by parliament, but the codes produced never passed into law and were not endorsed by the president (Botiveau 1993a:279–83). After the parliamentary election of 1984, in which the application of the *shari'a* constituted an important issue in the campaign, a Parliamentary Committee for Religious and Waqf Affairs was established and conducted six meetings on the question of the *shari'a*, with the participation of the prominent shaykh and Muslim Brotherhood leader Umar al-Tilimsani (since deceased), as well as the President of Parliament, Rifat Mahjoub, and the Minister of Awqaf, Muhammad Ali Mahjub. Tilimsani took a moderate and gradualist stance, while the ministers argued that the codification of the *shari'a* were merely studies and not a legislative programme. The committee finally reported to parliament in May 1985, to the effect that existing laws must be revised to contain nothing contrary to the *shari'a* (with implications for the crucial issues of interest dealings and of penal law). After a debate (in which Brotherhood deputies were not called) a government paper was accepted, which made it clear that there would be no wholesale abolition of existing laws, but that these should be studied carefully with a view to determining their conformity with the *shari'a* (Skovgaard-Petersen 1997:211–12). This was clearly a fudge, and government managers made sure that similar diversions were employed to prevent the issue being raised again. The only issues to be raised again in this respect were amendments to family law, which re-enacted some of the Jihan provisions, after they were successfully challenged in the Supreme Constitutional Court, then a further liberalization in 2000 (more below). Many Islamists saw these amendments as a departure from the *shari'a*.

As regards the constitutional imperative of applying the *shari'a*, in line with the clauses privileging it as the principal source of legislation, there were a number of attempts to test the matter in the courts. The Supreme Constitutional

Court was established in 1979. It rules on the constitutionality of laws, in cases arising or referred from lower courts, or from the Minister of Justice. It has the final word on constitutionality, and a law or practice declared unconstitutional by the court is automatically repealed. In 1985 it ruled the Jihan amendments on family law unconstitutional, not on the grounds of departure from the *shari'a* (as that would 'open a can of worms' regarding much of Egyptian law), but because of the manner of its promulgation by presidential decree under emergency provisions, thus bypassing parliament. In that same year it considered an appeal from al-Azhar against a lower court decision requiring it to pay back a loan with interest. Al-Azhar argued that the requirement to pay interest was unconstitutional in relation to the amendment specifying the *shari'a* as the principal source of legislation. The court ruled against al-Azhar, arguing that the amendments were not retroactive and did not invalidate preceding laws. They were addressed to the legislature for future enactments, and not to the courts with regard to existing law (Skovgaard-Petersen 1997: 204–5). This has been the general tenor of court rulings on the *shari'a* and existing law. Islamist lawyers and judges had to resort to elements of existing law as well as gaps in the law to pursue their cases on religious conformity in the public sphere and in cultural production.

Islamist judges and lawyers are engaged in manoeuvres to use various legal ruses within Egyptian law, as well as having a commitment to the *shari'a* in the constitution to bring cases or obtain judgements according to one or other Islamic principle. The most successful such manoeuvre was the use of the notion of *hisba* to prosecute a claim against the critical theologian Nasr Hamid Abu-Zayd for apostasy. There is no allowance for charges of apostasy in Egyptian law (though the conventional *shari'a* rule, confirmed in the draft codes by the assembly committees, specifies the death penalty for apostasy), and, therefore, no specification of what constitutes apostasy in a Muslim. However, a combination of the *shari'a*-based personal status law and the catch-all principle of *hisba* was used by Islamist lawyers to petition to divorce Abu-Zayd from his Muslim wife on the ground of his claimed apostasy – a non-Muslim man cannot marry a Muslim woman. Repeated attempts in the years 1992–96 in different courts and with appeals from both sides succeeded in obtaining a ruling from the Court of Appeal in 1994, then confirmed by the Court of Cassation in 1996, to uphold the petition and divorce the man from his wife. In effect the ruling confirmed judicially that Abu-Zayd was an apostate. While there are no criteria for determining apostasy in Egyptian law, the Court of Appeal determined that there was clear material evidence of apostasy in Abu-Zayd's writing which could not be disputed. He clearly denied the literal truth of so many elements of the holy book: he doubted the existence of angels, demons and the *jinn*, ascribing them to the realm of myth; he denied the literal truth of narratives, and argued that certain injunctions and rules were only valid for their time and place. Surely such brazen denial of revelation is clear indication to any Muslim of the impiety and apostasy of the author. By these criteria, of course, many Anglican bishops can be condemned as apostate. The court in this instance was making law where no legislation existed, on the basis of a general religious normativity and common sense.[4] This is the most prominent instance of the attempts to Islamize positive law through the normative judgements of an increasingly Islamized legal profession.

Having been legally declared an apostate, the taking of Abu-Zayd's life became licit to any sincere Muslim: he and his wife took refuge in Holland. Subsequently the executive judge (*hakim al-tanfidh*), under political pressure, ruled that the judgement to divorce Abu-Zayd and his wife could not be enforced. The Egyptian government brought in an amendment, not to abolish the catch-all ground of *hisba*, but to appropriate it: the amendment was to the effect that only public authorities, not private individuals or associations, can prosecute on those grounds.

There is one instance of a judge resorting to the penal provisions of the *shari'a*, against existing law in a controversial judgement that was subsequently quashed by higher authority. In 1982 Judge Ghurab, president of the district court of Abdin, south Cairo, tried a man accused of drunken behaviour in public and sentenced him to the *shari'a hadd* for drunkenness of 80 lashes. This is not only contrary to the existing law, but corporal punishment is not on the penal statute book for any offence (it was abolished in the nineteenth century). This brought Ghurab a reprimand from the higher judicial authorities and an administrative order relieving him of his judicial duties (Dupret 1995). While no other such cases have come to light since, many judges, as a preliminary to delivering their penal judgements according to the existing law have publicly regretted the fact that they cannot act according to the law of God, and are thus committing an impiety.

The general ambience of the Islamization of Egyptian society and politics has led to higher and more respectable tribunals, such as the one which tried the Abu-Zayd case, bringing in normative religious judgements which are then accommodated in permissive gaps in the law. Clearly, Sadat's political gamble has led to serious inroads into positive law in Egypt in favour of normative religious modifications, fitting in with the general mood of Egyptian society. This mood, as we have seen, does not go unchallenged, and there are important contests in the political and cultural fields. The *shari'a*, then, is now primarily a political issue, and its discourses that of political contest. We saw, however, that while the slogan of applying the *shari'a* elicits a public near consensus, politicians and legal professionals, fearing disruption, conflict and political fall-out, always fudge the issue when it comes to actually legislating the *shari'a*.

EPISODES OF LEGISLATION ON PERSONAL STATUS

These episodes in recent decades illustrate the terms of ideological controversies on legislation. As we have seen, the Egyptian personal status law of 1929 was an eclectic codification of *shariʿa* rules, and within these limits some degree of added protection for women and children. Liberal and feminist opinion, represented at high levels of Egyptian society and politics, became increasingly organized and vociferous in the 1970s in demanding reforms in the law to afford further protection for women in by now more complex situations of domestic society. Jihan, the president's wife, was the prominent sponsor of the legal reforms discussed above. Sadat, of course, asserted the perfect compatibility of the reforms with the *shariʿa*, and convened a meeting of al-Azhar *ulama* to endorse it. At that point in time official *ulama* were much more pliant to demands from the political leadership: as we have seen, all important decisions of Nasir and Sadat were endorsed by official *fatwas*. For that reason, official *ulama* often elicited the hostility and contempt of radical Islamists. In 1985, long after the death of Sadat, many of the official *ulama* 'jumped' on the Islamist 'bandwagon'. In the public debate on the legitimacy of the Jihan reforms, one of the *ulama* involved in endorsing the law in 1979, the then Minister of Endowments, Shaykh Abdul-Munʿim Nimr, declared that on that occasion the hands of the assembled *ulama* were forced, and that indeed several items of that law were contrary to the *shariʿa* (Botiveau 1993a:247–48). He and (according to him) other *ulama* present took special exception to the item allowing a married woman to work outside the home without the husband's permission and the item requiring divorce to be registered in court in front of witnesses, thus depriving the man of the right to verbal repudiation. The divorced wife's rights over the matrimonial home were also widely resented. In 1985, when the matter came to a head, Islamists organized demonstrations and protests to demand the full implementation of the *shariʿa*, while liberals and secularists cautioned against a return to the 'matrimonial anarchy' which preceded the law. Many religious legal professionals, however, including some *ma'thuns*, marriage registrars, were in favour of the reforms because they drastically reduced the frequency of divorce, and were conducive to more orderly conduct of the legal process. In 1985 a Fayoum judge declared himself unhappy with the application of these laws, doubting their constitutionality and for that reason referring the matter to the adjudication of the Supreme Constitutional Court. As we have noted, the objection to the law was not on the grounds of its incompatibility with the *shariʿa*, which was the contention of the Islamists, but the irregular procedure of its proclamation by the president, under emergency powers and without reference to the assembly, which had not been in session at the time. Of course, much of Egyptian legislation, including the 1929 personal status codes, were similarly promulgated by decree and without parliamentary process, but somehow this point was ignored. The Supreme Court ruled the amendments unconstitutional, as argued. Further legislation, however, was introduced in 1985, through parliament, which reintroduced some but not all of the provisions of the Jihan amendments. It still left women with many disabilities with respect to the capacity to initiate divorce, the consequences of divorce in terms of rights to custody of children and claims on the matrimonial home.

Reformist lobbies returned to the fray, and in 2000 introduced further amendment on the outstanding issues. The proposed reforms were introduced by the government for parliamentary approval, and included allowing a wife to obtain divorce without her husband's consent under the category of *khul'*. Another item was to allow a wife to travel abroad without her husband's permission, by petitioning a judge if the husband unreasonably withheld permission. After fierce debate, the first provision regarding *khul'* was passed, but the government had to concede defeat on the issue of travel.

The paradigm for divorce in the *shari'a*, as we have seen, is unilateral repudiation, *talaq*, by the husband, which is unconditional and does not require the wife's consent or even knowledge. The wife wanting to divorce her husband against his wishes has few options other than to obtain his agreement, usually by financial inducement. Under the 1929 Egyptian law, a wife can ask a judge to divorce her from her husband without the husband's agreement under specific and limited conditions, often hard to establish to the judge's satisfaction. This has resulted in considerable hardship for many women, who drag their cases through the courts over many years, often to no avail. The 2000 amendments were designed to remedy this situation by allowing a woman to obtain a divorce in the category of *khul'*. Under these provisions, a wife can obtain a divorce by returning to the husband all gifts and financial settlements given by the husband, and renouncing any further financial claims.

The amendments were widely debated, with support from liberal and feminist quarters, including the Shaykh of al-Azhar and some other religious figures, and opposed by religious conservatives. Supporters argued for the *khul'* provision in terms of its allowability in the *shari'a*, based on a *sunna* narration, according to which, the Prophet approved a woman's request for divorce on the grounds that she did not like her husband. The Prophet told her to return a garden given her as dower, then ordered the husband to divorce her (note, it is still the husband who has to take the initiative). Clearly, it was not sufficient for ministers, professors and social managers to argue in terms of the social necessities and in favour of alleviating the considerable hardships suffered by so many women and their families: the argument had to be clinched with a religious reference.

Opponents argued primarily in terms of incompatibility with the *shari'a*, dismissing the prophetic narration as an isolated case unsupported by any other argument or precedent. In the People's Assembly it was the leader of the supposedly liberal Wafd Party who was the most vociferous opponent and defender of the *shari'a* and social values. He anticipated severe strains on marriage as a result of this law: 'If a woman sees that her husband is less handsome than his friends, should she seek a divorce?' he asked. Others denounced the law as being at variance with the natural superiority of men over women, confirmed in the Quran and the *shari'a*.[5]

The liberal Shaykh of al-Azhar told the assembly that the draft law had been examined and revised and found, by a majority vote of the Islamic Research Academy, to be in conformity with the *shari'a*. This did not stop conservative *ulama* and their supporters from sending protest and petitions to the president objecting to the variance of this legislation from true religion and correct values. Family issues and their relation to the *shari'a* remain, then, contested in Egyptian society and politics. On the one side are the political elites and social managers, pointing to the exigencies and sensibilities of a modern society and economy, where the old legal provisions lead to considerable hardship and dysfunction; on the other are the social conservatives appealing to religion to arrest or reverse any measures of social liberalization. What is interesting, however, is that both sides appeal to religious sources and authorities: there seem to be no secularists.

THE CALL FOR THE *SHARI'A*: DIFFERENT STRANDS

The call for the application of the *shari'a*, as we have seen, comes from different Islamist quarters, with different ideas of the *shari'a*. Radical Islamists follow Qutbist ideas which reject the *fiqh* tradition and the historical *shari'a* (with the exception of Ibn Taimiya) in favour of a direct resort to the Quran and selected elements of the *sunna*. Their slogan: 'the Quran is our constitution'. They reject any form of democracy, which is the rule by the people through elected representatives in a legislature. Rule, they argue, is God's alone, and his law is the only law. There is no room for legislation and man-made law (Abdul-Fattah 1997:44–47).

A central element in radical Islamic thought is that of *takfir*, the charge that self-declared Muslims who do not adhere to the central tenets of Islam in their conduct and utterances are, in reality *kuffar* (plural of *kafir*), infidels. This is a charge applied in particular to the rulers, who pretend Islam but do not rule in accordance with its laws, which are what God has revealed. This is a controversial issue in Islamic discourse from medieval times. Any person who professes Islam, uttering the *shahdatayn*, the two affirmations of God's uniqueness and the prophecy of Muhammad, is considered a Muslim. This person may be a bad

Muslim and a sinner but still remain within the faith in the eyes of most orthodox authorities. For some, however, there is a limit to how bad a sinner one can be and remain a Muslim. When it comes to rulers, as we have seen, traditional Sunni political doctrines were almost infinitely tolerant of the deficiencies of rulers, and enjoined obedience to them in the interest of preserving the unity and order of the Islamic community and avoiding *fitna* or intrigue. The deeply conservative implications of this doctrine were, naturally, rejected by modern political Islamists, whether liberal or radical. For the radicals, they could find a historical root of their doctrine of *takfir* of the ruler in Ibn Taimiya.

We saw in Chapter 3 that Ibn Taimiya, while forthright in his upholding of the rule of the *shari'a* in all matters of government and society, was nevertheless mindful of the realities of power, and in practice critically supportive of the authority of his Mamluke masters. It was in his pronouncements on the Mongols, by his time formally Sunni Muslims, that he provided ammunition for the modern radicals. The Mongols were established in territories neighbouring the Mamluke domains in Syria and Anatolia. Ibn Taimiya declared that the Mongol rulers of Mardin were not real Muslims, not only because they disobeyed the religious commandments (equally true of his Mamluke rulers), but also because they did not rule in accordance with what God has revealed. His disciple Ibn Kathir (d. 1372) elaborated on this theme, referring to the Quran, he concluded that the adherence of the Mongol rulers to their *yasa* and privileging it over the *shari'a* constituted a return to *jahiliya*, barbarism and ignorance (Sivan 1985:97–98).

For the modern radicals, Ibn Taimiya's indictment of the Mongols served equally to condemn their current rulers as *kuffar* and apostates, and their societies as in a state of *jahiliya*. This served as justification for political assassinations, notably of Sadat in 1981. The assassin, Khalid al-Islambuli declared 'I have killed the Pharaoh', likening Sadat to worldly tyranny. The radicals differed between themselves as to whether the *takfir* applied to the ruler only or to the whole *jahili* society: some argued that the ordinary people were true Muslims who only needed to be awakened and directed to the righteous path.

This strand of thought has been primarily messianic and utopian, without much idea of a programme for social and political organization. It has made little, if any contribution to legal theory or reform, apart from the insistence on the application of the *shari'a*, coinciding with the Quran, to all aspects of life and rule. Progress towards the actual implementation of the *shari'a* was proposed by the mainstream and conservative Islamists, whose political campaigns in and out of parliament, as we have seen, seemed to bear fruit in the gradual Islamization of Egyptian society and aspects of the law. The mainstream of the Muslim Brotherhood is concerned with the practicalities of legislation. Politically it favours a democratic system of representation and has campaigned to be included within it as a political party. We have seen how it succeeded in getting its deputies into parliament. In parliamentary committees the deputies engaged in political negotiations, mostly with a moderate and gradualist approach to the application of the *shari'a*. Islamist lawyers and academics are part of this project and approach.

Another strand in the advocacy of the *shari'a* is a kind of cultural nationalism, a quest for authenticity, one which we noted as the romantic reaction to reform from the nineteenth century. For many Egyptians, and Muslims elsewhere, to be ruled by the *shari'a* is part of the cultural and spiritual heritage of Muslims. It is part of cultural and national authenticity, inspired by a kind of cultural nationalism: by the adoption of European codes, the argument runs, Egyptian society has been cut off from its most important and organic moorings to its Islamic essence and its history. As one Egyptian lawyer put it:

> [The *shari'a*] constitutes the spinal column of the Islamic civilizational project. If this spinal column were to be shaken, then Islamic civilization will disappear and become a transformed image of Western, Buddhist or some other civilization. No one in the world has the right to prevent a community from founding its legal, educational and cultural regime upon its heritage (*turath*) ...In our country it is colonialism which has, for a hundred years, suppressed the law founded upon the Islamic shari'a... As a community which has a history and a heritage, we have the right to be governed and educated in conformity with this heritage. [Dupret interview with Muhammad Salim al-Awwa: Dupret 2000:210]

Even liberals, seeking a legal system which upholds human rights, still hanker for some element of this authenticity. Abdullahi An-Na'im, the Sudanese lawyer, academic and human-rights activist, poses the problem as one of an impossible choice between the abandonment of the *shari'a* in public law (with respect to women and non-Muslims), or the full application of its historical forms, as advocated by many Islamists:

> I find the first option [abandonment of the *shari'a*] objectionable as a matter of principle and unlikely to be realistically available for much longer in practice. It is objectionable as a matter of principle because it violates the religious obligation of Muslims to conduct every aspect of their public as well as private lives in accordance with the percepts of Islam. Moreover, in view of the mounting Islamic resurgence [in the 1980s, book published in 1990], this option is unlikely to continue to be available for much longer in practice. I also find the second option [of full application of the historic *shari'a*] morally repugnant and politically untenable. It is morally repugnant, in my view, to subject women and non-Muslims to the indignities and humiliations of the application of shari'a today...given the concrete realities of the modern nation-state and present international order, these aspects of the public law of the shari'a are no longer politically tenable. [An-Na'im 1990:58–59]

The solution for him is the attempt to recast the religious sources and methods to arrive at a public law which enshrines modern conceptions of human rights, but within a semblance of religious derivation.

LIBERAL AND SECULARIST REACTIONS

On the liberal side, which is critical of the call for the application of the *shari'a*, there are few, if any, outright secularists. Even Faraj Fuda, who was assassinated by radical Islamists in 1992 for his supposed apostasy, argued against them in terms of Islamic history and precedent.[6] His main argument, echoed by many (see *infra*) was that Islam is primarily a religion and not a system of government and law, and that subsequent to the death of the Prophet his successors ruled pragmatically, following reasons of state. They altered and adapted legal principles in response to practical exigencies. The dynastic states of Islam were mostly oppressive tyrannies, which only drew on religious rhetoric to suit their requirements. As such, the caliphate, despite its religious pretences, was always worldly rule, and mostly tyrannical and corrupt. There are no historical or scriptural bases for Islamic government, and modern Muslims should seek a just and democratic state, which will be in harmony with the basic principles of their religion. The *shari'a*, it is argued consists largely of man-made laws which evolved historically, and that there is little in *fiqh* which is based on revelation. As previous generations of Muslims have adapted law to social needs and customs, so must contemporary Muslims. Egypt, it is argued, has developed a tradition of positive law over more than a century. To unravel this working institution in the name of some indeterminate *shari'a* would be at worst anarchic and at best an arbitrary substitution of an equally profane set of codes phrased in archaic language, as Judge Ashmawi has argued.

The critique from a historical angle is elaborated by Hussain Ahmad Amin, a distinguished intellectual and retired diplomat who wrote an interesting set of essays in the early 1980s, critical of the ideas and programmes of the Islamic current from a modernist and humanist Muslim point of view, including a critique of the call for the application of the *shari'a* (Amin 1987). Amin is in favour of following the holy book and prophetic example, but asks what it is in these sacred sources which may constitute law. If by the *shari'a* is meant the historical accumulation contained in the books of *fiqh*, then this is largely the product of human designs and judgements in accordance with contingencies, interests and needs, developed in a variety of social and historical settings, much of it deriving from diverse custom and practice. Rules and judgements derived directly from the Quran are few, and these, in any case, should not have the status of unvarying laws. The conduct of the Prophet himself and his close associates and immediate successors gives us an indication of the status of these maxims. Later Quranic verses, for instance, were deemed to have overruled earlier ones (on the matter of the allowability of wine, for example), all during the first twenty-odd years of the existence of Islam; what about the changes which occurred over 14 centuries (Amin 1987:189)? Wine-drinking and dealing in interest are both forbidden in the Quran, but is this prohibition in the nature of law, or is it a caution to the believer to work for the salvation of his or her soul? And why is wine-drinking subsequently made into a punishable offence, but dealing in interest only sanctioned by invalidating any contracts which stipulate it? And why other maxims, such as the verse 'Those who take ['eat'] the wealth of orphans unfairly, they are but eating fire in their belly', not translated into penal law? These are maxims to regulate people's relation to their maker, and have priority over the rules which regulate social relations. But worldly legislation is bound to advance the latter (Amin 1987:186–87).

When it comes to the *sunna* of the Prophet, we also see a readiness on the part of his companions and followers to change the rules in accordance with circumstances and contingencies. Regarding wine-drinking, for instance, it is related that at the conquest of Khyber, the Prophet ordered the destruction of the wine flasks found there, but one of the Muslims thought it a waste and greedily imbibed the stuff. Others shouted at him to desist and the Prophet hit him with his slipper, at which others followed suit. When Umar wanted to beat him further the Prophet forbade him, saying that the man loved God and the Prophet, and the man then sat with them amicably. The Quran does not stipulate punishment for drinking, but Abu Bakr, the first successor to the Prophet, then instituted the penalty of 40 strokes for imbibers, and the second caliph, Umar, raised the penalty to 80 strokes. Umar, who has the reputation of having been a puritan disciplinarian, also instituted the stoning of the adulteress, and forbade temporary pleasure marriage (*mut'a*), allowed by the Prophet. So, asks Amin, which tradition should we follow, that of the Prophet, Abu Bakr or Umar? The latter two clearly did not feel bound by the tradition of the Prophet, and adopted practices which suited their circumstances and inclinations. This, to Amin, sets a precedent for subsequent Muslims to do similarly (Amin 1987:189).

Many of the rules in the Quran, those relating to marriage and women, for instance, have to be considered in the context of contemporary practices in Arabia. Such is the concept of marriage as a sale contract giving the man rights in the woman's sex. Islam is a progressive religion and has to change rules and concepts in relation to the time. The Prophet was keen to improve the position of women in his time, and would be amazed to find the rules of *jahiliya* still prevailing today. He would certainly support the reformers who advocate equality and partnership in marriage (Amin 1987:208–9).

So what remains for Amin of the *shariʿa* and the dictates of the holy book and the Prophet's example? The *shariʿa*, he argues, was a set of stable and unchanging religious rules and principles, which at the same time, and within its limits did not ignore considerations of evolution and development, and allowed the adoption of novel systems which could serve the interests of individuals and society in ways which could not have been foreseen by the ancestors (Amin 1987:201). This is a vague and permissive formulation, which would give the legislator a free hand insofar as the claim can be made that the rules conform to the demands of piety and justice in the holy book and the example of the Prophet.

Similarly permissive and secularizing conclusions are reached by Muhammad Saʿid al-Ashmawi, lawyer and judge. Ashmawi is a tireless campaigner against political Islam, and a critic of the call for the application of the *shariʿa*. He is a thoroughgoing secularist, yet his numerous books are about Islam, history and law. He writes from a Muslim point of view, as a believing Muslim, but one who seeks to separate his faith from politics, and, in effect, from the law. Ashmawi is emphatic in the now common separation of *shariʿa* from *fiqh*, and in criticism and rejection of *fiqh*. In the process he engages with the intellectual bases and methodology of *fiqh* in order to expose its profane nature and difference from revelation and the sacred sources. Julian Murphy sums up his project well:

> In essence, Ashmawi argues that the only authentically Islamic *usul al-fiqh* which can be accepted are the Qur'an, selected *Hadith* (those that are in conformity with the spirit of the Qur'an), unfettered *ijtihad* in relation to those material sources and, finally, the consideration of the public good at any given time (*maslaha*, etc.). Given that Ashmawi rejects the idea that the Qur'an can be seen as containing specific legislative commands that are also eternally applicable, it is clear that his overall vision of the Islamic *usul* rejects the notion of the actual existence (within a true consideration of the Islamic message) of any such things as *usul al-fiqh*, or Islamic law. [Murphy 2001:128]

That is to say, Ashmawi enters into an extensive polemic against the Islamists, but as himself a Muslim concerned to derive rules of conduct from the sacred sources, only to arrive at thoroughly secularist conclusions.

This rejection of the historical corpus of *fiqh* as man-made law, the relativization of Quran and traditions to time and place, and the reduction of the legal requirements of religion to general principles of piety, justice and humanity, are common features of the secularist advocacy by men who at the same time insist on their adherence to Islam and the 'real' *shariʿa*. They maintain that Islam does not stipulate or legislate for a state and a government. It is primarily a religion and a culture, and its *shariʿa* a wide programme, a method, with values and principles, but not fixed law codes for all time. The caliphate in Muslim history, despite its religious pretensions, was no more than profane government, often tyrannical, with little if any religious content in its rules and procedures. The pretence of religion was endorsed by *fuqaha*, acquiescing in power and content with the sphere of authority allocated to them in private matters. Ashmawi also questions the cultural and historical distinctiveness of the legal system of *fiqh*. The *fiqh* schools, he argues, developed in a historical and geographical context of the ancient Near East where the practice of Roman law was common, and were inevitably influenced by it. Roman law is the basis for the Code Napoleon on which Egyptian legislation from the nineteenth century is based. French law could be introduced because it was not essentially very different from Egyptian custom and *shariʿa* principles. Indeed, there is much in common between different legal traditions because of the similarity of human problems. As such, modern Egyptian legislation is not at variance with the *shariʿa*, but, as we have seen, many of the principles of civil law are common to both traditions. The call for the application of the *shariʿa*, then, is no more than an ideological slogan, drawing unnecessary boundaries to emphasize Islamic distinctiveness from the West, and in the process attempting to introduce archaic formulations and practices (Shepard 1996:46–47).

It is precisely because the codified *shariʿa* in its mundane application to civil matters resembles other profane codes that those who seek the *shariʿa* as an identity and difference marker vis-à-vis the West emphasize those elements in it which are distinct and often disapproved in liberal contexts: the penal provisions, the patriarchal norms, the ban on alcohol and the interdiction of dealing in interest. These aspects, at the same time, bring a semblance of public law to what otherwise would be a *shariʿa* confined to its common historical limits to private law and civil transactions, which detracts from its centrality to a proposed Islamic state. The advocacy of enforcing these provisions as part of a truly Islamic state is common to conservative and radical Islamists, as we have seen. For those with liberal sensibilities or even a sense of what is possible in a modern state some of these provisions pose a dilemma. We have seen how this problem is posed by Abdullahi an-Naʿim in the quote above. While insistent that a *shariʿa*-based public law is a necessity for Muslims, he is troubled by the implications for women and non-Muslims. His resorts to special and selective reading of the Quran to arrive at a satisfactory solution would be rejected by most Islamists. But these concerns, to varying degrees, also figure in the writing and advocacy of many Islamists. Many of the Egyptian intellectual Islamists such as Adel Hussein, Fahmi Huwaydi, Tariq al-Bishry and Muhammad Amara, while forthright in advocating Islamization in all spheres, are liberal when it comes to non-Muslims, especially Copts, and ingenious in revising the usual *shariʿa* prescriptions regarding non-Muslims as *dhimmis*. They argue that full citizenship rights for Christians is fully compatible with the *shariʿa*, and cite texts and precedents to illustrate their arguments. These stances do not convince the majority of Islamists at the popular level, for whom Islamist sentiments are nourished and reinforced by communalist antagonism, as demonstrated by periodic attacks on Coptic communities in upper Egypt and elsewhere.

CONCLUSION

Egypt is the country which (along with Turkey) has the longest history of modernity in the Middle East. This modernity has included considerable measures of secularization in politics, society and culture over the course of the twentieth century. Under the *ancien régime* in the first half of the twentieth century it comprised a flourishing of commerce, culture, the arts, cinema and the media, few with any religious reference. Under Nasir's 'Arab socialism' it led the Arab world, and played a leading role in the 'Third World' in the vanguard of socialist and anti-imperialist struggles, largely without religious reference. This distance from religion also marked politics, the media and cultural discourses of the period. Was it the perceived failure of this 'national project' and the seeming persistence and reinforcement of Western hegemony backing an intransigent Israel that has enhanced the appeal of religious commitment and solidarity? Whatever the reason, Egypt seems to be in the grip of a powerful wave of Islamization. Radical and oppositional Islamism are on the retreat, unable to withstand overwhelming government repression, ceding ground to conservative and moralistic Islam straddling government and opposition and speaking the language of the *shari'a*. Yet the high visibility of this religious trend should not deceive us as to the continuing development of Egyptian society and economy in directions which cannot be controlled by these conservative, moralist forces, which makes the latter ever more vociferous in their assertion of authority. A current manifestation (at the time of writing) arousing the ire of the conservatives is what is called *'urfi* marriage, a kind of common-law attachment, unregistered in state records but concluded by a religious formula in front of witnesses and, maybe, a signed document. This form of marriage did not raise much interest in its old locations of secret second marriages, or rich Saudis seeking temporary partners. Recently, however, it is practised by university students and other young people, away from home and unknown to their families, getting over the expensive formalities and the parental involvement in proper marriage. Cries of indignation echo in press and broadcasting, denouncing the practice as immoral and a form of prostitution. The young, it would seem, now liberated from household bonds and patriarchal authority, are finding ways of overcoming sexual repression, but in Islamic forms. Veiled girls hold hands and whisper sweet nothings to their boyfriends on the Nile Corniche in Cairo, the veil serving as a legitimizing icon.

Are the efforts and measures to assert religious and moral authority, then, a losing battle against the effects of basic social and economic processes? The Islamic Republic of Iran has given a largely young population a taste of religious government, which they seem to be rejecting. Egypt has not undergone Islamic government, and religion retains an oppositional and solidaristic power. Yet the underlying social processes are similar, leading to resistance, especially by the young, but expressed in different terms. Will they converge?

6   THE POLITICS OF THE *SHARI'A* IN IRAN

HISTORICAL BACKGROUND

In the nineteenth century Iran was ruled by a decentralized and generally weak state under the Qajar dynasty. For most of the century it had little in the way of a standing army, and a limited court bureaucracy, with rudimentary offshoots of corrupt officialdom in the provinces. In these respects it was very different from its Ottoman contemporary, and attempts at reform were to come much later.[1]

Iran was, for the most part, ruled by local power elites, consisting of the Qajar aristocracy (members of the ruling dynasty), tribal chieftains, big merchants and religious magnates. Land was the property base for all these elites, who held villages in various property relations. Most of them commanded armed retainers, often forming a private army, by means of which they could enforce their interests and assure their revenues.

Within this configuration of power, the religious elites, the *mujtahids*, occupied a prominent position, both as players and as guarantors, mediators and adjudicators in the conflicts and struggles that inevitably followed from these arrangements. Religious chieftains were powerful and autonomous actors. Unlike their Ottoman counterparts their power did not derive, for the most part, from state office or stipend, but from their positions in the religious institutions and in the local power elites. Religious institutions were also decentralized: there was no overall 'church'. The rank of *mujtahid* was achieved by study culminating in an *ijaza*, a licence from a high-ranking teacher and patron. The status of a *mujtahid* would then be determined by the number of followers and 'emulators' (*muqallid*) he attracted, and who paid their religious dues to him. These considerations would, in turn, influence his evaluation by peers and superiors, who also gave due consideration to achievements of learning and piety, as demonstrated by writing and teaching, as well as lifestyle. Prominent *mujtahids*, until recently, tended to come from families of *mujtahids* and be married to women from similar households. These were often land-owning and merchant families, generally prosperous. In addition, successful *mujtahids* commanded considerable revenues from religious endowments and, crucially, from religious dues called *khoms* (one-fifth), paid by emulators who followed them. These were assessed as a percentage of certain categories of wealth. They were incumbent as a religious duty on every believer, who must follow a *mujtahid* of his or her choice, to whom the dues were paid annually. Some *mujtahids* were reputed to have employed their armed retainers in the collection of these dues (Algar 1969:19), but, for the most part, these payments were made voluntarily as an act of religious duty and piety. Titles, such as Hojattulislam, then Ayatollah and Grand Ayatollah, came into currency from the late nineteenth century to accord status and honour to the ranks of *mujtahids* and to suggest a hierarchy (Moin 1999:36–38). However, there is no formal system or procedure for the award or promotion to these ranks, to which individuals advance by an emerging consensus.

Madrasas were central to this system. *Mujtahids* were often teachers, and the *madrasas* were directed and financed by prominent *mujtahids* from the religious endowments and *khoms* revenues which they commanded. Many also paid stipends to students and managed bakeries to provide bread for students and the needy. These were important avenues of patronage and influence, as one's students and licencees constituted an important following, which would spread the fame and influence of their patron and recruit and maintain congregations of *khoms*-paying emulators. Historically, some *mujtahids* recruited their armed retainers, at least partly, from their students (Algar 1969:19).

These *madrasas* were located mainly in religious centres which tended to be shrine cities. Najaf, Kerbala and Samarra in Iraq, as well as the Iranian shrine cities of Mashhad and Qum. These are centres of pilgrimage, which provided job opportunities and revenues for religious personnel. The Iraqi centres were politically important because they were outside the reach of Iranian governments, and as such created further bases of autonomy for *mujtahids*.

The curricula of the *madrasas* followed three cycles, each typically requiring four years to complete. In the first cycle, the student learnt the basics of the Quran and Arabic language and grammar, at the end of which he would be qualified to practise as a low-level religious functionary in local mosques and to act as reader and reciter of the tales of martyrdom of Hussein at the ritual mourning ceremonies of the month of Muharram. The second cycle taught *fiqh*, and training in the intricacies of the *shari'a*, learning the appropriate texts, commentaries and methods of deduction. Graduates qualified as mollas in charge of mosques and congregations, and, presumably, as judges where *shari'a* courts functioned (which was not the case for much of the twentieth century, but revived in some ways more recently, as we shall see). The final cycle was training in *ijtihad*, to arrive at independent opinion on matters of law and interpretation. This was conducted through seminars and discussions of texts, traditions and commentaries, with the objective of training in the formation of independent judgement. When the student felt that he had reached that stage, then he could submit pertinent work to the teacher, who, if convinced, would issue a licence to practise *ijtihad*, and the student became a fully fledged *mujtahid*. Naturally, only a small minority of students pursue this third cycle and become *mujtahids*.[2]

Note the difference in ethos and culture between Shi'i Iran and the Sunni world. *Ijma'*, consensus, and the emulation of the accumulated *ijma'* of past generations, limits *ijtihad* in the Sunni world. When *ijtihad* is allowed and, indeed, required by the reformers and the radicals, it becomes permissive with few rules and procedures, and practised by any educated person with religious interests. In Shi'i Iran *ijtihad* is the regular practice of high *ulama*, who are explicitly exempt from the rulings of dead *mujtahids*, and who have to arrive at their own judgement. Of course, for the most part, the conclusions reached through *ijtihad* are seldom novel or revolutionary, and generally follow traditional lines and well-trodden paths. Indeed, the function of the doctrine of *ijtihad* appears to be a device to establish and buttress the authority and autonomy of the *ulama*, rather than an avenue for innovation. It does, however, under exceptional circumstances, give certain *ulama* room for flexibility and manoeuvre, allowing innovation to suit new conditions, as we see in both the Constitutional Revolution of 1906, and the more recent Iranian Revolution of 1979 and the Islamic Republic it generated. The craft of the law remains central to religious learning and practice for the Shi'a as much as for the Sunni world. Yet, Shi'i learning seems to have retained more of the philosophical, reflective and even mystical elements of medieval Islam than its Sunni counterpart, which has been more inclined to legalistic and textual limitations on reflection.[3]

THE POLITICAL BACKGROUND

The factors considered above have combined to give a fair degree of autonomy to high-ranking *ulama* in Iran: autonomy from government and its agents and autonomy with respect to other religious authorities and institutions. Each senior *mujtahid* has his own network of followers, his own endowments, institutions and revenues. It is in the interest of rivals not to challenge these aspects, as it concerns their own power and autonomy in turn. Political and personal conflicts and intrigues are inevitable products of such a system. These are managed and contained in times of stability, but exacerbated under turbulent conditions of social transformation, which have characterized many episodes since the late nineteenth century. The establishment of the modern state under Reza Shah in the 1920s witnessed similar processes of decline of religious authority and function as we saw for the Ottoman world.

The *ulama* played a prominent part in the political arena in Iran from the 1880s, with renewed concern over their status and power in relation to the mounting intrusion into the Iranian economy and politics of the European powers (mainly Britain and Russia) and their banks and merchants. These were acquiring influence and control, concessions and monopolies, through finance and credit to the bankrupt and revenue-hungry imperial treasury. The beginnings of modern education and culture (on a much more limited scale than in contemporary Turkey or Egypt) were also threatening, as was the intrusion of elements of European law for commercial purposes. The first major episode in which the *ulama* realized their power was that of the Tobacco Regie in 1881 (Keddie 1966). The shah had sold a monopoly on all trade in tobacco to the Imperial Tobacco Company, which would have been ruinous for many growers and merchants. The agitation which followed culminated in a *fatwa* from the most senior *mujtahid*, Mirza Hassan Shirazi, resident in Najaf, forbidding the consumption of tobacco on pain of eternal damnation. The successful boycott which followed ensured the cancellation of the monopoly. The *ulama* continued to play a part in the politics of transformation of Iran into modernity, and their role was not always 'reactionary': in fact, some were among the major supporters and theorists of the constitution, as we shall see. In their struggle against foreign domination and increasing centralization of government, which included more systematic taxation, the *ulama* had a natural affinity with the merchants of the bazaar, and they formed a close alliance, to be revived in many episodes, including that of the 1979 Revolution. Significantly, at that point at the turn of the twentieth century, other allies were the modern intellectuals, motivated by a nascent nationalism to oppose the traditional arbitrary tyranny of dynastic rule, especially when buttressed and exploited by foreign powers and financial interests. This, then, was the tripartite alliance which led the struggle for a constitution, culminating in the revolution of 1906. It is important to note at this point that the *ulama* were not, as we shall see, as one in support of the constitution, but were often divided by interests and theoretical outlook.[4]

Diverse forces and interests were involved in the campaign, first for an *adalet-khaneh*, House of Justice (a title for the rule of law and end to arbitrary rule), then crystallizing in the demand for a constitution (*mashruta*, literally conditional rule). Many of the *bazaaris* (market people) and *ulama* participated from a narrow and instrumental perspective, primarily to do with resisting the extension of taxes to themselves. Under previous regimes they were largely able to evade taxation, but now, with European personnel in charge of collecting revenues to service government debts owing to European banks, taxes were becoming more systematic and effectively collected. Worries over the corrosion of the *ulama*'s influence and control over law and education by the incursion of modern forms associated with the European penetration may also have been a background factor at that point. Few in these constituencies understood what the constitution was about, except as a limitation on royal power and the transfer of powers to some kind of assembly in which, they assumed correctly, they would have representation. This instrumental attitude did not, however, apply to all the *ulama*: some understood the issues and were moved to find religious justifications and arguments to theorize and sustain the constitution. Prominent among those was Mirza Mohammad Husayn Na'ini, who wrote a book, *Tanbih al-Umma wa Tanzih al-Milla*, published in 1909, theorizing the constitution. In the absence of Imam-ul-zaman, the Hidden Imam, he argued, it was incumbent on the community and its leaders to devise the means of just government. Government in accordance with law and by the representatives of the people was far superior, and more favourable to the rule of Islamic law than arbitrary tyranny. The main opponent of the constitution among the *ulama* was Fazlallah Nouri who argued that there is no room for legislation or legislatures in Islam, for whom divine law is the only law, with the *ulama* as its privileged guardians and interpreters. Although initially sympathetic to the *majlis* and to legal limits on the powers of the monarch, he soon turned against the constitution and eventually became its principal clerical opponent and supporter of the shah's attempt to restore absolutism. Nouri expressed strong doubts about the liberties and equalities specified in the constitution, such as freedom of expression which would include anti-religious expressions, compulsory education for girls and equality of non-Muslims with Muslims, all judged to be contrary to the *shari'a* (Enayat 1982:164–69; Martin 1989:165–200). We have seen that these lines of argument recur in religious stances against democracy, constitutions and legislatures to the present day, in Sunni and Shi'i Islam, advanced by conservatives and radicals, and was, indeed, taken over by Khomeini, who venerated Nouri as a principled jurist (although he ignored his support for monarchy). Nouri's militant alignment with the monarchist forces resulted in his public execution by the revolutionaries in 1909, when they returned to Tehran after an interlude in which the shah, with the aid of Russian troops, succeeded in banishing them and suspending the constitution temporarily.

In 1906 the shah was forced to ratify the constitution, which provided for an elected assembly, charged with legislation, and to whom ministers of state were responsible. Its legislative powers, however, were to be subject to clerical approval: a council of high clerics was to vet all legislation to assure its compatibility with the *shari'a*. In the early years after the promulgation of the constitution, some senior *ulama* tried to use this provision to retain control over legislation and judicial functions (Martin 1989:152–55). They were, above all, resistant to the idea of standardized law enacted and administered by the state, which would deprive the *ulama* of their autonomy and an important source of livelihood. They did not succeed and eventually, under Reza Shah, legal functions became etatized and centralized in parallel to the Ottoman example.

The Constitutional Revolution initiated a period of turbulence in Iran, with tensions and struggles between successive shahs and constitutionalist parties, with shifting alliances with different groups and forces in Iranian society. This period culminated in 1921 with the rise to power of Reza Khan, a Cossack officer, who turned after the Russian Revolution to serve in British-controlled forces and was supported by the British authorities in his bid for power. The last Qajar shah was deposed in 1924 by an assembly manipulated by Reza Khan. There had been a plan to establish a republic, which was strongly opposed by the *ulama*, who were fearful of the example of the Turkish Republic and the secularism of Ataturk. Reza thus took the crown and established the Pahlavi dynasty, with the blessing of the *ulama*, whom he at first cultivated. Reza Shah proceeded to build up an authoritarian modern state, subordinating parliament and bypassing the constitution, then subordinating or co-opting the centres of autonomous power one by one, starting with the old aristocracy and ruling cliques, then the tribes, then regional autonomies and all the modern political forces which supported his modernizing thrust. The *ulama* and the religious institutions as centres of power and social autonomy were also to be subordinated.

Although Reza had at first cultivated and flattered the *ulama*, once he had established his position he turned to control the religious institutions and personnel. In 1928 the Queen, on a visit to the shrine in Qom, unveiled her face during the proceedings, to general consternation. One Ayatollah Bafqi, present at the shrine, sent a message to the Queen: 'If you are not Muslim why did you come to the shrine? If you are then why are you not veiled?' When his message was ignored, Bafqi delivered a sermon denouncing the shah and inciting the crowd. In response, Reza Shah personally went to Qom, entered the shrine in his boots, horsewhipped Bafqi and had him arrested (Moin 1999:28). Reza Shah, ever the modernist nationalist, then mounted an assault against the 'backwardness' of Iranian society in which religion was the central pillar. In 1934 he visited Turkey, and was most impressed by the progress made by Ataturk, declaring on his return: 'We have been to meet a very great man. We must bring our people to the same level of development and progress as his' (Moin 1999:55). Notable in the programme of modernization was the regulation of dress: European hats for men were made compulsory, and the clergy had to apply for special dispensation, only granted to their senior members, others had to wear 'modern' dress. More significant was the ban on the *hejab* (veil) for women. The police were used to enforce these dress codes, and had orders to remove veils forcibly from the heads of women wearing them in public places. For many traditional and older women, this meant that they were confined to their homes.

The institution of the modern state and its associated organizations and processes inevitably brings into existence spheres of activity outside the control or pertinence of the religious sphere, as we have seen in the Ottoman case. Education, the press and publishing, broadcasting and the arts, are mostly part of a new secularized world that does not conform to religious authority and instruction. Under Reza Shah these developments were reinforced by propaganda, by government agencies as well as modern intellectuals, against the mollas and their institutions, presented as forces of reaction and obscurantism, holding back the progress of the country and its power and dignity among the modern nations. Any resistance or opposition from the clerics was forcibly repressed, with arrests and exile for recalcitrant clerks, and the majority of the religious classes retired to passivity, watching developments with mounting alarm, but helpless to resist. In the end, it was Ayatollah Borujerdi who emerged in 1946 after Reza Shah's abdication[5] as undisputed chief *marja'* of the Shi'i world, who worked out a *modus vivendi* with the state, based on the clergy keeping out of politics and opposition, but being assigned their niche in the religious institutions and general respect and dignity. In effect, the clergy under Borujerdi accepted the modern and secularized state and its culture, and the confinement of the religious sphere. Some, however, and certainly the then junior Khomeini, were seething with resentment against secularization and the subordination of religion and the clergy, but biding their time and keeping within the confines of the Borujerdi regime (Moin 1999:53–73).

The peculiarity of Iranian religion, however, ensured that it was never fully subordinated to government control, as it was largely in the Sunni world. The institutional autonomy of the *mujtahids* persisted, with revenues from their emulators, not only in Iran, but also in Iraq, Lebanon and India. The Iraqi Shi'i centres, though subject to Iraqi government interference and sometimes persecution, continued to furnish the Iranian *ulama* with extra-territorial refuge beyond the reach of their government. The shrine cities in Iran and their *madrasa* and religious culture continued to provide centres of autonomy for the *ulama* and a means of perpetuating their institutions and discourses. The *ulama* also found ready allies in the bazaars, some of whose interests and cultures were equally threatened by these policies and processes. These twin realms of social autonomy, the religious institutions and the bazaars, continued to pose challenges to the Pahlavis throughout their reign, despite repeated efforts to control and subordinate them. They were to be the major forces in the Revolution that ended that reign in 1979.

THE LEGAL SPHERE

Qajar Iran in the nineteenth century comprised the familiar duality of judiciary institutions, divided between the *shar'i* courts under *ulama* control, and the *'urfi* courts under the governors. Unlike the Ottoman example, however, the *shari'a* courts in Iran remained for the most part under the control of local *ulama*, and only the *'urfi* courts were in the sphere of government (Algar 1969: 11–14). Attempts by reforming shahs and their ministers to bring the *shari'a* courts under some form of government control were half-hearted and soon abandoned.

At the local level, legal disputes or complaints could be heard by any one of a variety of jurisdictions, from government officials to notables and warlords, as well as *ulama*. The *ulama* acted as notaries, drawing up and registering contracts, properties, marriages and divorces and matters of inheritance. They also ran *shari'a* courts, which ruled on civil and penal cases. These were often under the direct authority of senior *mujtahids*, outside the administration and control of government officials (Algar 1969:11–14). Many people did not resort to courts but to their chosen *mujtahid* to rule on family matters and civil disputes. Some trade guilds operated their own tribunals to adjudicate in disputes between members. Enforcement, punishment and police functions were carried out by various armed bodies of soldiers, tribal fighters and armed retainers, mostly private armies. Self-help, communal solidarities and protection by patrons and chiefs were the main guarantees of security.

Given the nature of *mujtahid*–emulator relationship, the function of *ifta'* became a component of that relation. There were no general state-appointed muftis, as in the Ottoman world, rather each *mujtahid* was a mufti for his followers. Each *mujtahid* could issue his own *fatwa*, which was binding on his followers, but not anyone else. Two *mujtahids* could, theoretically, reach opposite conclusions, and these could co-exist for their respective communities of emulators. On matters of public interest, which are increasingly features of modern political struggles, the *fatwa* of a senior *mujtahid* could be considered generally binding, as in the case of the boycott of tobacco noted above, or in many of the political *fatwas* of the twentieth century. The *fatwa* of a dead *mujtahid* ceased to have effect with his demise, though the authority and mode of reasoning of notable *mujtahids* remained as points of reference and precedent. This emphasis on living *ijtihad* is at variance with the Sunni veneration for the accumulation of the *ijma'* of previous generations.

The modern state followed a similar path to that of Iran's neighbours in modernizing the legal and the court systems along European models and with the adoption of European civil and penal codes, as well as public and administrative law. Criminal and commercial codes were based on French law. The civil code of 1928 was derived from the *shari'a*, but codified as state law and administered by a Ministry of Justice in modern court systems. That is to say, as in the Sunni world, *shari'a*-derived civil and family codes were withdrawn from religious institutions and *fiqh* practices and entrusted to government bureaucracies. The Ministry of Justice opened its own law school to train lawyers, replaced in 1928 by the Law Faculty of Tehran University, and a law degree became a requisite for legal practice. Clerics who wanted to practise law had to retrain in the new law schools. That is to say, *madrasa* education became redundant for a career other than that of strictly religious education and functions. The modern, secular education system qualified graduates for careers in the civil service, as well as for professional training.

THE HISTORICAL BACKGROUND TO THE REVOLUTION

Reza Shah was deposed by the allies (Britain and Russia) in 1941. They replaced him with his young son, Mohammad Reza, who remained on the throne till deposed by the 1979 Revolution. There then followed, under the allied occupation, a period of political and intellectual liberalization. Trade unions and political parties were licensed and operated openly, with some restriction, but nothing like the ruthless repression of Reza's regime. Nationalist, mostly liberal parties were eventually federated under the National Front in 1949 (Chehabi 1990:113). This included Muslim political elements which were reformist and liberal, sometimes critical of the religious establishment. Such were the personalities associated with Mehdi Bazergan, later to form the Freedom Party, and to be the first prime minister of the Islamic Republic. This was also the period of the formation of a communist party, with Soviet blessing, the Tudeh Party, which was to enjoy great popularity and support among the intellectuals and the young, as well as having grass-root bases in organized labour (Abrahamian 1982:326–82). The restrictions, especially the dress code that Reza imposed on the religious classes, could now be ignored. But this was little consolation for the clerics, who were further marginalized by the predominantly secular political and intellectual renaissance of the time. One religious movement came on the scene at that time, the Fedayan-e Islam, similar to the Muslim Brotherhood in Egypt, but without its wide popularity. It had tenuous connections with the religious establishment, which mostly disapproved of its radical and violent programme of assassinations.

This decade of political turbulence culminated in 1951 with the emergence, through parliamentary elections, of Muhammad Mosaddeq, the leader of the National Front, as prime minister. Mosaddeq embarked on the nationalization of Iran's oil, to the consternation of Western oil companies and their governments.[6]

There ensued a period of political turmoil, in which popular forces led by the National Front (with a grudging and oscillating role played by the Tudeh Party) came to the fore in support of the government, but pitched against conservative forces around the beleaguered shah, covertly supported by British and US agencies. In these confrontations, religious forces played little part. Ayatollah Kashani at first supported the Mosaddeq camp, then switched sides when his demands for religious law and authority were not met. The religious establishment, under the apolitical Borujerdi kept aloof from these struggles, and sidelined Kashani. Religion did not play an important part during this episode, confined largely to anti-Mosaddeq demonstrations led by Kashani and Fedayan-e Islam.[7] The issues and forces were identified primarily in terms of secular nationalism, the left, the right and the Cold War. In 1953, the CIA, allied with the conservative and monarchist forces, succeeded in staging a military *coup d'état* against the Mosaddeq government, restoring the shah to power and reversing the nationalization of Iranian oil. Mosaddeq was put on trial and imprisoned.

Religion was very much on the agenda in the next episode of turbulence in Iranian politics, in the events of 1961–63. It was then that Khomeini appeared on the scene, and many commentators considered these events as a prelude to the 1979 Revolution. Ruhollah Khomeini (1902–89) had by this time emerged as a senior *mujtahid* in Qom, one of four at the top of the hierarchy, but with no established order of seniority after the death of Borujerdi in 1961. Khomeini harboured a strong resentment against Reza Shah and his successor, and their secularizing measures which subordinated and often humiliated religion and the mollas. He had strong aspirations to the restoration of religious authority, and a faith in the basic religious allegiance of the Iranian people (Moin 1999:53–73) in support of their *ulama*. However, out of respect for Borujerdi's authority and his belief in the necessity of *ulama* solidarity, Khomeini refrained from open political challenges while Borujerdi was alive. He did, however, prepare the ground, in his writing and teaching, as well as in building up networks of popular following among his students and in the bazaars. He attacked all aspects of secularism and denounced Reza Shah and his collaborators among the clergy in a book, *Kshf al-Asrar* (*The Unveiling of Secrets*), which he published anonymously, probably in 1942 (Moin 1999:60–64). It was also in this book that Khomeini first advanced his views on the necessity of Islamic government, one in which the laws of God and the authority of the *ulama* were to be enshrined (Moin 1999:63). Khomeini also tapped the sources of support for religious militancy in the bazaars and their guilds by sending his representatives and deputies to the Tehran bazaar to organize networks in the form of study groups and charitable associations. From 1962 he sponsored the formation of the Coalition of Islamic Societies, which co-ordinated bazaar religious groups. These were to be crucial in channelling funds for Khomeini's projects and mobilizing popular demonstrations. These networks continued to play important parts in the 1979 Revolution and in the subsequent politics of the Islamic Republic (Moin 1999:78–81).

In 1961 the shah, under US pressure, embarked on a programme of reforms, which included proposals for land reform as well as the institution of elections to local government which enfranchised women and members of religious minorities into the electorate. Khomeini saw this as the opportunity to challenge the government and raise the banner of Islamic resistance. The *ulama*, including Borujerdi just before his death, were moved by lobbying from land-owners with whom they had close affinity, to declare land reforms to be against the *shari'a*, which upheld the sanctity of property. Khomeini, apparently, did not raise this issue, but opposed the enfranchisement of women and non-Muslims, which he declared contrary to Islam and an attack on its very bases (this is odd when seen in the context of the later Islamic Republic which he instituted, in which women's suffrage and standing for some political offices was a matter of course). Clerical and popular agitation succeeded in inducing the government to withdraw its proposals at that point, but the shah returned to the fray in 1963, with revived and more extensive proposals for land reform and distribution, labelled his 'White Revolution', and on extension of the franchise to women and non-Muslims for national parliamentary elections. There was clearly a decision to confront the clerical opposition full on and defeat it. The shah, who had cultivated the *ulama* and sought their support after the Mosaddeq episode in the early 1950s, by now felt sufficiently secure to challenge their pretensions. This was a version of the familiar strategy employed by so many governments and leaders in the region of mobilizing Islam against the left, but then confronting the religious challenge which could not be co-opted. The struggle which ensued pitched the security and paramilitary forces against the students and religious classes, as well as their popular and bazaari supporters in Qom and Tehran, claiming many casualties among the latter. This episode saw the rise of Khomeini to national prominence as a steadfast and charismatic figure who was forthright in his condemnation of the shah and his ungodly regime. From the other side, propaganda and press campaigns against 'black reaction' (a reference to the generally black garments of the clerics, and to distinguish them from 'red reaction', the leftists) were mounted. The clergy were presented as backwards, living in the dark ages, and embarking on a campaign to take the nation back to these primitive times, reversing the advances of modernity. The secular opposition, of nationalists and the left, thoroughly suppressed, deprived of leadership and organization and generally silenced at this point, may have admired the courage and organization of the religious forces, but could not go along with their religious and social objectives. In the years that followed, Khomeini, aware of the reservations of the secular opposition, shrewdly emphasized the anti-imperialist plank of his advocacy. He denounced the dependency and subordination of Iran and the shah to US dictates and the alliance with Israel, thus articulating Islam and the defence of religion to Iranian nationalism and Third-Worldist liberationism, striking a chord with the general sentiments of the left. These, as well as concerns with social and economic issues, were to be the means by which Khomeini appealed to the left in the campaigns leading up to the 1979 Revolution.

These anti-imperialist themes were to come to the fore in the stance that Khomeini took in 1964. The 1963 events culminated on the day of 'Ashura of that year, with a defiant speech made in Qom, in which Khomeini attacked the shah directly, adding satire and ridicule in humiliating comments made against the person of the monarch. In a charged atmosphere of mounting confrontation between the security forces and the religious students in Qom and elsewhere, retribution was swift: government forces laid siege to the city and to Khomeini's residence, and in the clashes that followed there was much violence and bloodshed. Khomeini was arrested, and spent the best part of a year in detention. The government, not knowing quite what to do with him, eventually released him in an attempt at reconciliation with the religious establishment. Most of the senior *mujtahids* were conciliated and reluctant to make any further stands against the shah. Not Khomeini: he soon found a pretext for a renewed campaign, this time against legislation granting US personnel in Iran extra-territorial legal immunity. In a speech in Qom, he denounced the shah's subservience to the US and Israel in the harshest terms. This time he was taken directly to Tehran airport, handed a passport, and sent to exile in Turkey, then to Najaf in Iraq, where he remained until the events leading up to the 1979 Revolution. Expelled to France for a short period, he returned triumphantly to Tehran to preside over the revolutionary republic.[8]

Khomeini's Doctrine of Government

Central to Khomeini's doctrine was the authority of the clergy in promulgating and enforcing the law of God. He was forthright and aggressive in his denunciation of critics of the clergy. Attacks on the clergy came from various quarters: official Pahlavi ideology presented them as 'black reaction' stuck in the dark ages, attempting to halt or reverse progress and modern life. Secular intellectuals, whether nationalist or leftist, did not dissent from this view. Of particular significance were the attacks and criticisms from modernist religious forces which appeared on the political and intellectual scene in the 1960s and 1970s, notably the Freedom Movement of Mehdi Bazargan, the leftist guerillas of the Mojahedin-e Khalq, influenced by Marxism, and the popular and charismatic Ali Shari'ati, whose lectures at the Hosseiniyeh Ershad attracted crowds of students and young activists, and circulated widely on cassettes. All these upheld modernized versions of Islam influenced by secular and Western political and social ideas, which converged in finding fault with traditional Islam and the reactionary clergy, who often left out the social and political message of Islam in favour of rules and rituals. Khomeini, while himself critical of conservative and quietist mollas, was ever vigilant in his defence of the clergy as a body and on maintaining an *esprit de corps* of the clerical establishment, as the bastion of religion and the law.

A regular theme in all Khomeini's writing is that in the absence of the Hidden Imam, the clergy have the special duty of acting as his deputies, and to rule the Islamic community in accordance with the law. In *Kashf al-Asrar* he argues that government can only be legitimate if it applies the *shari'a* of God, and cancels all laws incompatible with it. *Mujtahids* were to play a central role in such a state: if it were a monarchy, the king would be chosen by the *mujtahids* on the bases of his piety and probity and willingness to apply God's law. He goes on to argue that such a government would have a duty to protect Islam from its detractors, to censor publications which do not conform to its principles, and to prosecute, and if necessary publicly execute, detractors of the true religion as *mofsed fil-arz*, corrupters of the earth (a charge that was to be commonly used in the Islamic Republic against opponents) (Moin 1999:63).

Later in Khomeini's career, after his exile to Najaf, he was to deliver a series of lectures on Islamic government to students in that city in 1970 (Moin 1999: 153). It was there that he first advanced his concept of *velayet-e faqih*, which was to become a cornerstone of the Islamic Republic.[9] In this doctrine, Khomeini dispenses altogether with monarchy or any other rule in favour of rule by the *faqih*, the jurist or *mujtahid*. The argument runs as follows: Islam must include a government system. The separation of religion from government is completely alien to Islam: the Prophet established an Islamic government and made provision for its perpetuation by appointing a successor, a *khalifa*. Islam is above all divine law, and the law is not given merely to be studied and analyzed but to be applied and instituted in a state. It is a logical necessity that there must be a government to put the law into practice. Khomeini then seeks to establish the qualifications of a ruler who must undertake this task. Note that the idea of government is pinned on the qualifications of a ruler rather than institutional entities which constitute the modern notion of 'the state'. There are two qualifications for a just ruler upon which the Muslims are agreed: total knowledge of the law and total justice in its execution. The Shi'a believe these qualities to be among the attributes of the imamate, the imams enjoying the divine grace of infallibility. What are they to do, though, in the absence of this inspired guidance? The *shari'a* cannot remain in abeyance, and Muslims cannot live in anarchy, or under alien and godless government. Khomeini concludes that in the absence of the imam, the just *faqih*, while not sharing in the infallibility of the imam, can nevertheless endeavour to fulfil similar functions through his knowledge of the law, his justice, and his ability to fathom the meanings and intentions of the sacred text and the traditions of the Prophet and the imams (Zubaida 1993:13–20).

These seem to be simple and clear arguments. Why, then, did they constitute such a departure for the Shi'i doctrine of government? We have seen that Sunni Islamists have advocated the application of the *shari'a* and the institution of Islamic government, or even the caliphate. Most of these, however, privileged the law and the text, with little attention to the person of the ruler (except, perhaps, for Rashid Rida's notion of the future *khalifa* as a supreme *mujtahid*). In this respect, Khomeini's privileging of the *faqih* is very much within a Shi'i tradition regarding the centrality of a *marja'* for every believer to follow. Its novelty, however, is in postulating a supreme *marja'* as the head of government and an Islamic ruler.

Traditional Shi'i doctrine did assign authority or *wilaya* to the *mujtahid* over the affairs of his followers, and by extension, to the community of believers (although this normally admitted a plurality of authorities, each with his own following). Yet crucially, the community of believers did not constitute the state. Historically it was always assumed and implicitly accepted that the community existed within the territory of a government and a ruler, who ruled by the sword. The most that Muslims could hope for was a pious ruler who upheld the law and did not oppress the subjects too much. However, it was widely recognized that such a ruler was rare and that most were oppressive. But this was generally accepted, if not as legitimate, then as a fact, and order was better than rebellion, as we have seen. For the Shi'a, oppression was an inevitable product of *'asr al-ghaybeh*, the period of the occultation of the imam. Rule, in this view, was oppressive and illegitimate, but to be accepted and tolerated. In this scenario, the *faqih*'s domain was not government, but the affairs of the community.

I have argued elsewhere (Zubaida 1993:16–20) that the doctrine of *velayet-e faqih* is only plausible and thinkable in the context of the nation-state when the community of believers can be conceptualized as the 'nation'. The concept of the nation is tied to the concept of citizenship which, unlike the passive 'subject' of dynastic kingdoms, is active in deciding and shaping the destiny of the nation, through political action of reform and even revolution. Khomeini believed that 'the people' were the natural allies of the clergy in the defence of Islam and the establishment of the law. If only they could be awakened by the clergy and their agents and alerted to the dangers posed to Islam by imperialists and tyrants, they would rise to its defence. Islamic 'revolution' would inaugurate an Islamic 'Republic', concepts clearly borrowed from modern political vocabularies. As Abrahamian argued, Khomeini's ideas are better seen as modern populism rather than traditional 'fundamentalism' (Abrahamian 1993:13–38).

Khomeini's Islamic government, resting as it did on assumptions of the modern nation-state, was no democracy. Given the divine law and the authority of the ruling *faqih*, there was no room for legislation: every contingency could be catered for by the *ijtihad* of the *faqih* and his clergy associates. This 'theocratic' model was as much a feature of his early *Kashf al-Asrar*, as it was of the later lectures on Islamic government. However, while the principle of *velayet-e faqih* became enshrined in the constitution of the Islamic Republic, it had to co-exist, uneasily, with the full panoply of representative government, of an elected president and a legislature. This was mainly to do with the compromises that the clerical leadership had to make with the diverse forces, many secular, that made the Revolution.

The principle of *velayet-e faqih* and its application in government has important implications for the relationship of the *ulama* to government. It gives almost absolute power to the ruling *faqih* and his clerical associates. Indeed, in the case of the Islamic Republic, clerics have assumed power positions in all the institutions of state and society. What are the implications, however, for the autonomy of the senior *mujtahids* or *marja's*? We have seen that in the traditional system, each *mujtahid* enjoyed undisputed authority over his emulators, who were free to choose which *marja'* to follow. The assumption of one senior cleric of state power, including that of legislation and ultimate ruling on any issue, puts the autonomy of what should be his peers in question. This was clearly perceived by the *ulama*, and many of them rejected the principle of *velayet-e faqih*, some, such as Ayatollah Shari'atmadari, openly in the political arena, others quietly in their writing and teaching. Khomeini had his own entourage of mollas, including many senior figures, who participated in the Revolution and assumed positions of power and control in the ensuing republic. Shari'atmadari, a senior *mujtahid* with a wide following, especially in his native Azerbayjan, also participated in the Revolution, but independently from Khomeini, forming his own political party. He opposed Khomeini's project of clerical control of the state, favouring an Islamic democracy, and he challenged the theoretical credentials of *velayet-e faqih*. In the struggles of the first years of the Republic, Khomeini and his entourage eliminated all open opposition. In 1982 Shari'atmadari was implicated in a conspiracy to overthrow the regime, arrested, forced to recant and ask for forgiveness on television (his son was threatened with execution), then 'defrocked' from his clerical robes. This is completely unprecedented in Shi'i practice: an ayatollah is not appointed by any superior authority, and no such authority exists to dismiss him. The act scandalized the senior clerics not in Khomeini's entourage, but most kept silent. One, Ayatollah Golpayegani (d. 1993), apparently wrote to Khomeini to say that what had happened between him and Shari'atmadari was up to God and history to judge, but that that was no way to treat a venerable cleric and was a threat to the sanctity of religion (Moin 1999:252–53). This is clearly the view of many senior clerics in Iran, Iraq and Lebanon, most of whom keep their traditional authority over their followers, collect the religious dues from them, and run their own schools and institutions, but mostly keep quiet about the politics of the Islamic Republic.

THE CONSTITUTION AND THE POLITICS OF LEGISLATION IN THE ISLAMIC REPUBLIC

The Shari'a *in the Islamic Republic of Iran*

Iran presents us with a unique illustration of the problems of applying the *shari'a* in a modern state and society. This is a central plank in the platform of the Islamic elements of the Revolution which culminated in installing the clerical classes in a position of state authority. The *raison d'être* of clerical authority is their expertise in the legal sciences of *fiqh*, thus representing the authority of the sacred traditions emanating from revelation. However, as they proceeded to found and administer a modern state, the ruling clergy had to resort to many subterfuges to depart from the provisions of the historical *shari'a*, both in legislation and in practice, until they reached a point in 1988 when Khomeini issued a formal ruling exempting the government from the provisions of the sacred law.

The Iranian constitution of 1979 comprises two principles which may be considered contradictory: one, the principle of the sovereignty of the people through an elected legislative assembly, the other the sovereignty of God through the agency of the ruling *faqih*. It has often been stated by Khomeini and many of his followers and associates that the Muslim religion and its *shari'a* are perfect and complete, and can provide for all the needs of humankind at every time and place. Indeed such statements are frequently heard from Islamists everywhere. If this is the case, it may be asked, then why the need for an elected legislature, or the sovereignty of the people? There is no logical answer: the duality was dictated by political contingencies and compromises between the forces involved in the 1979 Revolution, which comprised many secularist and non-clerical Islamic elements. In the course of the first year of the revolutionary regime the clerics manoeuvred themselves into a position of supreme ascendancy, and were subsequently able to contain and subvert the democratic elements of the constitution. This was not difficult in a constitution which, despite its democratic provisions, gave the ruling *faqih* final powers and vetoes over decisions and policies. Nevertheless, it is noteworthy that the constitution is not the *shari'a*, and that the *shari'a* is given its place of prominence by the constitution.

The 1979 constitution was drafted, after many debates, by an elected Assembly of Experts (Majlis e-Khobragan), consisting overwhelmingly of pro-Khomeini mollas. The draft was then approved by a referendum. Its primary thrust was Islamic: an Islamic Republic, with leadership reserved for the ruling *faqih*, with almost unlimited powers, aided by other jurists of high rank and requisite piety. All law and legislation is tied to the *shari'a*: the explicit rules of the holy law are to be applied, others derived from it, and no law enacted that is not in conformity with its principles. To ensure this conformity, a Guardian Council (Showra-ye Neghaban), consisting of senior clerics, would be appointed by the leader to vet, approve or reject all parliamentary legislation. A Higher Judicial Council, consisting of senior mollas nominated by the leader, was to administer all judicial appointments and affairs. The 1989 constitution changed this provision to a single head of the judiciary. Thus, we have the dominant Islamic elements of the constitution providing for specifically religious centres of power, governed by the *shari'a* and the *ijtihad* of the senior government *ulama*. They consist of the office and the institution of leader (the ruling *faqih*), the Assembly of Experts, which was to oversee constitutional affairs and amendments, as well as rule on the succession to the office of leader, the Guardian Council, and the administration of the judiciary (Schirazi 1997:8–14; Ehteshami 1995:34–44).[10]

The constitution also made democratic provisions, based on the principle of the sovereignty of the people and deriving many features from a general model of the modern nation-state. An ideological link is made between the people and Islam. The preamble to the constitution states: 'that the state from the point of view of Islam…is the crystallization of a political ideal of a people who are united in religion and in their way of thinking'; and again: 'Islamic principles and guidelines' reflect 'the deepest wish of the Islamic community' (quoted in Schirazi 1997:14).

The constitution enshrines the principle of the separation of powers: legislative, executive and judicial. Legislation is to be carried out by a *majlis* (assembly), elected on the basis of geographical constituencies, with provisions for representation of the minority religious communities (only recognized 'religions of the book': Judaism, Christianity and Zoroastrianism) as distinct constituencies. Legislation, however, is to be carried out within the limits of Islamic law, as determined by the Guardian Council and the leader. The executive is to be headed by a president elected by universal suffrage, and a cabinet headed by a prime minister, all responsible to parliament, but also to the leader. The 1989 amendments abolished the office of prime minister and assigned his functions to the president, who assumed responsibility for forming a cabinet of ministers and having it approved by parliament. The judiciary was to form a separate and independent authority under a head of the judiciary (in the 1989 constitution), appointed by the leader, and serving a five-year term (Ehteshami 1995:40–41). This chief justice would then appoint the president of the Supreme Constitutional Court and the public prosecutor-general.

The effect of these arrangements is to create a duality of executive power: the leader and the president, each with a set of institutions and authorities. The leader has more powers and controls more institutions: he is commander in chief of the armed forces and appoints the chief justice, which gives him some control over the supposedly independent judiciary. As a supreme *mujtahid*, he also has almost arbitrary powers of direction over policy and law. While Khomeini held that position, he combined it with the charisma of the father of the Revolution and of being 'the imam', with the ambiguity of association with the Hidden Imam (explicitly denied, but acquiescing in the association). As such, any president or prime minister was in the shadow of this power. His successor, Khamene'i, by contrast, is a cleric of middle standing with little charisma. As such he becomes a politician like any other, and the aura of the leader has to be buttressed by institutional and forceful props. Another important structural factor in the politics of the Republic has been the multiplicity of centres of power following the different magnates and factions of the clerical establishment, entrenched in government departments, armed forces and the charitable foundations (*bonyad*), which control a large part of the economy. The role of these factors in the post-Khomeini politics will be explored further below with respect to the politics of law and justice.

The Shari'a

The codification of law and the rule by the courts in accordance with the codes have remained features of the law of the Islamic Republic. That is to say, the institution of the *shari'a* as the major part of the legal system did not explicitly include the restoration of the form of law as jurists' law or of *shari'a*-court procedures. However, there remained a tension, in some elements of the constitution as well as in the structure and procedure of the courts, between these elements of modernity and traditional forms. We shall see that these latter forms are arbitrarily and selectively followed in recent times in response to political contingencies. Article 167 of the constitution states that, in the absence of a clear written code to cover the matter in hand, judges must reach judgements in accordance with their *ijtihad* or follow authorities which they recognize and accept. The authority which is most explicitly followed is that of Khomeini's books on *fiqh*, and in particular *Tahrir al-Vasila* (Schirazi 1997:68). One report of the UN Commission on Human Rights expressed concern that 'It was reported that many sentences have been delivered only on the basis of fatwa and authoritative Islamic sources, ancient usage, precedent or doctrine, without due consideration to positive and codified law' (A/49/514 October 1994:48). In criminal law, witness testimony and confessions seem to be the predominant forms of evidence required and accepted. The prominent part played by the courts in political repression reinforces the tendency of the courts to eclectic application of whatever comes to hand. I shall expand on this theme in discussions that follow.

The Court System

We have seen that at first a Supreme Judicial Council was appointed by the leader – later, in 1989, changed to the office of the chief justice. This office has the ultimate authority in the appointment, promotion, suspension and dismissal of judges. The chief justice is answerable only to the ruling *faqih*. The court system which he administers divides courts into the following categories.

The Supreme Constitutional Court is charged with supervising the proper application of the law in lower courts, and for consistency of judgements. It can also act as a court of appeal for serious cases judged by lower courts. In practice, appeals are seldom considered or granted. Which seems to reflect the traditional *shari'a* absence of appeals, as well as the Shi'i principle of autonomy of judgement of each *mujtahid*, which we noted above.

General Courts (*'umumi*) judge in civil and criminal cases. In the criminal section these courts are divided into first- and second-class categories, depending on the gravity of the offence and the range of punishments.

Revolutionary Courts are political courts, first instituted in the early days of the Revolution as a temporary measure to deal speedily with counter-revolutionary offences and the offenders from the *ancien régime*. Subsequently they became a permanent fixture of the Republic, dealing with a range of offences, including crimes against state security, drug offences, economic crimes of embezzlement, hoarding and profiteering. It also deals with a catch-all category of *mohareb ba khudah*, 'warring against God', used to define political and religious opposition. This will be further discussed below. Many of these offences are not specified by law, in that it is not clear in the legislation what acts precisely constitute the infractions. These matters are, then, left largely to the judge's arbitrary discretion.

The Special Court for the Clergy was instituted in 1987 for trying dissident and oppositional members of the clergy. It consists of a jury of senior clerics and does not seem to operate under any specific codified laws. It has come to prominence in recent political struggles.

The Press Court is another political court aimed at muzzling the press, and operating without clear legal mandate.

Special Civil Courts and Family Courts will be fully discussed in the section on family law.

Court procedure seems to vary with the category of the court (see family courts below) as well as with changes over time, not always authorized by legislation. The constitution and the law provide for the right of defendants to employ lawyers of their choice, and for guarantees to the independence and security of these lawyers through an independent professional association. UN International Human Rights and Amnesty Reports repeatedly express concern about the absence or weakness of these provisions in actual practice.[11] A UN report of 1993 laments the fact that a bill approved by the Council for Determining the Interests of the System (Expediency Council, more below) refers to the right of any Muslim to appoint an agent (*vakil*) who need not be legally qualified or a professional lawyer (Commission on Human Rights E\CN.4/1993/41:126). This designation and procedure, as we have seen, was a feature of *shariʿa* courts historically. Successive UN reports express concern on the weakness and subservience of the Bar Association, and the intimidation and persecution of lawyers of political defendants.

A public prosecutor was appointed in the 1980s, indicating, presumably, that court procedure included the modern adversarial elements of having a prosecutor and a lawyer. In 1994, however, in a reform of Revolutionary and General Courts, the functions of investigator, prosecutor and judge were all combined in the judge (Amnesty International: MDE 13/045/2001). This is a clear compromise of the impartiality of the judge, and a constant theme of concern in reports of international human-rights organizations. This is another aspect of the reversion of the Iranian court system to the traditional *shariʿa* mode of procedure, in which the *qadi* assumed all these functions. A more recent UN report indicates that its concerns on this matter are shared by the current head of the judiciary, who had promised reform. A UN report dated August 2001 states that the re-establishment of the procuracy had been approved by the *majlis* judicial affairs commission in June of that year. However, the establishment of the procuracy was rejected by the Guardian Council in December.

The administration of justice, court procedure, the independence of the judiciary and the autonomy of the legal profession all continue to be issues of concern and debate in Iran between reformists and conservatives (more below), as well as for the international human-rights organizations.

Legislation

The basic conceptual and institutional problem facing the Islamic government with regard to the *shari'a* is that, historically, it has operated primarily as private law, and its historical location was in non-centralized religious institutions in which the judgement of individual *mujtahids* was autonomous and final, not subject to appeal. Cases were brought to *shari'a* courts by private parties, and there was no public prosecuting authority in that sphere. The implicit project of the Islamic Republic was to develop the *shari'a* into public law, capable of accommodating the exigencies of public policy, and to codify and centralize it as state law, much like earlier developments in the Sunni world.

In the early years of the Republic, until 1982 or 1983, the Islamic government's commitment to implementing the *shari'a* remained largely theoretical. The obvious basic provisions which symbolically distinguished an Islamic regime from its predecessor, such as banning alcohol and bars, forcing the veil on women and segregating the sexes in public places, were immediately implemented. Significantly, however, the earlier (1960s) opposition by Khomeini and the clergy to voting rights for women as contrary to the *shari'a* was discarded. Similarly, long-standing rulings forbidding or restricting consumption of television and cinema, games such as chess and caviar (because the sturgeon is a *makrouh*, detested, fish) were all quickly reversed. Banks continued to operate with interest calculations till 1982, after which they had to disguise interest under other categories and procedures.

In general, much of the legislative heritage from the *ancien régime* was maintained. To do otherwise would have led to a legal vacuum. Meanwhile new laws for a vast range of provisions were enacted. In any case, as Schirazi (1997: 161–74) shows, there was much political manoeuvring between Khomeini as the leader, the National Assembly, the Supreme Constitutional Court and the Guardian Council. This latter remained ever jealous of its powers and spheres of competence and control, and refused to allow procedures by which the courts could decide on the compatibility of existing laws with the *shari'a*. In order for the council to rule, however, the proposed legislation had to be referred from the assembly, and could, therefore, only apply to new legislation. Decisions on Islamicity of laws got bogged down in these manoeuvres, which left many of the old laws in operation.

New legislation, first by decree of the Revolutionary Council, then by the *majlis*, was largely non-relevant to the *shari'a*. Schirazi (1997:171) calculates 1022 bills approved by the Revolutionary Council and 1383 bills passed by successive parliaments till 1995. Despite careful scrutiny, the Guardian Council, with few exceptions, did not establish any relationship between these bills and the *shari'a*. He concludes: 'For the new legislation regulates social [...] relationships which are foreign to the mercantile, agricultural or nomadic societies in which the *shari'a* came to exist' (Schirazi 1997:171).

> The absence of the shari'a from much legislation was felt by some leading clergy as an embarrassment which had to be addressed. Ayatollah Montazeri declared that these provisions followed the shar' injunction, 'Regulate your affairs', and in so far as these regulations are approved by the Guardian Council, then they become Islamic. In effect, all legislation by the Islamic government becomes by definition Islamic! [Schirazi 1997:171–72]

Some issues, however, were the subject of extensive conflict and debate with reference to the *shari'a*, and a consideration of these will be especially pertinent to our concerns. These issues were to do with questions of the *shari'a* protection of private property as against public policy dictating state controls and appropriations. This applied to urban land in relation to public housing and urban planning, and agrarian land reforms. Land reforms had already been enacted by the shah in the early 1960s, and provisions for state control of urban land were also in effect. Another issue was that of laws and regulations regarding the labour contract, pay, conditions of work and rights of workers. The conservative *shari'a* position was that the labour contract was entirely a matter for the contracting parties, and that public authority had no right to intervene. That is to say, it was an assertion that contracts are private and not matters of public policy.

The context for these conflicts is the radical commitment and rhetoric of the Revolution: the populist appeal to the masses, the slogans regarding the protection of *mustazefin* (the oppressed), the denunciation of capitalism ('Neither East nor West, only Islamic Revolution'). Many revolutionary mollas, most notably Ayatollahs Beheshti, Taleqani and Montazeri, were committed to statist planning and redistribution, on the model of the then prevalent Third-Worldist state socialism, such as that of the Nasirist state. The radicals of the Revolution were vociferous in their advocacy of nationalization of the main sources of wealth, including foreign trade. At the same time, the constitution empowered some of the most conservative elements in the religious establishment to exercise a power of veto on legislation in these directions. A committee of high-ranking revolutionary *ulama* drafted a land reform bill for the Revolutionary Council in 1979 (the most prominent, Taleqani and Beheshti, were to meet an untimely death soon after). Yet, parliamentary bills to that effect were repeatedly vetoed by the Guardian Council throughout the 1980s, on the grounds that the *shari'a* holds the private property of Muslims to be sacred, and any attempts at expropriation or redistribution would clearly be illegitimate. Many clerics, in and out of parliament, however, were advocating state interventions. What, then, were their grounds in legal argument?

The main grounds for advocating state appropriations were that of *zarurat*, necessity or emergency. It was argued that the needs of the Muslim people for housing and urban planning constituted an emergency, which, according to the Quran, justified the suspension of ordinances. Another argument was that property acquired under the *taghut*, the anti-God, was, in any case, illegitimate, which would entitle the Islamic government to take it over in the public interest of Muslims. Both these arguments accept the *shari'a* near absolute protection of private property and attempt to get around it in terms of exceptional conditions (Schirazi 1997:175–202). These arguments were consistently rejected by the Guardian Council, which returned bills on these matters passed by parliament in spite of repeated efforts by parliament to compromise and attempt to satisfy the council's objections.

Regarding the Labour Law, regulations of contracts and conditions of labour were enacted in Iran in the 1950s and remained on the statute books at the time of the Revolution. In 1982, a conservative Minister of Labour, Tavakkoli, introduced a draft bill to parliament with the intention of making labour law conform to the *shari'a*. This consisted in the conception of the labour contract as a form of hire or rent, by which the employer agreed to pay the worker a certain sum for specified work. Pay, work hours, vacations, duration of contract, dismissal and so on, were all to be specified in the contract, which would be an entirely bilateral contract between the parties in which a third party, such as the state, had no business. The draft bill, therefore, only made provision for state intervention to ensure safety and hygiene at work, and in exceptional circumstances determine minimum wage by order of the minister.

This proposal aroused strong opposition from labour leaders and their supporters on the left in and out of parliament, and the bill was abandoned. It became imperative then to introduce 'Islamic' labour laws which would protect the workers. Throughout the 1980s reformers were faced with the dilemma of how to justify, in *shari'a* terms, the intervention of the state in the labour contract, and how to make it acceptable to the Guardian Council. The favoured formula was to include the state in the contract by virtue of the services it rendered to employers, such as energy, raw materials, infrastructural facilities, foreign exchange, bank credits and so on. The state could then be a party to the labour contract in requiring the employer to observe its ordinances regarding employment conditions in return for the provision of services. At the appeal of the government, Khomeini himself issued a *fatva* (*fatwa*) in 1985 approving this formula (and contrary to his earlier judgements on the labour contract in his writings on *fiqh*) (Schirazi 1997:210–11). In spite of this authoritative support the Guardian Council, ever jealous of the powers of the state, prevaricated. Ultimately, Khomeini's declaration in 1988 (see *infra*) which, in effect, granted the Islamic government absolute powers to determine policy regardless of *shari'a* provisions, allowed the Labour Law to go ahead with few modifications imposed in 1990 by the newly formed Expediency Council (see *infra*). Schirazi concludes: 'The Labour Law of the Islamic Republic which finally emerged from this lengthy process has many points in common with the old, non-Islamic, law of 1958 as well as with the labour laws of other countries' (Schirazi 1997:214).

Family Law

The Family Protection Law of 1967 introduced radical reforms to previous, largely *shari'a*-based legislation on personal status. The reforms were further extended in 1975. Minimum age at marriage was fixed at 18 years for females and 20 years for males. All divorces had to be decided by courts, and the husband's right to unilateral divorce was revoked; women could equally petition for divorce; divorced women were entitled to maintenance; the custody of children was to be decided by the court; the right of men to multiple wives was ended. These laws were administered by Family Protection Courts, presided over by judges trained in modern law schools, and following the procedures of modern courts, with lawyers representing the parties (Mir-Hosseini 2000b: 24–25). The legislators were careful to retain an element of *shari'a* legitimation by writing these conditions into the standard and obligatory marriage contract (Mir-Hosseini 2000b:55), a device which was to be used later by the Islamic regime. Most *ulama* saw this legislation as a flagrant departure from the *shari'a*, and Khomeini condemned it as such, declaring divorce under its provisions void (Mir-Hosseini 2000b:55; Schirazi 1997:216).

The triumphant clergy declared this legislation void after the establishment of the Islamic Republic, and proceeded to rule in accordance with Shi'i *fiqh*. The Family Protection Courts continued to operate for some months after the Revolution, and were then replaced by Special Civil Courts dealing with all familial disputes. These courts, which continued to operate until 1994 (see *infra*), were special in that they operated outside the law of evidence and procedure of the ordinary civil courts, and were presided over by religious judges. The judge summoned the parties to his chambers, listened to their respective cases, then engaged in lengthy discussions and probing with them, partly to ascertain the facts of the case, partly in attempts at reconciliation, and finally rendered his judgement. This was in line with the procedure and the ethos of traditional *shari'a* courts.

The repeal of the Family Protection Law restored the earlier (pre-1967) provisions of the civil code based on Shi'i *fiqh*. However, many elements of the reform were reintroduced, partly through amendments, but mainly through the new marriage contract: these are primarily to do with the right to divorce and its consequences. The husband's right, enshrined in the old civil code, to repudiate his wife at will, is restricted in the 1979 act: if he does not have the wife's agreement to the divorce he must petition the court and make a case for the divorce. This is only granted after the failure of mediation initiated by the judge (Mir-Hosseini 2000b:55–56). The 1982 official marriage contract contains two crucial provisions in favour of the wife regarding divorce. The first allows a wife divorced through no fault of her own to claim up to half the wealth accumulated by her husband over the course of their marriage. The second allows a wife to petition the court herself to divorce if she can establish one of a number of conditions, such as the failure of the husband to support her, his insanity, drug addiction, conviction and imprisonment, impotence or failure to father a child, bad treatment or repugnant occupation (Mir-Hosseini 2000b:57). The husband's signature is required on each of these clauses in the contract, and he can choose to withhold his signature. Mir-Hosseini, in a study of the operation of the divorce courts in the 1980s, found that in practice the judges were reluctant to grant women's divorce petitions on these grounds, made attempts at reconciliation, drew out the proceedings over long periods of time, until the case was abandoned, or some settlement reached between the parties (Mir-Hosseini 2000b:57–72). Court proceedings, in effect, became arenas of negotiation and manoeuvring between the parties, in which financial consideration of the payment of the dower and other monetary compensations figured prominently. Mir-Hosseini (2000b:58) found no cases of claims to portions of matrimonial wealth by wives. An important factor entering these negotiations was the question of custody of children. This is one aspect in which no element of the previous reforms survived. The law reverted to the *shari'a* provision that children belonged to their father and his kin. The mother retains custody until the age of two for a boy and seven for a girl, and can claim maintenance for the duration. After that the father is entitled to assume custody, and the issue often features in the divorce and monetary negotiations and settlements.

The commitment to the *shari'a* by the rulers of the Islamic Republic did not, then, result in the return to a traditional regime of family law, in the style of Saudi Arabia, Afghanistan under the Taliban or even Pakistan. Many elements of pre-revolutionary reforms were retained or re-enacted. This reflects the influence of many reformist elements within the revolutionary establishment, not least women's lobbies in parliament and government, as well as the general sensibilities and exigencies of a complex society and economy, especially one shaken by popular revolution in which many elements of that society, by no means all religious, participated. The reformist thrust of the 1990s, leading to the election of President Khatami, included further legislative and institutional reforms. Court reforms in 1994 included the abolition of the Special Civil Courts, and the transfer of family matters to the jurisdiction of General Courts, which dealt with all civil and criminal cases, presided over by religious or lay judges. This step led to chaos, and soon family cases were dealt with by specialized courts again. In 1997 legislation was enacted, at the instigation of the Parliamentary Women's Commission, to institute Family Courts. One of the provisions of this law is that judgement should, as far as possible, be passed in consultation with a female legal advisor. An Amendment to Divorce Regulations, passed in 1992, tightened requirements for the registration of divorce, requiring a court certificate, only obtained after a process of arbitration, to be followed even when the couple consented to the divorce. This provision reinstated another element of the rejected pre-revolutionary reforms (Mir-Hosseini 2000b:ix–x). A man can only register a divorce after he has settled all dues to his wife, of dower and maintenance for the *'idda* period. Another law enables the court to allow a woman, if divorced through no fault of her own, to claim monetary compensation for the work she has performed in the marital home, called *ujrat al-mithl*, wages in kind.[12] A law passed in 1997 allows for revaluation of the *mahr*, dower, in line with inflation, thus increasing the cost of divorce for the man (Mir-Hosseini 2000b:x).

Starting from the *shari'a* model and assumptions of marriage, sexuality and gender roles, the legislators of the Islamic Republic have made considerable advances in liberalizing provisions for women within marriage, as we have seen. The central area of these advances are the rules and procedures of divorce: the right to unilateral divorce given to a husband in traditional *fiqh*, and the wife's inability to initiate divorce, except in limited circumstances. This imbalance is ameliorated to a degree, by legislation as well as the framing of the marriage contract, but not eliminated. Courts are reluctant to follow the legislation fully, and judges are liable to present obstacles to women who have initiated divorce. Rules pertaining to financial compensation after divorce seem not to be implemented. One consideration which seriously handicaps women is that of custody of children, on which the law favours the husband, giving him crucial bargaining advantage against a divorced wife. Nevertheless, liberalization has occurred, and pressure continues for further measures. Part of the motive for liberalization comes from realization of policy-makers of the changed circumstances in society, especially with the increasing demands, both by family finances and the national economy for women's work outside the home. Another source of pressure is the increasing importance, activity and political awareness of women. The Revolution brought women onto the political and public stage, and the conservative mollas, hard as they tried, could not send them back to domestic isolation. Women, including those with Islamic credentials, continue to exert pressure for their rights and interests, often against powerful resistance, as we shall see in connection with the ideologies of reform.

Penal Law

The Islamic Republic abolished the penal code of the *ancien régime*, which was derived from European models, and replaced it with an Islamic code. This was accomplished in legislation enacted in 1982 and 1983 culminating in the Law of Islamic Punishments. These codes follow the *shari'a* classification of crimes and punishments into: *hudud*, crimes against God's rules, such as theft, adultery, *qazf* (calumny), intoxication and rebellion against religion and authority. Punishments for these crimes, of death, amputation and lashes, are specified in the Quran, and seemingly leave little discretion to the judge (though, historically, as we saw, jurists and judges found formulations and conditions which allowed them wide discretion). *Qisas* is the law of *tallion* and covers crimes against the person: murder, injury and mutilation. Punishments for these crimes are in the nature of compensation to the victim and his family, who can choose between inflicting a similar loss upon the perpetrator or seeking a monetary compensation, *diya*. This category retains the concept of the private transaction between the parties, only facilitated and enforced by public authority. Finally, *ta'zir* is a residual category of offences not specified in the Quran, and whose punishment was traditionally left to the discretion of the judge. In Iranian law, the *ta'zirat* are specified in law codes, defining the crimes and the punishments. These became the widest category, comprising most of the offences faced by the courts. The punishments under this heading comprise terms of imprisonment, execution and fines, as well as corporal punishments of specified numbers of lashes.[13]

Legislation on *ta'zir* raised a number of interesting conflicts and debates in the 1980s between the *majlis* and the Guardian Council. The issue of the conflict was the right of government to institute penal codes which are binding on court decisions, as such depriving the *shari'a*-given right of the judge to use his own discretion to judge each case on its particularities. That is to say, the Guardian Council was expressing the *shari'a* tradition's resistance to codification in an area in which the rules which precluded codification were clear and explicit. The principle of fixed penalties was passed by parliament in 1983, ostensibly for a trial period of five years, somehow bypassing the Guardian Council, which only expressed its extensive objections subsequently. On the expiry of the five years, the council objected to additions to this law, such as the specified penalties for fraud, embezzlement and bribery. Its grounds were that interfering with a judge's discretion, and fixing penalties which exceed the *hudud*, was contrary to the *shari'a* (Schirazi 1997:224–26). The resolution to these conflicts only came in 1996 when the Islamic Penal Code was finally approved.

It is difficult to ascertain the scope and manner of application of the penal codes in the courts. The picture is complicated by political considerations.

Political offences, mostly in Revolutionary Courts, are often framed in terms of the penal law, and severe punishments are applied. However, this is not the only effect of the political. There are episodes in which corporal punishments are applied, sometimes in public, just to underline the power and Islamic nature of the courts when political challenges are being posed to the religious authorities and the judiciary in the wider political field. It is difficult to find information on how 'ordinary' cases are judged 'normally'.

Most information on the application of penal laws in Iran comes from reports of the human-rights organizations such as the UN Commission on Human Rights and Amnesty International. A constant theme in these reports is the difficulty of obtaining detailed information and statistics on the frequency of application of various penalties. One UN reporter quotes the response of Ayatollah Yazdi, head of the judiciary until 1999, to his questions on this issue. Yazdi states that many conditions had to be met before the corporal punishments could be carried out, and that in his six years in office he knew of only two or three proposals for amputation. He also says that he had authority, which he often used, to intervene in cases of *qisas* to press the complainant to accept financial settlement (UN Report E/CN.4/1996/59:42). Other observers have remarked on the rarity of application of penalties of amputation. There seems to be no such restraint, however, when it comes to the death penalty, including stoning to death of adulterers (mostly women) and homosexuals, as well as beatings in specified numbers of lashes. The UN Special Representative was informed that under the penal law the death penalty could be applied for the following offences: spreading corruption on earth, *mofsed* (primarily political offences), assassination, armed robbery, kidnap, rape, adultery or incest, coerced sexual relations of a non-Muslim man with a Muslim woman, sodomy, apostasy (apparently not specified in the law codes, but decided on the basis of *shari'a* authorization of *ijtihad* by the judge), drug-trafficking and armed mischief among the people. Murder and injury, as we saw, come under the law of retribution, in accordance with which execution or amputation are at the discretion of victims or their families, who may settle instead for monetary compensation. In a law of 1995 the death penalty was made applicable to additional crimes: attempts against the security of the state, outrage against high-ranking officials, and insults to the memory of Imam Khomeini and against the leader of the Republic (UN Report E/CN.4/1996/59:44–45). These are vague categories which give wide discretion to police and judges in categorizing offences. Regarding stoning for adultery, UN reporters have difficulty ascertaining numbers, but a 1998 report states that, based on press accounts, there seems to be a substantial number of applications, spread through the country, and that each case had been endorsed by the Supreme Court, so they cannot be regarded as random excesses (UN Report E/CN.4/1998/59:21).

Given the high level of proof, in the form of number of direct witnesses to the offences, demanded by the *shari'a* rules, the police and judges have to rely predominantly on confessions, mostly coerced through systematic use of torture. This is sometimes supervised by judges in their capacity as investigators.

THE JUDICIARY, THE LAW AND THE POLITICS OF THE REPUBLIC

The Shari'a *and the Exigencies of the Islamic Republic*

We have seen how government policy and legislation on diverse matters came into conflict with the Guardian Council as the enforcers of conformity with the *shari'a*. Ultimately, Khomeini was moved by representations from pragmatic politicians close to him (reportedly, Ayatollah Hashemi Rafsanjani, later to become president) to broadcast a ruling which, in effect, liberated government decisions and policies from the limits of the *shari'a*, employing the same concept of *maslaha* or utility as the Sunni reformers we examined in the previous chapters.

In January 1988, in a letter to President Khamene'i commenting on a speech by the latter, Khomeini declared that the Islamic state is a 'branch of the absolute trusteeship of the Prophet... and constitutes one of the primary ordinances of Islam which has precedence over all other derived ordinances such as prayer, fasting and the pilgrimage' (Schirazi 1997:213). This was a clear and explicit empowerment of the state freely to pursue its legislation and policy-making in the belief that the Muslim ruler as an ordinance of God stands above all other divine ordinances, and could abrogate even the most basic of rules if it was judged to be in the interest of the Muslim people and their state.

This ruling was immediately given institutional effect in the creation, at Khomeini's instigation, of the Council for the Assessment of the Interests (*maslaha*) of the System (*nizam*), commonly designated the Expediency Council. It was given wide powers, not only to resolve matters of dispute between parliament and the Guardian Council in the light of the interests of the Islamic regime, but also to take initiatives in legislation. Its membership consists of the Guardian Council plus members nominated by parliament and the president. Within this arrangement the Guardian Council constituted a minority, and decisions are reached by majority voting. Since its inception this council has been a powerful influence on legislation, and has in some instances acted as the legislative body. After the presidential election in 1997, the outgoing President Rafsanjani became president of the Interest Council, making it his institutional power base, and bringing his considerable political skills and wide influence to this body.

It is interesting to note here that the term used to designate this council is *maslaha*. We have encountered this concept before and noted its widespread use by Sunni reformers as the cornerstone of *ijtihad*, in terms of which the *shari'a* provisions can be brought into conformity with modern conditions and sensibilities. We have also noted the criticism that this concept can lead to arbitrary deductions, not subject to any rigorous methodology of derivation from the sacred sources. The concept of *maslaha* did not have a systematic standing in Shi'i *fiqh*, yet it came to the rescue in much the same way as it did for the Sunni reformers: to make *shari'a* provisions more malleable for modern adaptations or outright evasion.

Khomeini's ruling grants unlimited discretion to the Islamic government, but, it is important to note, it does not extend this permissiveness with regard to the law to any other quarter. The authorities, then, can suppress dissidence and reform in the name of strict adherence to the *shari'a*, while they have licence to revoke or suspend any of its provisions.

The Judiciary

The subordination of the judiciary and the law to political considerations is a common feature of many (perhaps most) regimes in the modern world, and especially common in the authoritarian regimes of the Middle East. Exceptional courts operating special security or emergency laws are common, and in this sense the Egyptian State Security Courts and the Iranian Revolutionary Courts are similar. What makes Iran exceptional is the way these features are related to the peculiarly bifurcated nature of executive power and the multiplicity of institutional centres of power. The use of Islamic rhetoric and of practices derived from the *shari'a* tradition also distinguish the Iranian case.

The Iranian political field has been particularly lively since the election of Khatami as president in 1997. A reformist and relatively liberal president was thus pitched against the clerical establishment headed by the leader, Khamene'i, and all the institutions under his control, notably the judiciary. This conflict was reinforced in 1999 with the election of a new *majlis*, with a predominant reformist majority, largely in sympathy with the president. The line of division of authorities, then, fitted in neatly with the two principles of sovereignty in the constitution of the Republic: that of the ruling *faqih*, in accordance with the principle of *velayet-e faqih*, as against the authority of elected representatives of the people. Clearly, the 'will of the people', assumed by Khomeini and the formulae of the constitution to accord with the theocratic authority of the *faqih*, had in fact fallen out with clerics, frustrated by their arbitrariness, repression, corruption and incompetence. Khatami, though himself a cleric, and careful to adhere to an Islamic vocabulary, advocates the rule of law and respect for rights (implying their weakness in the Republic), the empowering of civil society, as well as economic and other policy reforms. Though he himself avoids reference or explicit questioning of *velayet-e faqih*, this can be read into his positions, and is articulated by some of his followers. These stances of the presidency and the legislature have opened the way for some degree of freedom of expression and organization, manifested in political, cultural and religious fields. In particular, after the 1997 presidential election, a large number of newspapers and magazines appeared, many with outspoken support for the reformist agenda, highly critical of the clerics and the leadership, and carrying reports and exposes of corruption, repression and incompetence. This included a high-profile case of the involvement of high-ranking security officers in the assassination of secular intellectuals. Many sectors of the population were emboldened to defy the repressive moralization of public spaces and impositions on women and youths. Dissident clerics and Islamic intellectuals came on the scene with novel interpretations and formulations of religious and legal discourses favouring liberalization – especially on family issues and women (see *infra*). These challenges to theocratic authority and to the power and interests of clerical establishments, elicited fierce responses from the leader and his followers. The judiciary play a central role in the repressive responses of the clergy. The reformist press which came to prominence after Khatami's election was ruthlessly pursued by the courts on a variety of improvised charges, the publications banned and the journalists imprisoned. The head of the judiciary and the judges of the Supreme Court are appointed by the leader and are responsible to him. As such they are centres of clerical authority, protecting its interests against these challenges. We saw how penal law and court procedure play an important part in assimilating political offences to vague and elastic criminal categories. The Revolutionary Courts, now a permanent feature, operate with exceptional powers. To these were added specialist Press Courts and a court to try dissident clerics. Court procedure in all the courts seem to have abandoned guarantees written into the constitution regarding the role of prosecutors, investigators and lawyers, with judges assuming all these functions. In this respect, they have the sanction of traditional *shari'a* models of procedure. These also give the judge wide latitude in resorting to his own *ijtihad* and choice of religious authority to follow, which tends to bypass the written law codes. That is to say, the arbitrariness of repressive courts which are commonly found in the region and elsewhere, are here reinforced by Islamic models and principles of justice, derived from traditional practices. At the time of writing, these are central issues in the conflicts between the reformist and the theocratic sides of the Iranian government, as well as of the political fields. The leader and the clerics dominating the institutions under him have by far the most powerful positions, and ones they use effectively to repress opposition. Yet the existence of rival centres of power, however weak, have emboldened wide sectors of opinion to persist in their opposition and challenge.

Law and Shari'a *in the Ideologies of Reform*

The Revolution and the Islamic Republic, while empowering the mollas, their discourses and rules, over government and society, also posed unprecedented challenges to them. While the clerics were excluded from state and legislative powers and functions, they could afford to be theoretical, and to promulgate rules which believers can follow or not depending on their consciences and circumstances. In any case, the circle of believers and emulators was limited, and perhaps shrinking. When assuming the power of government, however, they had to face the challenges and the pressures emanating from a variety of sources. 'The convergence of religious and political authority has opened a new door from within, which no longer can be closed' (Mir-Hosseini 2000a:273).

The most important challenge and notable response was that of the role of the *shari'a* in government policy and legislation. We have seen how *shari'a* rules and judgements, as defined by the Guardian Council, impeded government policy and legislation, and attempts to surmount these obstacles by loose reasoning in terms of *zururat* and *maslaha* became cumbersome. Ultimately Khomeini, with his claim to almost absolute religious authority, issued his momentous ruling in 1988 in which he exempted the Islamic government from provisions of religious law by investing it with the authority of the Prophet. This step was a further empowerment of the government and the ruling clergy and as such had the potential for greater authoritarian and arbitrary powers. These, however, faced challenges from below.

While the conservative and authoritarian government clerics asserted their wide authority, many of their shrewder colleagues perceived and reacted to these challenges. Take gender issues, for instance. The Revolution mobilized women in street demonstrations and general political activism in the name of Islam. It empowered them through participation in elections, and even in being elected to parliament, in itself a major transformation from clerical positions of the 1960s when women's suffrage was a *casus belli* for Khomeini and others, and restoring their political status to many of the rights enjoyed under the *ancien régime*. They could not then be ordered back into the home and the kitchen without major resentments and oppositions. Women from prominent clerical and political families, including Khomeini's own daughter, but most notably Fa'ezeh Rafsanjani, daughter of Hashemi, became active in the political and cultural fields (such as sport for Fa'ezeh) and championed women's presence and participation in these fields. Successive reforms had made it possible for women to be appointed as junior judges in family courts and as ministers (one or two), and there was one vice-president of the Republic (though not nominated for president) (Mir-Hosseini 2000b:274–75). Another structural consideration was one of economics: women were needed in the job market, and most families needed the wages of a working mother to make ends meet. Confining women to the home was a luxury which the Islamic Republic could not afford. The liberal and reform measures were often opposed, and there were many setbacks, and women are still subject to draconian restrictions, prominent among which is the imposed *hejab*, which has become emblematic of the Islamic Republic, and which no-one dares challenge. But the overall trend is towards some amelioration of traditional *shari'a* rules in favour of women.

The duality of executive power, between leadership and presidency, as well as the elected legislature, added to the multiplicity of centres of power in the clerical-state institutions and foundations, have generated a degree of latitude in political and cultural expressions. The balance of power strongly favours the leader and the state clerics, but the fact that they find it necessary to clamp down periodically on critical expressions in the press shows that though they can obstruct and repress these expressions, they cannot stop them altogether. Elections for the presidency and the *majlis* show the overwhelming popular support for the reformist positions, and express widespread discontent and frustration, especially among women and the young, with the Islamic regime. The wiser heads among the state clerics realize that you cannot react to these trends with repression alone, and that an amelioration of the rigours of the regime is in order.

In response to all these factors, new currents of religious and political thought contend for attention and support, not least in the hub of clerical thought and authority, the city of Qom. The elevation of its *madrasas* to centres of religious and political authority, required to pronounce on law and policy, has opened up the city to the currents of argument and debate, and opened up some of its quarters to new ideas and methods. A new concept in the *fiqh* circles is that of dynamic jurisprudence (*fiqh-e puya*), which is contrasted to *fiqh-e sonnati*, traditional jurisprudence. The latter refers to pre-revolutionary *fiqh*, along traditional lines, while 'dynamic' *fiqh* refers to *fiqh* seeking innovation and reformulation in relation to new circumstances (Mir-Hosseini 2000a:17). Mir-Hosseini divides these reformers into neo-traditionalists and modernists. With respect to gender issues, the first are those who attempt to develop new formulations of *fiqh* to take account of changing position of women in society. They follow in the footsteps of the late Ayatollah Motahhari, a 'modernist' molla who wrote a book advancing new *fiqh* formulations on women.[14] The basis of the argument is the 'naturalization' of *fiqh* prescriptions on family relations, arguing that it follows the biological and natural differences between men and women.

The two sexes are equal in religious worth and value, but different, and complementary to one another, in their rights and obligations. The thrust of their effort is to legitimize women in public life, which has some implications for liberalizing aspects of family law, such as rights of wives to work outside the home and liberal attitudes to divorce and maintenance. However, they retain many of the traditional concepts of gender roles within the family, emphasizing 'balance' and complementarity between them rather than equality. The modernists, on the other hand, are those posing challenges to the *fiqh* tradition and seeking radical innovation in religious thought, in line with the requirements of modern society and in conformity with science and reason. Let us consider the most prominent example of this trend in the figure of Abdulkarim Soroush.[15]

Soroush (b. 1945) is not a cleric: he had a scientific education in pharmacology, followed by postgraduate work (in England) in philosophy of science. He was a student activist in the Islamic movement in opposition to the shah, participated in the Revolution and assumed a leading position in the 'cultural revolution' which followed. From the late 1980s Soroush came to prominence as an Islamic critic of the clerical establishment and the author of challenging ideas on religion, philosophy, law and politics.

A basic theme in Soroush's thought is that *fiqh* is not the only, nor the highest, Islamic science. *Fiqh* and the *shari'a* are central to clerical thinking and claim to authority, and the cornerstone of the Islamic Republic and its ruling principle of *velayet-e faqih*. This centrality of *fiqh*, argues Soroush, has relegated theology, ethics and mysticism to subordinate positions. His attempt to prioritize these aspects, of both 'inner' faith and public religion is a direct challenge to the authority of the *ulama* and the principle of *velayet-e faqih*.

Soroush makes a distinction between religion as such, as divine revelation, eternal and unchangeable, and religious knowledge, which is a human product, and as such variable and relative to the understanding of particular societies and historical periods. In modern society, religious knowledge must relate to science, philosophy and culture. Religious education of the clerics insulates them from these modern currents, and as such they are least qualified to develop the religious thinking on faith and ethics to fit into these modern paradigms. *Fiqh* and law must follow from these new understandings and be open to innovation in their terms in line with the requirements of society and culture, in a symbiosis between reason and revelation. This reasoning diminishes the authority of the *ulama* and opens up religious knowledge to discussion between lay intellectuals of scientist, including social scientists as experts on society, philosophers and religious thinkers, operating in terms of theology and mysticism rather than the mere assertion of rules (Schirazi 1997:281–88).

Soroush's discourses draw on figures and traditions in the history of Islamic thought. His main support for ethics and theology against the primacy of *fiqh* is Ghazzali, the medieval (eleventh-century) author of *Ihya' 'ulum al-din*, the renaissance of the religious sciences, as well as prominent Shi'i and Iranian figures such as Molla Sadra and Molla Mohsen Feiz Kashani (from seventeenth-century Iran). He also draws on themes in poets and mystics, his favourites being Jalal al-Din al-Rumi and his *Mathnawi*, and Hafiz, the revered poet of Iran. His approach to the Quran and the *hadith* of the Prophet and the imams is to subject them to reasoning and deduction relating to the context of revelation and of the *hadith* in question. In a lecture on women, for instance, he subjects some notoriously misogynist pronouncements of the Imam Ali (a most sacred authority for the Shi'a) to scrutiny, pointing out fallacies in his reasoning, as well as engaging in contextual analysis of the conditions which prompted the *hadith*. The result is a thorough historical and social relativism: a *hadith* which presents an argument and reasoning can be subjected to analysis to determine its validity. As to the *hadith* which enunciates general principles and rules: '[t]hese hadiths are "pseudo-universal propositions" (as logicians have it); that is, they reveal the conditions of women of their time. In addition, since what an Imam or a sage says is in line with the society in which he lives, we need a reason to extend it to other epochs' (quoted in Mir-Hosseini 2000a:225). The reasoning required must come from outside the sacred text, in terms of the relation of the *hadith* to modern conditions and thought.

This radical challenge to religious authority ultimately puts into question the very notion of Islamic government, and there are elements in Soroush's pronouncements favouring the separation of religion from politics, in the interest of religion. One consequence of the access of the clerics and their academies to political power has been 'that they now speak the language of power and have abandoned the language of logic' (quoted in Schirazi 1997:284). The participation of religious authority in government power, he argues, brings about the stagnation and ossification of religious thinking and knowledge, which can only be revived in the participation and dialogue with many sectors of society and modern thought. 'Emulation', the key concept of traditional religious authority is, for Soroush, defunct. Addressing students, he proclaimed: 'Your task is firstly to inform the ulama about the serious problems of the day, and secondly to engage in a critical dialogue with them ... As long as you are simply imitators, you will not be able to move the ulama to educate themselves about matters outside the realm of fiqh' (quoted in Schirazi 1997:285). The public are no longer tributaries and imitators of the *ulama*, but their educators: a thorough democratization of religious authority, totally at variance with the founding principles of the Islamic Republic.

While out-and-out secularist advocacy has not been tolerated by the Islamic authorities, criticisms of that authority in Islamic language is possible, though precarious. Soroush's challenge to clerical authority and to *velayet-e faqih* has led to threats and attacks. Frequent attacks on Soroush were made in the Iranian press: he is accused of using the language of the enemy, and to being complicit in conspiracies to undermine the clergy, the academies, the Islamic sciences and the Republic. Some clerics have presented more reasoned refutations of his arguments (Schirazi 1997:288). The attacks did not stop at press denunciations but assumed violent forms. The paramilitary gangs of Ansar Hizbullah, enforcers for the state clergy, started disrupting his lectures and attacking him and his audience in 1995. This was after an article in *Kiyan*, a paper closely associated with his ideas, in which he argued that the clergy function as a guild, with religion as its source of livelihood, which limits its freedom and that of others. This article was widely denounced, and violent attacks upon him in effect prevented Soroush from giving public lectures until 1997, and he spent various periods of time lecturing abroad to Iranian and other audiences in Europe and America. It is significant, however, that despite the attempts to silence Soroush, he has survived and continues to write and lecture to wide audiences.

It is interesting to note the differences between the Iranian Muslim critics, such as Soroush, and the Sunni modernists in Egypt. They both sideline *fiqh*. The Sunnis, however, continue to place the *shari'a* and its application at centre-stage. They resort to a selective reading of the products of the 'sacred history' of early Islam, giving themselves licence for free interpretations following the examples of those holy figures. We have also seen the centrality of the notion of *maslaha* for their permissive formulations. In Iran it is the government itself and the ruling *faqih* who have resorted to this concept, invoking the authority of the Prophet. Soroush, by contrast, demotes *fiqh* in favour of the other Islamic sciences of theology, philosophy and mysticism, and his inspiration is historical figures from the medieval and the early modern periods. Other Iranians, such as the cleric Hojjat ul-Islam Mohsen Sa'idzadeh, who collaborated in Mir-Hosseini's work, and to whose work she devotes a chapter (Mir-Hosseini 2000a:247–72) mined the *fiqh* tradition itself, using its sources and methods to reach startlingly liberal conclusions. These differences may be related to the status of *fiqh* and its institutions in Iran, and its centrality to the Islamic Republic, as well as the different intellectual and educational traditions of Shi'ism, which assigned a greater role to philosophy and mysticism than in the Sunni canon.

CONCLUSION

The Islamic Republic of Iran is a uniquely interesting case study for the present discussion. It is a republic instituted by a popular revolution, culminating in clerical rule precisely on the grounds of their expertise and authority in religious matters, primarily in the legal sciences of *fiqh*. We have seen first how most matters of legislation and administration in a modern state are not pertinent to *shari'a* provisions. In matters central to the *shari'a*, such as property, its provisions are in the form of private law incompatible with the requirements of modern states and societies, and ultimately bypassed. Family matters remain, in Iran, as in most other parts in the region, subject to *shari'a* provisions, but considerably attenuated and modified in line with modern problems and sensibilities, to the extent of the effective restoration of some of the extra-*shari'a* provisions of the 1967 legislation by the *ancien régime*, and in some respects, like 'wages for housework' for divorced women, going further.

In nineteenth-century Iran the religious institutions were separate from the state. The state was decentralized and the high *ulama*, alongside tribal chiefs, aristocrats and other land-owners, constituted autonomous centres of power and social organization. These *ulama* administered and ruled their local communities. This is where the *shari'a* was located and practised, in the private affairs of community. The Constitutional Revolution of 1906 saw the uncertain beginnings of the modern state. In theory, the *ulama*, who were among the leaders of the Revolution, were the guardians of the constitution, and ensured the conformity of legislation to the *shari'a* (although there was no suggestion that the legislation, other than on personal status matters, should be derived from the *shari'a*). Given the abeyance of the constitution for most of the twentieth century, this provision remained theoretical. In practice, Iranian law codes were lifted from European examples with the usual exception of family and personal status law, which was a codification of a reformed version of *shari'a* provisions, as we have seen. The project of the Islamic Republic has been to take the private law of communities and make it state law. We have followed the course of this project and seen that it has largely failed. The failure was officially signalled by Khomeini's 1988 ruling exempting the Islamic government from *shari'a* provisions: as heir of the privileges of the Prophet it could enact its own legislation in the interest of the community and following a *raison d'état*.

Did the Islamic state, then, take over the authorities and functions of the old religious institutions? Clearly not. Many of the high-ranking *mujtahids* in Iran, as well as in Iraq and Lebanon, did not follow Khomeini's revolutionary doctrines, and many expressed reserve, if not outright rejection, of *velayet e-faqih*. Kho'i (d. 1999), Galpangyani (d. 1993) and Marashi-Najafi, to name the most prominent, continued to enjoy authority and revenues from their networks of followers in Iran, Iraq, Lebanon and India, and their successors are perpetuating their functions.[16] The fact that Khamene'i, successor to Khomeini as leader (ruling *faqih*), is a lower-ranking cleric with little authority or charisma, has further widened the gap between the government and religious legitimacy.

A crucial issue in the early days of the Islamic Republic was the question of taxes: were they to be confined to the religiously specified dues of *zakat, khoms* and *jizya*? And if the state was to take over the religious revenues, then the religious institution would have to be merged into the state. Khomeini, who in his pre-revolutionary writing advocated the confinement of taxation to the religiously sanctioned dues, very quickly changed his mind when faced with the fiscal requirements of a state. In effect, the issue was buried, and the *status quo ante* restored: state taxes continue as before, and the *mujtahids* continue to draw *khoms* revenues from their followers. This is yet another, and crucial, indication that the Islamic state, under the constraints and necessities of rule, is increasingly 'secularized', and the religious institutions continue to thrive alongside distinct boundaries from the state. State personnel at the higher levels are predominantly clerics, but are their functions clerical? Increasingly they look like an entrenched interest group clinging on to state power, legitimizing their control in terms of religious formulae, which to many Iranians ring hollow.

CONCLUSION

Calls for the 'return to Islam' and the application of the *shari'a* in the modern world presuppose a historical Muslim society that was ruled by the holy law, only disrupted by colonial incursions and irreligious reforms. We have seen that this view cannot be supported in its entirety. Yes, the *shari'a* has always been an important feature of Muslim societies and governments, but it has been assigned particular niches of operation, mostly in the private matters of the subjects. The sphere of the state, public finance and administration largely bypassed the *shari'a*. As a body of law, the *shari'a* co-existed with customary law, which it sometimes incorporated, as well as the statutes of government promulgated by the rulers. Under the Ottomans the *qadi* of the *shari'a* court was entrusted with the application of these different laws. Even then administrative, police and military tribunals operated side by side with the *qadi* courts, not always with a clear differentiation of jurisdictions. Criminal cases were often heard in these latter, partly because of the high level of evidence required for conviction under the *shari'a*. And contrary to the current image of the *shari'a* and its courts based on its functioning in some modern authoritarian regimes, *shari'a* judges historically tended to be sparing in the application of corporal punishments of amputations and executions. These were undertaken more freely by the rulers.

The *shari'a* always enjoyed ideological resonance as a high, indeed sacred, standard of justice. Rulers claimed legitimacy in its terms, and rivals and rebels employed its rhetoric in indicting unjust or illegitimate rule. Scholars and jurists, the guardians of the *shari'a*, enjoyed high positions of wealth and influence in most periods, often through the patronage of the rulers. Some of the most innovative, such as Ebussu'ud in the court of Suleiman the Magnificent (see Chapter 3) devised formulae by which existing fiscal practices were brought into the ambit of the *shari'a*. This was done not by making these practices conform to the holy law, but by extending the concepts and vocabularies of the law to cover existing practice, thus giving them religious legitimacy and at the same time maintaining the competence of the jurist in their management. The *shariʿa*, then, displayed considerable flexibility over time and place. The insistence in modern pronouncements on its fixed and unvarying nature as the law of God for all time is not supported by an examination of its history and function.

The fate of the *shariʿa* in the legal systems of modern nation-states is a complex matter. Many of the modern states, as we have seen, have adopted or developed law codes which depart from the *shariʿa*. Most of them, however, have based some of their codes, notably on family and personal status, on *shariʿa* sources. Yet even in these instances its codification into state law has radically transformed the *shariʿa* and its logic. We have seen that its incorporation into the state has separated the *shariʿa* from its religious locations, from the books and traditions of *fiqh* and into state manuals, from the custody of the scholars to that of bureaucrats and legislators, from the religious training in the *madrasa* to the modern law faculty, from the judicial procedure of the *qadi* court to modern adversarial court systems. Legislation and judgement are now subject to bureaucratic and political logic and not to the ratio of *fiqh* tradition and method. The judge rules in accordance with law codes, and not the books of *fiqh*. His responsibility is to the state and the law, not to God and his conscience.

We have considered exceptions and resistance to these developments, notably in the case of Saudi Arabia, which has attempted to retain the law in the hands of the scholars and to continue with some of the old procedures. Yet we have also seen (in Chapter 4) the strains that these produce in the modern spheres of the economy and government, and the repeated attempts at bypassing these procedures, and ultimately the pressure for codification. The Islamic Republic of Iran has codified the *shariʿa*, its *raison d'être* as an Islamic state, into modern law and instituted a modern judicial system. But we have seen how the powerful clerical judiciary are attempting to subvert these steps and return to traditional procedures. These would give them greater discretion and arbitrary powers. In Egypt, where there is a great clamour for the application of the *shariʿa*, few of its advocates would wish to reverse codification and modern procedures. Given that many of its advocates are lawyers and bureaucrats, reversion to traditional forms would undercut their training, competence and employment opportunities.

The case of modern Iran, considered in Chapter 6, illustrates the difficulties encountered by a modern government in a complex society in attempting to institute the *shariʿa* as the law of the land. The great bulk of legislation on practical matters of day to day administration and regulation is irrelevant to the *shariʿa*. On matters that are relevant, such as social and welfare policy and family law, the traditional prescriptions of *fiqh* have obstructed policy-making. *Fiqh*, as historically developed, is largely private law regulating inter-personal relations, as we have seen in the case of the labour contract. As such, it cannot easily accommodate public policy, which is essentially about public responsibility and regulation. On family matters and the status of women, the Islamic government started by repealing all the modern reforms undertaken by the *ancien régime* and restoring *shari'a* provisions. Yet they were soon forced by the exigencies and sensibilities of a modern society into restoring many of the repealed elements, but with labels derived from the vocabulary of *fiqh*. It is on birth control and family planning that we see the most dramatic reversal of policy. At the inception of the Republic, Khomeini condemned family planning as un-Islamic and an imperialist conspiracy to limit Muslim populations. The dramatic rise of population numbers in the early 1980s forced a change of policy, restoring family-planning centres and mounting a publicity campaign, with prominently displayed posters showing happy families with two children, one of each. Crucially, however, Khomeini found it necessary to make his momentous pronouncement in 1988 declaring that the Islamic government enjoys the prerogatives of the Prophet in suspending the provisions of the *shari'a* in the public interest.

The application of the *shari'a* in modern states and societies is understood in different ways by the various interested parties. We have seen how both radical Islamists (so-called 'fundamentalists') and liberal reformers tend to jettison the historical traditions of *fiqh* and its logic and methodology in favour of a return to the pristine sacred sources of the Quran and the traditions of the Prophet. Yet the radicals and the conservatives read these sources differently from the liberals. The latter tend to adopt a historical relativism, reading the sources in terms of time and place, asserting that while the Quran is the word of God, God spoke to people in terms which they could understand, which makes the utterances relative to the milieu of their reception. As such, we have to understand the holy text in our own terms, interpreting it in accordance with its spirit and intentions. For the radicals, and conservatives, such relativism is heresy, and those who utter it should be punished as apostates, hence the assassination of the Egyptian Farag Fuda in 1992 and the persecution and exile of Abu-Zayd in the following years (see Chapter 5).

The *shari'a* and the call for its application in the modern world are moved by ideological and political logic and dynamic, based on a number of perspectives which we have considered in Chapters 4, 5 and 6. One perspective is that of social conservatism: the quest for the restoration of patriarchal authority, of order and hierarchy and the moralization of public space and cultural activity. It is the strand which is currently dominant in Egyptian Islamism and among the Iranian conservatives. The *shari'a* then is an expression of this quest for authority. Given the nature and dynamics of a modern economy and society, this is a losing battle. Another dominant and overlapping perspective is that of cultural nationalism and the quest for authenticity. Islam and the *shari'a* in this perspective are the markers of authentic national heritage for Muslims. As the Egyptian jurist said to Dupret (see Chapter 5), the *shari'a* is the essential component of an Islamic civilizational project and the spinal column of that civilization, and without it the whole edifice would collapse, and Muslim society would be no different from Christian or Buddhist. It was colonialism and its aftermath which deprived Muslims from the *shari'a*, and true independence is to restore it. These are common sentiments, and in one form are expressed in the contrast drawn between a totalized Islam with an equally totalized and hostile West, Christian or secular. Western dominance is blamed for all corruption and irreligion in the Muslim world, and for modern cultural products of disapproved literature, film and entertainment. All these are products of a 'cultural invasion' alien to Islam and undermining the fabric of society and civilization. The application of the *shari'a* is seen as a decisive step in halting and reversing these processes, and the restoration of the authenticity of Muslims as a distinct and independent civilization. Even liberals such as Abdullahi An-Na'im (see Chapter 5), while seeking the protection of human rights and democratic values, seeks to do so in terms of the *shari'a*, in the name of authenticity and appeal to the populace.

To return to Iran, the attempt of the authorities to impose these religious and social virtues and to root out Western corruption is proving highly unpopular, especially with a large majority of the population who are young. This resistance, as well as that of intellectuals and artists against censorship and repression, are at the base of the reformist campaign in that country, and its consistent electoral successes. In Egypt the campaign for Islamization, mor-alization and censorship coincides with a deep chauvinism which includes many of the 'secular' intellectuals. It is increasingly directed against a mythical, homogeneous West which is seen as hostile to Islam and the Arabs, politically and culturally. Yet even in this charged atmosphere the 'corruption' seems to continue, especially among the young, orientated as they are to consumer culture and personal liberties.

In the public mind in the West and elsewhere, the hallmarks of the *shari'a* are the few dramatic manifestations of corporal punishments, especially amputations and stoning, the veiling and other restrictions on women, the banning of alcohol and the prohibition on dealing in interest. We have seen that historically these elements were unevenly applied, and the punishments were more likely to be meted out by administrative tribunals than by *shari'a* courts. On interest the scholars showed considerable flexibility, and on occasion con-tracts involving fixed and reasonable rates of interest were recognized in the courts. The drinking of alcohol was and continues to be widespread in Muslim societies, and has given rise to extensive literature of poetry and *belles-lettres*. It is in modern times that political advocacy and the practice of some governments have insisted on the application of these elements, precisely as a marker of Islamicity and distinction from the West, as well as a means of intimidating opponents. It is ironic that the so-called Quranic punishments are described by commentators as 'medieval', when in fact medieval jurists and judges showed great restraint in their application, while modern dictators flaunt them as a sign of religious legitimacy.

Notes on the Text

Notes on Chapter 1

1   Max Weber's formulations of types of rationality and forms of rationalization in the law are contained in his *Economy and Society*. The sections dealing with law are compiled (in English translation) in Max Rheinstein (ed. and annotated) (1954), *Max Weber on Law in Economy and Society*, translated by Edward Shils and Max Rheinstein, New York: Simon and Schuster. Chapter VIII (224–55) is on 'Formal and Substantive Rationalization in the Law (Sacred Laws)', and includes a few pages (237–44) on Islam. This is one of many occasional references to Islam in Weber's work, usually in a comparative context, and with various degrees of accuracy.

2   Weber distinguishes the rationalization of sacred law in such priestly theoretical contexts from the formal rationalization of law in separate, secular contexts. 'Its casuistry, inasmuch as it serves at all practical rather than intellectual needs, is formalistic in the special sense that it must maintain, through reinterpretation, the practical applicability of the traditional, unchangeable, norms to changing needs' (Weber 1954:205). This formulation does describe part of the *fiqh* enterprise, as we shall see. This enterprise, however, also included intellectual pursuits for their own sake, following a logic of theoretical games which it invented.

3   All references and quotes from the Quran, unless otherwise stated, follow Arberry 1964.

4   Mu'tazila or Mu'tazilites were a philosophical school in Abbasid Iraq (Basra and Baghdad), from the eighth to the eleventh centuries, distinguished by a kind of rationalist approach to religion, interpreting revelation and tradition in accordance with notions of justice beyond the literal statements of texts and traditions. As such they were opposed to the literalist subservience to the text. In theology they were the antagonists of Ash'arism, which favoured the traditionalist legalism of *fiqh*. They were the protagonists of the doctrine of the 'createdness of the Quran' which featured so prominently in the Mihna episode with Ibn Hanbal, discussed in Chapter 3. See Watt 1973, where discussions of different aspects of Mu'tazilite ideas are dispersed in the text.

5   There is a prevalent view that philosophy was marginalized and persecuted by religious authority and that little significant philosophical contributions were made after the great Ibn Sina (Avicenna) (d. 1037). This view is convincingly challenged by Dimitri Gutas (2002), who shows the vitality of Arabic philosophy ('Arabic' to distinguish it from 'Islamic') into the later middle ages, then in Ottoman times.

6   Tim Mitchell (1988:151) quotes this example from Richard Bulliet (1972), *The Patricians of Nishapur: A Study in Medieval Islamic Social History*, Cambridge: Cambridge University Press: 45–57.

7   The Khawarij, or Kharijites, are a sect which developed in early Islam at the time of the war between Ali and Mu'awiya in 657, who refused the authority of the caliphs in favour of a community ruled in accordance with the scriptures.

8   Van den Berg, the translator into French, did not render a literal translation, but to make the text more intelligible, paraphrased and drew upon two sixteenth-century commentaries on the *Minhaj, Tohfat al-Mohtaj* and *Nihayat al-Mohtaj*. These multiple translations and paraphrasing have, no doubt, effected many mutations of the original. It serves here merely as an illustration of themes and contents.

Notes on Chapter 2

1   See Tyan 1960.

2   Mawardi (d.1058) is the foremost theoretician of 'Sunni realism' in developing *shari'a* concepts and vocabularies to cover the institutions and acts of power. His book, *Al-Ahkam al-Sultaniya, the Statutes of Government,* is 'a treatise composed at the request of the authorities to defend the legitimacy of the Abbasid caliphate and restore, as far as possible, its prestige and power'; H. Laoust (1968), 'La pensée et l'action politique de al-Mawardi, 947–1058', *Revue d'Etudes Islamiques* XXXVI:11–12. See Hanna Mikhail (1995), *Politics and Revelation: Mawardi and After*, Edinburgh: Edinburgh University Press. Further discussion in Chapter 3.

3   The *muhtasib* is the functionary charged with the inspection and regulation of markets, guilds and professions, as well as supervising public morality. See *infra*.

4   On the Shurta, see Tyan 1960:567–616. The term 'Shurta' continued to be in use in some countries, for example Iraq, until the first half of the twentieth century, later substituted with '*amn*', security.

5   We shall see in Chapter 5 that Islamist lawyers in Egypt have recently resorted to the concept of *hisba* to bring cases against individuals accused of deviating from the correct religion, as in the case against Abu-Zayd, when Islamists petitioned the court to divorce him from his Muslim wife on the grounds of his apostasy.

6   The account of Ottoman judicial institutions draws on Gibb and Bowen 1950/57 II.

7   For a study of the urban politics of *waqf*, see Richard van Leeuwen (1999), *Waqfs and Urban Structures: the Case of Ottoman Damascus*, Leiden: Brill.

8   The editor (Max Rheinstein) of *Max Weber on Law in Economy and Society* (1954), explains the term '*khadi* justice' as used by Weber as 'the administration of justice which is orientated not to fixed rules of a formally rational law but at the ethical, religious, political or otherwise expediential postulates of a substantively rational law':213 fn. 48.

Notes on Chapter 3

1   Crone and Hinds (1986) is a lively and controversial treatment of the subject, and particularly suitable for bringing out the issues of the articulation of religion, legislation and political authority. See also Watt 1973:82–85; Hawting 1986:13.

2   Al-Mawardi, the tenth-century jurist who wrote an authoritative treatise on the statute of government, explicitly prohibits the use of the term *khalifat Allah* as illegal and impious, see Gibb 1962a:158.

3   Watt (1973) cites Umayyad authors and poets with pronouncements making their caliphs the pillars of religion and the intermediaries between God and his worshippers, such as: 'We have found the sons of Marwan pillars of our religion, as the earth has mountains for its pillars', and 'were it not for the caliph and the Quran which he recites, the people had no judgements established for them and no communal worship':83.

4   This is a formative episode in early Muslim history, the battle of Siffin in 657 between Ali and Mu'awiya. The battle culminated in agreement on adjudication in accordance with the Quran as to the rights of each party, which resulted in an ambiguous verdict favouring Mu'awiya and establishing the Umayyad dynasty (Watt 1973: 12–14). This episode was to give rise later to the schism between Sunnis and Shi'is, but many among the Sunnis (and especially some Sufi orders) continued to view the triumph of Mu'awiya as one for worldly kingship as against the righteous rule of the first Muslims, Al-Rashidun (the rightly guided) caliphs. Ali and his descendants continue to enjoy a kind of sanctity, and not just among the Shi'a.

5   See Hawting 1986:11–20, 123–28.

6   The Shi'a are the Muslim sects who maintained the sanctity of the lineage of Ali and their right to the imamate, the leadership, of the Muslim community. Their charisma is God-given, and as such they are privileged interpreters of God's commands. The Imami or Ithna'ashari (Twelver) Shi'a are the mainstream grouping in Iran, Iraq, Lebanon and India, who trace a succession of 12 descendants from Ali, culminating in the twelfth Imam al-Mahdi, who 'disappeared' in 873, depriving the community from his direct guidance though he remains *Imamul-Zaman*, the imam of all time, until his return in Messianic time. Other sects, such as the Zaydis and the Ismailis, split off at various times over the line of succession, and continue to enjoy the guidance of living imams.

7   This view is elaborated by Crone in her *Slaves on Horses* (1980). It is also taken up by Ernest Gellner in his various writings on Muslim society (Gellner 1983; 1992). For a critical account see Zubaida 1995. I shall return to these questions at the conclusion of this chapter.

8   On Ghazzali, see Watt 1963.

9   On the rise and history of the Abbasids, see Hugh Kennedy (1981), *The Early Abbasid Caliphate: A Political History*, and Kennedy (1986), *The Prophet and the Age of Caliphates*, Chapters 5–8.

10   On Kharijite thought, see Watt 1973:9–37.

11 In relating the narrative of the Mihna, I draw on the classic account of Walter M. Patton (1897), *Ahmad Ibn Hanbal and the Mihna*, Leiden: Brill. This account is highly sympathetic to Ibn Hanbal and needs qualification in places.

12 Notably Ernest Gellner; see Zubaida 1995.

13 Dimitri Gutas (2002) has argued convincingly that philosophical work continued uninterrupted throughout Muslim history, but separately from the religious sciences, and that philosophers only got into trouble when, like Ibn Rushd (Averroes, d. 1198) they brought philosophical discourses to bear on the religious sciences.

14 For expositions and commentaries on al-Ahkam, see Gibb 1962a, 'Some Considerations of the Sunni theory of the Caliphate' and 'Al-Mawardi's Theory of the Caliphate', in *Studies in the Civilization of Islam*, 141–75; D.P. Little 1974; Mikhail 1995.

15 Ibn Taimiya, *Al-Siyasa al-Shar'iya (Arabic) Dar al-Ma'arif*, n.d.

16 See Sivan 1985:94–102.

17 For a discussion of the influence of Ibn Taimiya on Wahhabi Islam and religious and legal thought in modern Saudi Arabia, see Vogel 2000.

18 Mamluke means 'slave', and the Mamlukes were a dynasty of slave soldiers who ruled in Egypt and Syria in 1250–1517, but continued sporadically to be part of the military equation in these lands after the Ottoman invasion of 1516–17, and until they were finally liquidated by Muhammad Ali in the early years of the nineteenth century. See Robert Irwin 1986; Ira Lapidus 1967.

19 For an account of the historiography of the formative period of Ottoman rule, see Cemal Kafadar 1995.

20 On the Safavid dynasty in Iran, see Arjomand 1984.

21 For an account of the penetration of Sufism into Ottoman life, including the religious institutions, see J.K. Birge (1937), *The Bektashi Order of Dervishes*.

22 Halil Inalcik 1978.

23 *Diya* as a monetary transaction, was always considered a private matter between the parties, and as such fully within the sphere of *shari'a* courts.

24 For an account of this deep penetration of religion in European life, see Lucien Febvre 1982.

25 A popular Turkish joke asks: how often does a Bektashi drink? Answer, every evening; how often does he pray? Answer, every *bayram* (religious feast).

26 See Crone 1980, especially 82–91.

27 Ernest Gellner 1983.

28 For a critique of Gellner's arguments, see Zubaida 1995. For a critique of essentialist arguments on Islamic politics, see Zubaida 1993:121–82.

Notes on Chapter 4

1 For accounts of these episodes see U.Heyd 1961; R.L.Chambers 1978; Niyazi Berkes 1964/1998:23–50.

2 On the Abdul-Hamid era, see Deringil 1998.

3   This section draws on the important work of Niyazi Berkes 1964/1998. See also Mardin 1989, especially Chapter 3.

4   On the history of the Tanzimat reforms, see Roderick Davison 1973.

5   '*Millet*' was the term used in general for 'nation', but was a more specific designation of religious communities. The '*millet* system' of the Ottomans was the designation of Christian and Jewish communities as corporate units under the authority of their religious hierarchies and churches, which ruled on the private and family affairs of the community. They were often corporate taxation units.

6   Under 'capitulations' the nationals of the European powers had special legal privileges, including the right to be judged by their consuls in accordance with their own laws, and as such were not subject to Ottoman jurisdiction.

7   Aspects of Azhar reforms will be discussed in Chapter 5.

8   For a history of the Young Ottomans and an analysis of their politics and ideas, see Mardin 1960.

9   Ashmawi 1983; Hallaq 1997:231–41; Shephard 1996.

10 Qasim Amin 1899; see also Hourani 1983:164–70.

Notes on Chapter 5

1   Sanhoury, a prominent jurist, was the architect of the Egyptian civil code of 1948. His project was the 'Egyptianization' of law, incorporating elements from the *shari'a*, and resulting in an eclectic mix. See Botiveau 1993a:148–50.

2   On Islam in politics and society in modern Turkey, see the contributions in Tapper 1991 and Zubaida 1996.

3   On the Egyptian political scene and the pretence of democracy, see Kienle 2001 and Kassem 1999.

4   For an account of the Abu-Zayd affair and the legal arguments, see Dupret 1995 and Balz 1997.

5   Information on this episode is drawn from an unpublished paper by Enid Hill, based on Egyptian press reports.

6   See his book, *Al-Haqiqa al-Gha'iba* (1996). It is a critique of an Islamic tract entitled *Al-Faridha al-Gha'iba, The Absent Obligation*, meaning *jihad* in the sense of armed struggle.

Notes on Chapter 6

1   For pertinent accounts of Iran in the nineteenth century, especially in respect of religion and the state, see Hamid Algar 1969; Arjomand 1984; Keddie 1966, 1972, 1981.

2   On *madrasas* and their curricula, see Fischer 1980; Moin 1999; Mottahedeh 1987.

3   On the place of mysticism and illumination in the Shi'i tradition, see Mottahedeh 1997, Chapter 5.

4 For accounts of the Constitutional Revolution see Abrahamian 1982:50–101; Keddie 1981:63–112; Enayat 1982:164–9; Martin 1989.

5 Reza Shah was forced to abdicate in 1941, when British and Russian forces occupied Iran and put an end to Reza's attempted neutrality. He was succeeded by his young son, Mohammad Reza.

6 On the Mosaddeq and oil nationalization episode, see Abrahamian 1982:261–80; Keddie 1981:119–41.

7 On Kashani, see Akhavi 1980:61–69; on Fedayan-e Islam, see Kazemi 1984.

8 For the episodes of Khomeini's career I draw on Baqer Moin's comprehensive biography (Moin 1999).

9 A version of Khomeini's lectures outlining his concept of Islamic government and the doctrine of *velayet-e faqih* was published in Arabic, Persian and translated in English; see Ayatollah Khomeini, *Al-Hukumah al-Islamiya: Wilayat al-Faqih*, Beirut: *Dar al-Tali'a*. Expositions and analyses are many, see Moin 1999; Zubaida 1993:1–37; Abrahamian 1993:17–26.

10 In this section I draw extensively on Schirazi (1997), *The Constitution of Iran*.

11 Much of the information on the structure and operation of the judicial system is drawn from Human Rights reports issued by the United Nations and Amnesty International, as indicated in the text.

12 *Ujrat al-mithl* and *thaman al-mithl* are traditional *fiqh* categories for 'fair rent' and 'fair price' (Johansen 1993:38). This is an example of the extension of traditional vocabularies to cover novel situations which are not provided for under the *shari'a* or even contrary to its specifications.

13 Information on penal law and procedure is drawn from a variety of sources, including UN reports and some unpublished papers, including Hedayat Matine Daftary, a distinguished Iranian jurist, 'The New Law of Islamic Punishments of Ta'zirat and Preventative Punishments'. Other material comes from the cited sources.

14 For an analysis of the ideas of Motahhari and other Iranian ideologues on the question of women and the family, see Parvin Paidar 1995.

15 On Soroush, see Matin-asgari 1997; Boroujerdi 1994; Cooper 1998; Mir-Hosseini 2000a.

16 Some leading *mujtahids* have formalized and institutionalized their functions and revenues. Kho'i, for instance, instituted a modern foundation registered and functioning in Europe and North America. This constitutes a 'globalization' of organization and function beyond the reach of the nation-states in the region.

References

Abdo, Geneive (2000), *No God But God: Egypt and the Triumph of Islam*, Oxford: Oxford University Press.

Abdul-Fattah, Nabil (1997), *Al-Nass wal-Risas* (*The Text and the Bullets*), Beirut: Dar al-Nahar.

Abrahamian, Ervand (1982), *Iran Between Two Revolutions*, Princeton NJ: Princeton University Press.

— (1993), *Khomeinism: Essays on the Islamic Republic*, London: I.B.Tauris.

Akhavi, Shahrough (1980), *Religion and Politics in Contemporary Iran: Clergy-State Relations in the Pahlavi Period*, Albany NY: State University of New York Press.

Algar, Hamid (1969), *Religion and the State in Iran, 1785-1906*, Berkeley CA: University of California Press.

Amin, Hussain Ahmad (1987), *Hawl al-Da'wa ila Tatbiq al-Shari'a al-Islamiyya* (*On the Call to Apply the Islamic Shari'a*), Cairo: Madbuli.

Amin, Qasim (1899), *Tahrir al-Mar'a* (*The Liberation of Women*), Cairo: no mention of publisher.

Amnesty International (2001), *Iran: A legal system that fails to protect freedom of expression and association*, AI-index: MDE 13/045/2001.

Anderson, J.N.D. (1976), *Law Reform in the Muslim World*, London: Athlone Press.

An-Na'im, Abdullahi Ahmad, *Towards an Islamic Reformation: Civil Liberties, Human Rights and International Law*, New York: Syracuse University Press.

Arberry, Arthur (1964), *The Koran Interpreted*, Oxford: Oxford University Press.

Arjomand, Said Amir (1984), *The Shadow of God and the Hidden Imam: Religion, Political Order and Societal Change in Shi'ite Iran from the Beginning To 1890*, Chicago IL: Chicago University Press.

Asad, Talal (2001), *Thinking about Secularism and Law in Egypt*, ISIM papers, Leiden: ISIM.

Baer, Gabriel (1969), 'Tanzimat in Egypt: the Penal Code', in G.Baer, *Studies in the Social History of Modern Egypt*, Chicago IL: University of Chicago Press, 109–32.

Balz, Killian (1997), 'Submitting Faith to Judicial Scrutiny Through the Family Trial: The Abu Zayd Case', *Die Welt des Islams* 37: 135–55.

Berkes, Niyazi (1964/1998), *The Development of Secularism in Turkey*, London: Hurst.

Birge, J.K. (1937), *The Bektashi Order of Dervishes*, London: Luzac.

Black, Antony (2001), *The History of Islamic Political Thought from the Prophet to the Present*, Edinburgh: Edinburgh University Press.

Boroujerdi, Mehrzad (1994), 'The encounter of post-revolutionary thought in Iran with Hegel, Heidegger and Popper', in Serif Mardin (ed.), *Cultural Transformation in the Middle East*, Leiden: Brill.

Botiveau, Bernard (1993a), *Loi islamique et droit dans les sociétés arabes: Mutations des systèmes juridiques du Moyen-Orient*, Paris and Aix-en-Provence: Karthala-IREMAM.

— (1993b), 'Contemporary Reinterpretation of Islamic Law: the Case of Egypt', in Chibli Mallat (ed.), *Islam and Public Law*, London: Graham and Trotman: 261–77.

Bulliet, Richard (1972), *The Patricians of Nishapur: A Study in Medieval Islamic Social History*, Cambridge: Cambridge University Press.

Calder, Norman (1993), *Studies in Early Islamic Jurisprudence*, Oxford: Clarendon Press.

Chambers, R.L. (1978), 'The Ottoman Ulama and the Tanzimat', in Nikkie Keddie (ed.), *Scholars, Saints and Sufis*, Berkeley CA: University of California Press.

Chehabi, H.E. (1990), *Iranian Politics and Religious Modernism: The Liberation Movement of Iran Under the Shah and Khomeini*, Ithaca NY: Cornell University Press.

Cole, Juan (1993), *Colonialism and Revolution in the Middle East: Social and Cultural Origins of Egypt's Urabi Movement*, Princeton NJ: Princeton University Press.

Cooper, John (1998), 'The limits of the sacred: the epistemology of Abd al-Karim Soroush', in John Cooper, Ron Nettler and Mohamed Mahmoud (eds), *Islam and Modernity: Muslim Intellectuals Respond*, London: I.B.Tauris.

Crone, Patricia (1980), *Slaves on Horses*, Cambridge: Cambridge University Press

Crone, Patricia and Martin Hinds (1986), *God's Caliph: Religious Authority in the First Centuries of Islam*, Cambridge: Cambridge University Press.

Davison, Andrew (1995), 'Secularization and Modernization in Turkey: the Ideas of Ziya Gokalp', *Economy and Society* 24:2.

Davison, Roderick (1973), *Reform in the Ottoman Empire, 1856-1876*, New York: Gordian Press.

Deringil, Selim (1998), *The Well-Protected Domains: Ideology and the Legitimation of Power in the Ottoman Empire, 1876-1909*, London: I.B.Tauris.

Dupret, Baudoin (1995), 'Entre le droit et la loi: Le juge et le jeu de la normalisation islamique du droit positif', *Droit et Culture* 30: 48–64.

— (2000), *Au nom de quel droit*, Paris: Maison des Sciences de l'Homme.

Ehteshami, Anoushirvan (1995), *After Khomeini: The Iranian Second Republic*, London: Routledge.

El-Nahal, Galal H. (1979), *The Judicial Administration of Ottoman Egypt in the Seventeenth Century*, Minneapolis MN and Chicago IL: Bibliotecha Islammica.

Enayat, Hamid (1982), *Modern Islamic Political Thought: The Response of Shi'i and Sunni Muslims to the Twentieth Century*, London: Macmillan.

Faroqhi, Suraiya, Bruce McGowan, Donald Quataert and Sevket Pamuk (1994), *An Economic and Social History of the Ottoman Empire, Volume Two 1600-1914*, Cambridge: Cambridge University Press.

Febvre, Lucien (1982), *The Problem of Unbelief in the Sixteenth Century: the Religion of Rabelais*, Cambridge MA: Harvard University Press.

Fischer, M.M.J. (1980), *Iran: From Religious Dispute to Revolution*, Cambridge MA: Harvard University Press.

Fuda, Farag (1986), *Al-Haqiqa al-Gha'iba* (The Absent Truth), Cairo: Dar al-Fikr.

Gellner, Ernest (1983), *Muslim Society*, Cambridge: Cambridge University Press.

— (1992), *Postmodernism, Reason and Religion*, London: Routledge.

Gibb, H.A.R. (1962a), *Studies in the Civilization of Islam*, Stanford J. Shaw and William R. Polk (eds), London: Routledge.

— (1962b), *Mohammadanism*, London: Oxford University Press.

Gibb, H.A.R. and H.Bowen (1950–57), *Islamic Society and the West*, Vol. 1, Parts I (1950) and II (1957), Oxford: Oxford University Press.

Goldziher, Ignaz (1910/1981), *Introduction to Islamic Theology and Law*, translated by Andras and Ruth Hamori, Princeton NJ: Princeton University Press.

Gutas, Dimitri (2002), 'The Study of Arabic Philosophy in the Twentieth Century: An Essay on the Historiography of Arabic Philosophy', *British Journal of Middle Eastern Studies* 29, 1: 5–26.

Hallaq, Wael (1984), 'Was the Gate of Ijtihad Closed', *International Journal of Middle East Studies* [*IJMES*] 16:1: 3–41.

— (1993), 'Was al-Shafi'i the Master Architect of Islamic Jurisprudence?' *IJMES* 25: 587–605.

— (1997), *A History of Islamic Legal Theories: an introduction to Sunni usul al-fiqh*, Cambridge: Cambridge University Press.

— (2001), 'From Regional to Personal Schools of Law? A Reevaluation', *Islamic Law and Society* 8:1: 1–26.

Hawting, G.R. (1986), *The First Dynasty of Islam: The Umayyad Caliphate AD 661-750*, London: Croom Helm.

Heyd, Uriel (1961), 'The Ottoman Ulama and Westernization in the time of Selim III and Mahmud II', in U.Heyd (ed.), *Studies in Islamic History*, Jerusalem: Magnus Press.

— (1973), *Studies in Old Ottoman Criminal Law*, Oxford: The Clarendon Press.

Hobsbawm, Eric (1992), *Nations and Nationalism Since 1780: Programme, Myth, Reality*, Cambridge: Cambridge University Press.

Hourani, Albert (1968), 'Ottoman Reforms and the Politics of Notables', in W.R.Polk and R.L.Chambers (eds), *Beginnings of Modernization in the Middle East*, Chicago IL: Chicago University Press: 48–61.

— (1983), *Arabic Thought in the Liberal Age, 1798-1939*, Cambridge: Cambridge University Press.

Imber, Colin (1997), *Ebu's-Su'ud: the Islamic Legal Tradition*, Edinburgh: Edinburgh University Press.

Inalcik, Halil (1973), *The Ottoman Empire: the Classical Age, 1300-1600*, London: Weidenfeld and Nicholson.

— (1978), 'Suleiman the Lawgiver and Ottoman Law', in *The Ottoman Empire: Conquest, Organization and Economy, Collected Studies*, London: Variorum Reprints.

— (1994), *An Economic and Social History of the Ottoman Empire: Volume 1 1300-1600*, Cambridge: Cambridge University Press.

— (1998), 'Islamization of Ottoman law on land and land tax', *Essays in Ottoman History*, Istanbul: Eren: 155–72.

Irwin, Robert (1986), *The Middle East in the Middle Ages: The Early Mamluke Sultanate 1250-1382*, London: Croom Helm.

Johansen, Baber (1988), *The Islamic Law on Land Tax: The Peasants' Loss of Property Rights as Interpreted in the Hanfite Legal Literature of the Mamluke and Ottoman Periods*, London: Croom Helm.

— (1993), 'Legal Literature and the Problem of Change: The Case of Land Rent', in C.Mallat (ed.), *Islam and Public Law*, London: Graham and Trotman: 29–48.

Kafadar, Cemal (1995), *Between Two Worlds: The Construction of the Ottoman State*, Berkeley CA: University of California Press.

Kassem, May (1999), *In the Guise of Democracy: Governance in Contemporary Egypt*, Reading: Ithaca Press.

Kazemi, Ferhad (1984), 'The Fed'iyan-e Islam: Fanaticism, Politics and Terror', in Said Amir Arjomand (ed.), *From Nationalism to Revolutionary Islam*, Albany NY: State University of New York Press.

Keddie, Nikki (1966), *Religion and Rebellion In Iran: the Iranian Tobacco Protest of 1891-1892*, London: Cass.

— (1972), 'The Roots of the Ulama's Power in Modern Iran', in N. Keddie (ed.), *Scholars, Saints and Sufis*, Berkeley CA: University of California Press.

— (1981), *Roots of Revolution: An Interpretative History of Modern Iran*, New Haven CT: Yale University Press.

Kepel, Giles (1985), *The Prophet and the Pharaoh: Muslim Extremism in Egypt*, London: Al-Saqi.

Kerr, Malcolm (1966), *Islamic Reform: The Political and Legal Theories of Muhammad Abduh and Rashid Rida*, Berkeley CA: University of California Press.

Kennedy, Hugh (1981), *The Early Abbasid Caliphate: A Political History*, London: Croom Helm.

— (1986), *The Prophet and the Age of the Caliphates: the Islamic Near East from the Sixth to the Eleventh Century*, London: Longman.

Kienle, Eberhard (2001), *A Grand Delusion: Democracy and Economic Reform in Egypt*, London: I.B. Tauris.

Lapidus, Ira (1967), *Muslim Cities in the Later Middle Ages*, Cambridge MA: Harvard University Press.

Laoust, Henri (1939), *Essai sur les doctrines sociales et politiques de Taki-d-din Ahmad b. Taimiya*, Cairo: Institut Français d'Archéologie Orientale.

— (1968), 'La pensee et l'action politique de al-Mawardi (974-1058)', *Revue d'Etudes Islamiques* XXXVI.

Mallat, Chibli (1993a), *The Renewal of Islamic Law: Muhammad Baqer as-Sader, Najaf and the Shi'i International*, Cambridge: Cambridge University Press.

— (1993b) (ed.), *Islam and Public Law*, London: Graham and Trotman.

Marcus, Abraham (1989), *The Middle East on the Even of Modernity: Aleppo in the Eighteenth Century*, New York: Columbia University Press.

Mardin, Serif (1962), *The Genesis of Young Ottoman Thought: A Study in the Modernization of Turkish Political Ideas*, Princeton NJ: Princeton University Press.

— (1989), *Religion and Social Change in Modern Turkey: The Case of Bediuzzaman Said Nursi*, Albany NY: State University of New York Press.

Marsot, A.L. (1984), *Egypt in the Reign of Muhammad Ali*, Cambridge: Cambridge University Press.

Martin, Venessa (1989), *Islam and Modernism: The Iranian Revolution of 1906*, London: I.B. Tauris.

Masud, Muhammad Khalid (1995), *Shatibi's Philosophy of Islamic Law*, Islamabad: Islamic Research Institute.

Matin-asgari, Afshin (1997), 'Abdolkarim Soroush and Secularization of Islamic Thought in Iran', *Iranian Studies* 30: 1–2, 95–115.

Memon, Muhammad Umar (1976), *Ibn Taimiya's Struggle Against Popular Religion*, The Hague: Mouton.

Mernissi, Fatima (1991), *The Veil and the Male Elite: Feminist Interpretation of Women's Rights in Islam*, New York: Addison-Wesley.

Messick, Brinkley (1993), *The Calligraphic State: Textual Domination and History in a Muslim Society*, Berkeley CA: University of California Press.

Mikhail, Hanna (1995), *Politics and Revelation: Mawardi and After*, Edinburgh: Edinburgh University Press.

Mir-Hosseini, Ziba (2000a), *Islam and Gender: the Religious Debate in Contemporary Iran*, London: I.B.Tauris.

— (2000b), *Marriage on Trial: a Study of Islamic Family Law*, London: I.B.Tauris.

Mitchell, Richard P. (1969), *The Society of Muslim Brothers*, Oxford: Oxford University Press.

Mitchell, Tim (1988), *Colonizing Egypt*, Cambridge: Cambridge University Press.

Moin, Baqer (1999), *Khomeini: Life of the Ayatollah*, London: I.B.Tauris.

Mottahedeh, Roy (1987), *The Mantle of the Prophet: Religion and Politics in Iran*, Harmondsworth: Penguin.

Murphy, Julian (2001), *An Analysis of the Writings of Muhammad Sa'id al-'Ashmawi and Their Significance within Contemporary Islamic Thought*, DPhil thesis, St Catherine's College, Oxford.

Mustafa, Hala (1995), *Al-Dawla wal-Harakat al-Islamiya al-Mu'aridha: bayna al-muhadana wal-muwajaha fi ahdai al-Sadat wa-Mubarak* (*The State and the Islamic Movements of Opposition: Between Truce and Confrontation, Under Sadat and Mubarak*), Cairo: al-Mahrousa.

Nawawi, Muhyi al-Din al- (1914), *Minhaj al-Talibin*, trans. E.C. Howard, *A Manual of Muhammadan Law According to the School of Shafii*, London: Thacker and Co.

Nicholson, Reynold Alleyne (1921), *Studies in Islamic Mysticism*, Cambridge: Cambridge University Press.

Paidar, Parvin (1995), *Women and the Political Process in Twentieth Century Iran*, Cambridge: Cambridge University Press.

Patton, Walter M. (1897), *Ahmad Ibn Hanbal and the Mihna*, Leiden: Brill.

Peters, Rudolph (1997), 'Islamic and Secular Criminal Law in Nineteenth Century Egypt: the Role and Function of the Qadi', *Islamic Law and Society* 4, 1: 70–90.

Quataert, Donald (1994), 'The Age of Reforms, 1812-1914', in Suraiya Faroqhi, Bruce Mcgowan, Donald Quataert and Sevket Pamuk (eds), *An Economic and Social History of the Ottoman Empire, Volume II, 1600-1914*, Cambridge: Cambridge University Press: 759–943.

— (2000), *The Ottoman Empire, 1700-1922*, Cambridge: Cambridge University Press.

Qutb, Sayid (1980), *Ma'alim fil-Tariq* (*Landmarks Along the Path*), Cairo: Dar al-Shuruq.

Rosen, Lawrence (1989), *The Anthropology of Justice: Law and Culture in an Islamic Society*, Cambridge: Cambridge University Press.

Schacht, Joseph (1953), *The Origins of Muhammadan Jurisprudence*, Oxford: Oxford University Press.

Schirazi, Asghar (1997), *The Constitution of Iran: Politics and the State in the Islamic Republic*, trans. John O'Kane, London: I.B.Tauris.

Shepard, William E. (1996), 'Muhammad Sa'id Al-'Ashmawi and the Application of the Shari'a in Egypt', *IJMES* 28: 39–58.

Sivan, Emmanuel (1985), *Radical Islam: Medieval Theology and Modern Politics*, New Haven CT: Yale University Press.

Skovgaard-Petersen, Jakob (1997), *Defining Islam for the Egyptian State: Muftis and Fatwas of Dar al-Ifta*, Leiden: Brill.

Tapper, Richard (ed.) (1991), *Islam in Modern Turkey: Religion, Politics and Literature in a Secular Society*, London: I. B. Tauris.

Tyan, Emile (1960), *Histoire de l'organisation judiciaire en pays d l'Islam*, Leiden: Brill.

United Nations: Commission on Human Rights, Reports on the situation of human rights in the Islamic Republic of Iran: E/CN/1993/41; A/49/514 1994; E/CN.4/1996/59; E/CN.4/1997/63; A/52/475 1997; E/CN.4/1998/59; E/CN.4/1999/32; A/54/365 1999; A/55/150 2000; Report by the Special Representative, January 2001 and August 2001.

Van Leeuwen, Richard (1999), *Waqfs and Urban Structures: The Case of Ottoman Damascus*, Leiden: Brill.

Vogel, Frank (2000), *Islamic Law and Legal System: Studies of Saudi Arabia*, Leiden: Brill.

Wardi, Ali (1954), *Wa"az al-Salatin*, Baghdad (no publisher mentioned).

Watt, W. Montgomery (1973), *The Formative Period of Islamic Thought*, Edinburgh: Edinburgh University Press.

Weber, Max (1954), *Max Weber on Law in Economy and Society*, trans. Edward Shils and Max Rheinstein, ed. Max Rheinstein, New York: Simon and Schuster.

Zubaida, Sami (1993), *Islam, the People and the State: Political Ideas and Movements in the Middle East*, London: I. B. Tauris.

— (1995), 'Is there a Muslim society? Ernest Gellner's sociology of Islam', *Economy and Society* 24:2.

— (1996), 'Turkish Islam and National Identity', *Middle East Report* 199, 26:2: 10–15.

Glossary

adab: literature, *belles-lettres*
'adl: justice
'aql: reason, rationality
a'yan: notables
bay'a: declaration of allegiance to a ruler
caliph/*khalifa*: deputy, used for the ruler as 'Deputy of the Prophet'
caliphate/*khilafa*: the office of caliph, headship of the Islamic community
dawla: 'dynasty' in historical usage; 'state' in modern usage
derbey: local chief/landlord, in Ottoman usage
diya: material restitution made by an offender or his or her kin to the injured party
faqih: jurist, legal theorist
fardh kifaya: obligation fulfilled on behalf of the community by qualified members
    such as *jihad* in war or scholarly *ijtihad* in formulating religious and legal judgements
fatwa: ruling on matter of law or worship, usually issued in response to a question
ferman: royal decree, in Ottoman usage
fiqh: jurisprudence, legal theory
ghazi: warrior for the faith
ghazu: holy war
hadith: a narration of the Prophet's proclamations and judgements, as transmitted by
    trusted companions and witnesses
hakam: adjudicator, arbitrator
hijra/hijri: Muslim calendar, dated from the *hijra*, flight of the Prophet from Mecca
    to Madina
hisba: accountability, a responsibility to ensure religiously correct conduct
hudud: a class of punishments, postulated as the limits or rights of God
hukm: ruling by a judge or adjudicator; modern usage, to govern
'ibadat: rules of rituals and worship in the *shari'a*
'idda: a period of time during which a divorced wife is not allowed to remarry and is
    maintained by the ex-husband
ifta': the function of issuing a *fatwa*
ijma': consensus
ijtihad: the exercise of reason in the derivation of legal judgements from the canonical
    sources
imam: generic usage as religious leader, including a prayer leader; Shi'ite special
    usage to designate charismatic descendants in the line of the Prophet through Ali
    and Fatima
Imam-ul-zaman: 'the imam of all time', referring to the Hidden Imam in Shi'ite belief
isnad: chains of narration of *hadith*
jahiliya: ignorance or barbarism, designating the time preceding the coming of Islam,
    but used to denigrate disapproved groups and societies, deemed irreligious

jizya: poll-tax levied on protected non-Muslims

khanga: Sufi lodge

kharaj: land-tax, at first levied on land acquired by conquest, later generalized

Khawarij/Kharijism: radical sect in early Islam, which vested authority in the Quran and the community as against the caliphate

khoms: religious tax paid by the Shi'i faithful to their chosen *mujtahid*

khul': a form of divorce, in which the wife takes the initiative

madhhab: doctrinal school of law (plural *madhahib*)

Mamluke: literally 'slave', designates the slave dynasties which ruled in different parts of the Middle East

marja' al-taqlid: the 'source of emulation', a title applied to the highest authority among the Shi'ite clergy

maslaha: utility of interest, usually 'public interest'

ma'thun: marriage registrar

matn: original text of legal treatise, distinct from the *sharh*, exegesis, written in its margin (plural *mutun*)

mazalim: a tribunal presided over by the ruler or his deputies, to receive petitions from subjects

Mecelle/Majalla: Ottoman legal statutes codifying the civil law elements of the *shari'a* in modern forms, published in 1876

mihna: hardship, torment; used in the sense of 'inquisition'

miri: state or royal land

mu'amalat: transactions; rules in the *shari'a* which cover them

muhtasib: the official charged with the functions of *hisba*, to monitor public spaces, especially markets, and ensure correct conduct

mujtahid: a high-ranking member of the clergy, qualified to practise *ijtihad*

nizamiya: a term applied to state schools and law courts emerging in the nineteenth century as distinct from the religious counterparts

qada': the function of judging

qadiaskar: two high religious dignitaries in the Ottoman court; literally, military judge

qanun: law ordained by a ruling authority, as distinct from *shari'a* as religious law

qanun-name: the book of ordinances issued by the Ottoman sultans

qisas: retribution or *tallion*, a class of punishments requiring equivalent damage to the perpetrator, or material restitution

qiyas: analogy, part of legal methodology

Rashidun: 'rightly guided', applied to the first four caliphs succeeding the Prophet

ra'y: opinion, in the process of legal reasoning

re'aya: common people, subjects of the sultan

sahih: accurate or sound; refers to compilations of attested *hadith*, sayings of the Prophet

sharh: commentary of exegesis, usually on the Quran or other canonical sources (plural *shuruh*)

shaykhulislam: the highest-ranking cleric in the Ottoman court, Mufti of Istanbul

Shi'i/Shi'a: 'Shi'i' is a singular noun as well as an adjective; 'Shi'a' is the generic plural, as in 'the Shi'a'; they refer to a section of Islam that championed Ali, the fourth caliph and his descendants as the rightful rulers of Muslims *shura*: consultation, usually applied to the ruler consulting the ruled

siyasa: administration, applied to tribunals, judgements and punishments effected by the ruler and his deputies, as distinct from *shariʻa*; in modern usage, politics

sunna: the norm established by the exemplary conduct of the Prophet (and, to a lesser extent, his companions); also applied to the mainstream congregation of Muslims, as distinct from what they consider to be sectarians

Sunni: adjective, referring to the mainstream congregation of Muslims

takfir: to declare another (disapproved) Muslim to be an infidel

taqlid: emulation; lay believers are said to emulate learned scholars, and later generations of scholars to emulate illustrious predecessors

tariqa: path, referring to a Sufi order (plural *turuq*)

taʻzir: punishments imposed at the discretion of a judge

tekke: a Sufi lodge; see also *zawiya* and *khanga*

ʻudul: professional witnesses; in practice, court functionaries with notary functions

ʻurf: custom, referring to customary law

ʻushr: tithe, land-tax on Muslims

usul al-fiqh: the principles of legal theory

velayet-e faqih: 'the guardianship of the jurist', Khomeini's doctrine of government, assigning authority to a ruling *faqih*

Wahhabi: rigorist sect founded by Muhammad bin Abd al-Wahhab in the eighteenth century, now the official doctrine of Saudi Arabia

wali-amr: guardian, a term applied to one in authority (plural *awli-amr*)

waqf: endowment (plural *awqaf*)

zakat: alms-tax due from Muslims

zawiya: a Sufi lodge

Index